YES YES YES

ALEX GREENWICH led Australia's marriage equality movement for over a decade. He served as co-chair of both Australian Marriage Equality and the YES campaign that successfully delivered marriage equality in 2017. In addition to being the Independent Member for Sydney in the New South Wales Parliament, he is internationally respected as a leader in LGBTIQ rights, having addressed legislatures and global conferences in Europe, Asia and North America.

SHIRLEENE ROBINSON has volunteered with Australian Marriage Equality since 2012. During this time, she served as New South Wales co-convenor, national spokesperson and board director. She is a historian with a PhD from the University of Queensland and the author and co-author of many books, including *Serving in Silence: Australian LGBT Servicemen and Women* (2018). She has been a Rydon Fellow at King's College London, has taught Australian Studies in China and has been an Associate Professor at Macquarie University. In 2017, the *Conversation* named Shirleene as one of Australia's top fifty Australian thinkers.

YES YES YES

Australia's Journey to Marriage Equality

Alex Greenwich and
Shirleene Robinson

NEWSOUTH

A NewSouth book

Published by
NewSouth Publishing
University of New South Wales Press Ltd
University of New South Wales
Sydney NSW 2052
AUSTRALIA
newsouthpublishing.com

A catalogue record for this book is available from the National Library of Australia

ISBN   9781742235998 (paperback)
          9781742244402 (ebook)
          9781742248844 (ePDF)

Design Avril Makula
Cover design Sandy Cull, gogoGingko
Cover image Australians gather to hear result of marriage equality survey, photograph by Scott Barbour. Getty Images
Printer Griffin Press

Contents

*For Victor Hoeld, Alex's husband
and Sarah Midgley, Shirleene's wife.*

Introduction

Australia's path to marriage equality was never perfect or smooth. Most countries with marriage equality achieved it through parliament, the courts or a public vote. We had all three. Thanks to the incredible efforts of determined supporters, on 7 December 2017 marriage equality became the law of the land. There had been 22 unsuccessful parliamentary attempts to pass marriage equality before 7 December. The journey had been long but it was finally done. We were both lucky enough to be there watching Parliament make history after so many of us had fought such a long campaign. People unfurled rainbow flags and the crowd of spectators who had been waiting in the galleries all day burst into non-stop applause, then broke into song. Politicians from all sides reached across the aisles, hugging and shaking hands. More than anything the mood inside that building, the mood we felt, reflected the sentiment of people watching across the country. It was a mix of euphoria, relief, exhaustion and pure happiness that senseless discrimination against a section of the Australian community had finally ended.

Less than a month earlier, on 15 November, the results of an unprecedented postal survey on the question of same-sex marriage had been announced. On an extraordinary Wednesday morning that few will ever forget, the nation stopped to hear that Australia had returned an emphatic YES. Every single state and territory had shown majority support for marriage equality. While the survey process was a gruelling experience for the lesbian, gay, bisexual, transgender, intersex and queer (LGBTIQ) community and their supporters, the nation's tremendous and widespread support for equality was a message that could no longer be ignored in the halls of parliament. Advocates had always maintained that the question of marriage equality should not be put to a public vote. In 2013, the High Court of Australia had very clearly said this was an issue that could be resolved through a vote in Federal Parliament. Our own research suggested that the Parliamentary numbers to pass legislation were there in 2015. That year, to avoid a conscience vote that opponents of marriage equality would lose, Prime Minister Tony Abbott proposed a compulsory plebiscite. The LGBTIQ community and allies so effectively fought against this, by pointing out the damaging impact a vote could have on people, that it was blocked by the Senate.

In 2017, though, the Turnbull Government put forward a new means of circumventing parliament by polling the Australian public directly on the issue of marriage equality. The Australian Bureau of Statistics would administer a national survey through postal ballots. In an unprecedented step, every single Australian voter would be asked their opinion on whether the law should be changed to allow same-sex couples to marry. The process was to be not only anonymous but also non-compulsory, and the results would not be legally binding on the parliament. This subjected same sex couples to intense public scrutiny while betting that public apathy would result in a negative vote. Two High Court challenges failed to stop this postal survey and advocates had less than three months to convince Australians to show their support for equality and post their YES.

The roots of the marriage equality movement were built on the efforts of brave pioneers from the LGBTIQ community who had been working for equality since the 1970s and earlier. When the Netherlands became the first country in the world to introduce marriage equality in 2000, there was little sense that such change would be replicated in Australia at any time in the near future. Indeed, in 2004, then Prime Minister John Howard introduced legislation to amend the *Marriage Act of 1961* to prevent same-sex marriages from being recognised in this country. It was quickly passed by the Federal Parliament with scant opposition.

Even before the 2004 amendments were passed, courageous individuals stood up publicly to point out the great injustice looming. We both have had the privilege of working alongside some of them and getting to know many others. Over time, the marriage equality movement evolved from something driven by a small group of committed individuals into something that depended on the efforts of hundreds of thousands of people from all across the continent. The great majority of these volunteers and advocates were everyday Australians determined to rectify a significant wrong and change the course of history. They were joined along the way by champions from many other spheres, including the political, celebrity and corporate worlds. All were united in their resolve to make marriage equality a reality. They wanted to send a powerful message about who Australians were as people and how LGBTIQ people should be treated.

Since 2004, advocates and supporters have had to negotiate a constantly evolving terrain. There have been a great many setbacks and sacrifices along the way. We have both felt them deeply and we know so many others who have as well. Back in 2004, there were some in the LGBTIQ community who questioned whether marriage equality should even be a goal. The gay liberation and feminist movements of the 1970s had both critiqued marriage as patriarchal and oppressive. But society moves on and institutions evolve. Flaws in systems become apparent and possibilities emerge to create positive change. Until marriage equality was passed as law, there were clear legal differences in how relationships between same-sex and opposite-sex couples were recognised. Marriage means something socially. It also instantly confers legal rights upon both partners. De facto status takes longer to establish and rights for same-sex couples vary across state and territory borders.

Like so many marriage equality advocates across the country, we have heard far too many accounts from individuals in same-sex relationships who struggled to have their relationships recognised during or after the illness or death of a partner. Discrimination has compounded grief far too many times in this country, sometimes preventing people from spending their last hours with their long-term partner, or arranging or taking part in funerals. Unequal marriage laws also had an impact on a younger generation, contributing to the sense of exclusion and isolation many felt as they came to understand their sexuality or gender identity. These injustices drew many advocates to the cause and they developed new strategies and methods of outreach to communicate why equal marriage matters. Over thirteen years, through nationwide advocacy, organising and action, they succeeded. They raised public awareness and formed the networks that would become crucial when Australia faced the challenge of the postal survey.

Throughout Australia's journey to marriage equality, there have been moments of triumph and hope. Over time, public and political support increased. There have been inspiring scenes when some politicians stood up for Australian same-sex couples. Senator Sue Boyce was the first Liberal politician to vote YES for marriage equality when she crossed the floor in Federal Parliament over this issue back in 2013. Federal politicians such as Sarah Hanson-Young from the Greens and Penny Wong and Louise Pratt from Labor, along with many others, have also delivered moving speeches at times when inspiration and leadership was desperately needed.

In 2017 though, supporters of marriage equality needed the entire country to back them in a way never before tested. There was one particularly difficult issue to face. How would a marginalised community deal with being subjected to a public judgment of their personal lives by their fellow Australians? No-one should ever minimise how difficult this experience was for many LGBTIQ Australians. They were placed in a position where they were treated as fundamentally different to heterosexual Australians. Many literally had to knock on their neighbours' doors to ask them to vote YES, so they could achieve equality under the law. It was a cruel, anxiety-inducing process. In 2004, when the *Marriage Act* was amended, it was done by parliament, not after an expensive survey to canvass the views of the entire nation. It is an enormous credit to the decency and empathy of many Australians that people reached out to support those who were hurt by the process and those still dealing with the hurt today.

Throughout the survey we also saw and experienced something else that was without precedent. That is, people from all across Australia joining together on a scale never before seen to support their family and friends in the fight for marriage equality. LGBTIQ Australians also organised on a level that amazed us. During the survey, Australians delivered a clear message that, though parliament might fail us, marriage equality would unite us as a country.

Questions haunted us as the postal survey began. Would younger voters, the keenest supporters of marriage equality, who have always been under-represented on the electoral roll, sign up? How could grassroots campaigners be empowered? Would people from across the country have the energy to keep up the momentum and work like never before? Would the one million Aussies living overseas vote? Would the Australian people fill out and return their postal ballots by the deadline? Yet, despite all the odds being stacked against us, supporters of marriage equality succeeded and did so spectacularly. The postal survey results delivered the biggest mandate any social issue has ever received in this country.

The 2017 campaign saw thousands of volunteers, many of whom had never campaigned for any cause before, come out when they were needed most. Australian advocates ran one of the most effective digital campaigns ever seen. While the NO campaign propagated untruths and misdirection, the YES campaign stayed focused and positive. An astounding volume of creative content encouraged Australians to keep sharing their personal stories about why marriage equality mattered – a method that had guided the movement since its formal foundations in 2004. The largest rallies ever held for LGBTIQ rights occurred across the country. In Sydney alone, over 30 000 people joined together to show their support by marching. Advocates knew that it was important to emphasise what this process was really about – the dignity and equality of fellow Australians. People opened their hearts and returned their surveys. Parliament could not ignore the resounding YES announced on 15 November.

Allowing same-sex couples to marry sent a powerful message that resonated across the country: that the love LGBTIQ people feel is equal to the love felt by heterosexual couples and deserves to be treated this way. The YES vote on marriage equality will not solve all the issues that LGBTIQ people face. Much still needs to be addressed. However, the achievement of marriage equality under Australian law was a landmark moment in our history and points the way forward. We are one step closer to a fairer and more equal Australia. The movement showed that love matters in this country and that through perseverance, with hope to sustain the momentum, discrimination can be overturned.

This book tells a story about Australia's journey to marriage equality. It is an account of profound social change, the type that occurs once in a generation. It describes how we achieved a once-inconceivable victory and how this came to transform a country. The marriage equality movement was driven from the grassroots up and the victory belongs to the Australian people. It was a long journey and it was difficult. We believe there are lessons activists can learn from such a successful campaign run in the face of considerable adversity – from the resilience built during the extreme lows of political stalemates to the triumphs of community-driven campaigns in regional and rural towns. We have both been privileged to be a part of this movement. It will never be possible for us to know all the names of the countless Australians who worked so hard across this continent to achieve marriage equality but we owe them a debt we can never repay. We regret that we cannot tell more of their stories in this book.

But we are very grateful that we can introduce you to just some of the incredible people we do know, who gave their all in different ways. Through this spirit and commitment, we hope to capture the feeling of the movement we lived through and share some of our personal reflections along the road to marriage equality.

We are writing this book to pay tribute to all the marriage equality supporters who contributed so much to achieving this reform. We were privileged to be part of the Australian Marriage Equality (AME) team and through that, we both saw the movement grow over time, formed a close friendship and shared many highs and lows. This movement broke our hearts at times but it gave us the great privilege of witnessing the most extraordinary events unfold. We bring shared, but at times quite different, perspectives. We were both volunteers, we worked predominantly in AME and we have always loved grassroots campaigning the best. But we grew up in different cities and our perspectives are informed by the different cultures of each. Alex is a gay man and Shirleene is a lesbian. Alex brought his instinctive advocacy skills into the political sphere as a state parliamentarian in NSW. Shirleene is an Australian historian with a passion for driving social change through better understandings of our past. Along with so many other organisations and individuals, we completed thousands of marriage equality miles and shared unforgettable, cherished moments with people across the country in the pursuit of equality. In the chapters ahead, we share our personal stories, the political and social context that guided the movement and its strategies and also describe the efforts of so many others that were crucial to love finally winning when Australia said YES.

It is the millions of Australians who showed their support for YES who are the heroes of this book. We hope the voices we share will provide a small glimpse of just some of the amazing people who have given so much. At its heart, it is an account of an incredible social transformation. We hope that by telling this story we might inspire others to know that it is possible to play a part in creating a fairer and more equal society for all. Extraordinary social change starts from individual acts of courage. As Australia's marriage equality journey shows, even when all the odds are stacked against you, if you can use hope to motivate you, triumph is ultimately possible. This book shows how social change can be driven from the grassroots and how sustained effort can eventually move an entire nation and change the course of history.

The journey begins

In 2017, the Australian campaign for marriage equality was all-consuming and inescapable. The pressure was unrelenting and the stakes extremely high. Media scrutiny was intense as advocates embarked on a High Court challenge to stop a postal survey and then had to campaign across the country to win an untested national postal vote on human rights. Losing would have been devastating, setting back the cause of LGBTIQ rights for, arguably, at least a decade. Under this pressure, more Australians than ever before came forward, determined to do all they could to see marriage equality achieved.

It would do a disservice to history, though, to suggest that marriage equality was achieved solely as a result of the events of 2017. Its success was built on the efforts of those from across the LGBTIQ community and our allies who gave so much in earlier decades and those who laboured tirelessly to build community support for marriage equality from 2004 onwards. Through persistence and heroism over time, the world that gay men and lesbians occupied began to change. While reform for transgender, gender diverse and intersex people has been much slower, and there is still more to be done, we have been encouraged by witnessing increased awareness and advocacy across these areas.

In 2018, as we had a conversation in the aftermath of the marriage equality campaign, Peter Black, the Queensland director of Australian Marriage Equality (AME), emphasised this point. 'There is no way that we would have won this campaign, or this campaign could have even made sense, were it not for those people who fought so hard, particularly in the 1980s and 1990s, but even going back before that. We always need to remember that.' We owe an enormous debt to those who came out and were open about their sexuality or gender identity in earlier decades, and to our allies who have stood alongside us while working for equality and challenging social and legal prejudice.

The origins of the marriage equality movement drew from the efforts of those who had courageously been advocating for the most basic of rights since the 1970s and even earlier. Until the 1960s and 1970s, homosexuality could potentially result in forced medical treatment such as aversion therapy. Male homosexuality was criminalised in parts of Australia until 1997 and Queensland Premier Joh Bjelke-Petersen even tried to criminalise lesbianism and ban gay bars in the state in the 1980s. The arrival of AIDS on Australian shores in the 1980s meant a generation of the LGBTIQ community – and particularly gay men – lost friends and lovers. Larry Galbraith, former editor of the *Sydney Star Observer* and senior policy officer to Sydney's lord mayor, Clover Moore, remembers:

> Many gay men who fell ill found that their families refused to
> acknowledge their partners. Their partners were denied access
> to them in hospital, were not welcome at their funerals and, as a
> result, were not able to properly grieve. This lack of recognition
> had concrete impacts as well. Surviving partners frequently

faced challenges in accessing their partner's estate. This could leave them in a precarious financial position, and in some cases, forced out of their shared home.

Marriage as an issue became publicly visible in Australia later than many other matters that affected the LGBTIQ community. Through necessity, earlier activists had to focus on decriminalisation, the struggle against prejudice and discrimination at work and in the community, the fight for relationship recognition under a range of state and federal laws, and contending with the HIV and AIDS epidemic. Larry Galbraith believes that these campaigns were all-important in leading to the marriage equality movement. He says, 'The experience gained in campaigning for same-sex relationship recognition was invaluable in achieving marriage equality. De-facto same-sex relationship recognition also highlighted the inequality that remained and galvanised those who refused to accept this unequal status'.

The movement towards marriage equality took time to develop in Australia. There were many activists who did not view marriage as a priority or saw it as contradicting gay liberationist and feminist thought, which had emphasised the oppressive nature of marriage as an institution. Australian legislation recognising same-sex relationships was far from perfect but it was further progressed than United States legislation. Australia was actually one of the earliest countries to allow migration on the basis of de-facto same-sex relationships.

LGBTIQ couples have engaged in marriage-like rituals well before same-sex marriage was legally possible. There are examples of male couples using the language of commitment and eternal bonds in convict and colonial society.[1] There are recorded accounts from as early as the 1920s of LGBTIQ people engaging in ceremonies akin to marriage in Australia.[2] Many activists from the 1970s remember attending same-sex commitment ceremonies. The Metropolitan Community Church in Sydney conducted several in this era. As greater emphasis is put on uncovering previously hidden histories of LGBTIQ people, more and more accounts from the past will be unearthed.

Many Australians first considered the issue of marriage equality in February 1998. A journalist from the *Daily Telegraph* had threatened to out high-profile doctor Kerryn Phelps and her partner, Jackie Stricker, after finding out the two women had recently married in a deeply meaningful but legally unrecognised Jewish religious ceremony in New York. Rather than hide their relationship or refuse comment, the couple decided that by being open about it and discussing it with the media, they could push for social reform and provide young LGBTIQ people with a positive example of a happy same-sex relationship. This took real courage and it had costs for them both. However, they tell us that they received many heartfelt and moving letters from across the LGBTIQ community from people who had been given hope after they shared their story. The visibility of Kerryn and Jackie's relationship was a very important step in growing mainstream support.

It was in 2004, though, that a formal and organised marriage equality movement emerged in this country. The legislation of marriage equality in provinces in Canada, starting with Ontario, from 2003 onwards, was a particularly significant turning point as Canada did not require couples who wished to marry to be residents. Once this option was available, Australian couples began taking it up.

In 2004, two Melbourne-based couples, Jacqui Tomlins and Sarah Nichols, and Jason and Adrian Tuazon-McCheyne, who had married in Canada, prepared to take a case to the Victorian Family Court in order to clarify whether their marriages were recognised in Australia. The existing Australian *Marriage Act* at that time did not specifically preclude the recognition of same-sex couples.

On 27 May 2004, before the Victorian Family Court hearing, which had been scheduled for 23 August 2004, the Howard Government introduced the Marriage Amendment Bill 2004 into the House of Representatives to define marriage as between a man and a woman and to prevent same-sex marriages conducted overseas from being recognised in Australia. Indeed, the Howard Government was so keen to alter the existing legislation that it introduced two Bills. The second came after Labor indicated it would not support a clause in the first piece of legislation to prevent same-sex couples from adopting overseas and a Senate Inquiry had been proposed.

On 8 August 2017, John Howard told the *Australian* that he had been motivated to change the *Marriage Act 1961* after realising that couples who had married overseas might be able to have their marriages recognised in Australia. 'What we didn't want to happen in 2004 was for the courts to start adjudicating on the definition of marriage because that was a real threat in 2004 because some people who had contracted same sex marriages in another country had the capacity to bring their issues before courts in Australia.'[3]

Some more perceptive observers had been concerned that this change was coming and in some ways, Howard's actions were the catalyst for the marriage equality movement. Bob Brown, an openly gay Greens Senator from Tasmania, was in Federal Parliament as the change loomed. He remembers an early meeting with Rodney Croome, who had led the campaign to decriminalise homosexuality in Tasmania, which achieved victory in 1997. Regarding marriage equality, Bob Brown recalls:

> The feeling was that even the LGBTIQ community wasn't
> ready for it yet. They'd been taken by surprise and hadn't
> had time to have a debate so we had to get that debate.
> I knew that in Parliament, you are always outflanked if
> you don't have a community that's up and campaigning.
> That goes back to my environmental campaigning in
> the 1980s. We needed to get the crowd roaring about
> equal marriage.

Rodney had been arrested and gaoled as part of his advocacy in Tasmania and had also taken a case to the High Court of Australia and to the United Nations to push for the reform. When it appeared that the LGBTIQ community was going to be targeted with anti-marriage legislation, Rodney took the lead in organising a response. From the start of 2004, he had publicly argued that opposition to same-sex marriage was going to be used an issue to unite conservative politicians and wedge Labor.[4]

In the early 2000s, Rodney's internet blog on LGBTIQ issues was one of the few ways that activists within Australia were able to communicate with each other and keep informed about issues that affected them. In 2004, a number of people from across Australia made contact with Rodney about the issue of marriage. He organised a telephone conference for 22 June from the offices of Labor's Duncan Kerr, the Federal Member for Hobart.

A handful of advocates from across Australia – and the LGBTIQ community – dialled in to the call with Rodney, including Damien and Graham Douglas-Meyer from Perth; Peter Furness, Luke Gahan, Morrison Polkinghorne, Robert Carmack, Peter Fitzpatrick and Michael True from Sydney; Iain Clacher, Geraldine Donoghue and Neil[5] from Brisbane; and Jen Van-Achteren and Martine Delaney from Hobart.

On that first phone call, the participants decided to form a national lobby group to advocate for marriage equality. This decision took real courage. Not only was mainstream support for marriage equality still elusive, there were many in the LGBTIQ community who were yet to be convinced. There were some on that call who would be immediately affected by any possible changes to legislation. Damien and Graham Douglas-Meyer had married in March 2004 at Toronto City Hall.[6] Luke Gahan was also planning to marry his partner.

On that first phone call, Luke Gahan from Sydney and Geraldine Donoghue from Brisbane were elected as the first national convenors and media spokespeople. Geraldine had needed a little prompting from Rodney, as she was concerned that she did not have any political experience, but he convinced her that being passionate without being partisan about an issue was actually an advantage. Luke also had to break the news to his partner, whose first reaction was 'How am I going to tell my parents this?' Luke remembers coming up with the group's name, Australian Marriage Equality, 'on the floor of my bedroom in my apartment in Sydney with the landline sitting on the floor writing down possible acronyms'.

Geraldine emphasises that Rodney was central to establishing an organised movement. He was 'so generous with his time' and they 'relied on him so much. It would not have been possible without him. He started conversations, pulled us together, got the ball rolling and kept it rolling'. We have both worked with Rodney as part of the campaign for marriage equality and acknowledge the tenacity and deep conviction that kept him working on this cause from 2004 all the way through until 2017.

During the course of writing this book, we had the opportunity to sit down and talk to Luke and Geraldine about what their journey and involvement was like. Both were young when they assumed the roles of national convenors but they treated the cause in front of them very seriously. Luke was only twenty-three at that time and Geraldine twenty-seven. Luke had grown up a Baptist with a keen appreciation of the social meaning of marriage. He had some experience with lobbying, having previously been a member of the Labor Party and having served the NSW Gay and Lesbian Rights Lobby as treasurer. A cruise to the west coast of Mexico with his partner in 2004, with a number of North Americans on board the ship, had first exposed him to the concept of marriage equality. At the time of AME's first telephone meeting, he was engaged and was planning to travel to Canada to marry.

Geraldine had spent most of her childhood on the Gold Coast before moving to Brisbane for university. She had gone to a school where it was 'the worst thing in the world to be called lesbian'. At the age of twenty, though, she started to become aware of her sexuality. Although her extended family had a conservative background, she had developed an awareness of social justice growing up. She had known gay men through her family's friendship circles as a child and although she saw these men were in some ways treated differently to others, it helped her enormously later as she dealt with her own sexuality to know that other gay people existed.

In 1997, while at university, she met Beck, the woman who is still her partner today, after asking to borrow a pen. The two ended up falling madly in love. Having previously been in heterosexual relationships, Geraldine soon realised that many people viewed her same-sex relationship as something lesser. She had always been vocal within her friendship circle about marriage and equal rights but 'wouldn't have called [herself] political before the Amendments in 2004'.

On 28 June 2004, after the phone hook-up earlier in the week and the election of Luke and Geraldine as the two national convenors, AME announced its formation with a press release. Luke remembers 'that was the founding of AME. Very casual. Very sort of grassroots really'. Luke is also pleased that the group included representation from across the LGBTIQ community.

The first press release AME issued announced that the group intended to campaign for equality under Australia's marriage laws. It listed two major tasks that lay ahead. The first was to gather submissions for the planned Senate Inquiry. The second was to 'build strong representative structures for AME so that it has the support and resources necessary to advocate, lobby and educate effectively during what will be a long-haul campaign'.[7] Few could have estimated just how drawn out the journey would be. Luke remembers the press did not cover the release in 2004. 'I don't think anyone thought it was interesting.'

From the outset, even before the *Marriage Act 1961* was amended, advocates knew a positive tone was essential if they were going to convince others that marriage equality mattered. In one of his earliest speeches, at a rally organised by Community

Action Against Homophobia in Sydney on 25 July 2004, Luke conveyed the message that the best way to counter attacks is to 'go out this week to your places of work, education, your places of entertainment, shopping and even worship and let people know about your friends and our special message of love, family, commitment and equality. As you have heard, our message is a positive message, rather than a message of fear and hate'.[8]

Tanya Plibersek, the Federal Labor Member for Sydney, also spoke at this rally and asked the crowd to make submissions to the pending Inquiry. Sydney Lord Mayor Clover Moore also spoke, pointing out that the federal government's claims of protecting traditional marriage were similar 'to the idea last century that denying women the vote protected democracy'.

As well as introducing a positive tone from the outset, the AME team was influenced by international LGBTIQ rights developments, particularly in the US. Iain Clacher, one of the founding members, would produce an e-journal opinion piece only two days after the first phone meeting, considering the conservative case for marriage equality. His piece concluded: 'As much as our politicians hope it will go away, gay marriage is an issue that's here to stay'.[9] Iain made a significant contribution to the community in Queensland, and continues to be remembered fondly after he passed away of a heart attack in 2009.

Efforts to prevent the *Marriage Act 1961* from being amended were ultimately unsuccessful. On 4 August 2004, before the planned Senate Inquiry could proceed, Nicola Roxon, Labor's shadow attorney-general, appeared at a conference for an organisation called the National Coalition for Marriage and announced that the Labor Party would support Coalition changes to the *Marriage Act* of 1961 to prevent marriage equality.

The National Coalition for Marriage's conference had been arranged just three weeks earlier with the intention of lobbying politicians to support changes to the *Marriage Act* to prevent same-sex marriage. John Howard spoke for twenty minutes at the conference, receiving a standing ovation at the end. Ironically, given the postal survey that would later be imposed upon the Australian people, Howard told the assembled crowd that if there was to be a change in the understanding of marriage in this country, 'it is a change which is to be legislated by an expression of will of the Australian people through the national parliament'. He continued 'if the law in this instance is to be remade, it can only and should only be remade by parliament'.[10]

Other speakers at the conference included the deputy prime minister John Anderson, David van Gend, Fred Nile and former tennis player Margaret Court. Pastor Ron Brookman, who told the crowd he had been a 'practising homosexual for 31 years' but had left the 'homosexual lifestyle' and was now happily married with children, also spoke. The Australian Christian Lobby press release noted approvingly that 'his story clearly challenged the common myth that homosexuals are born that way and cannot change'.[11] A number of MPs, including Kevin Andrews and Bronwyn Bishop, were in attendance.

The conference organisers, clearly not short of funding, launched a new booklet against marriage equality entitled *Twenty-One Reasons Why Marriage Matters*. They had printed 15000 copies, which they intended to distribute to all parliamentarians and across the country as part of their campaign against marriage equality. There was only one minor interruption to the conference, when the Democrats unfurled banners with the slogan 'Hate is not a family value' from the galleries.

Like AME, the National Coalition for Marriage was also established in 2004. However, it had much greater financial resources than AME, who were a newly emerging group funded by small donations and driven entirely by the efforts of a small band of volunteers. The three founding groups of the National Coalition for Marriage were the Australian Christian Lobby, the Australian Family Association and the Fatherhood Foundation. Representing these groups were Jim Wallace, Bill Muehlenberg and Warwick Marsh. It was also supported by an evangelical church, Catch the Fire Ministries. Many of those who attended the National Coalition for Marriage conference would spend the next thirteen years attempting to prevent marriage equality in this country.

Luke remembers how grating it was that the National Coalition for Marriage was given such a warm welcome into the Great Hall of Parliament. 'Something we could never get into. We couldn't even get to meet with MPs and they got this hearing and they talked about marriage being between a man and a woman and we knew straight away both Labor and Liberals were going to support this legislation.'

Bob Brown was particularly disappointed that Nicola Roxon opted to speak at this conference. He recalls her addressing 'a thousand or so during a vote from the Christian lobby in the Great Hall to announce that Labor would be opposing same-sex marriage. And they did. They were patently out there to try and grab some of the oxygen out of John Howard'. He told us, 'It was demoralising that Labor was trying to outdo John Howard and it wasn't an unprecedented thing for Howard to do. He was always looking ahead to see what the progressives might do and moving to legislate to block it'.

There is some debate over whether Roxon followed proper Australian Labor Party (ALP) process in making this announcement. In August 2004, Tanya Plibersek went on the record, telling the *Sydney Star Observer*, 'I think it's terrible. It doesn't reflect the decision we made in the Labor Party caucus to send this legislation off to a committee. I've told Nicola in the strongest terms that I feel betrayed by what she said yesterday and I take very seriously the fact she's not followed proper caucus procedure'.[12] It was also reported that Anthony Albanese had argued vigorously within the Labor Party against changing the *Marriage Act*.

Penny Wong, Labor Senator for South Australia, also argued strongly against supporting the changes. Although she was gay and directly affected herself by the proposed amendment, it was the principle of parliament introducing new forms of discrimination that concerned her greatly. She remembers, 'We had the caucus debate on that, although the position had already been clear. And I thought at the time the most important thing was to invest in where we wanted to go, and so I thought the best thing to do was to just label what was happening'. She courageously spoke out within her party. 'I said something like, "If the discrimination that is proposed were on the basis of any other attribute, age, race, disability, not a single person in the caucus would countenance it, but you're prepared to do it to people who are gay".'

Regardless of internal debates within the Labor Party, the proposed changes to the marriage laws ultimately did receive bipartisan support. Penny Wong remembers thinking, '"Oh, we're going to fix this up" but it did take us a bit longer than I thought it might'. She would spend the next thirteen years working within the Labor Party and across the Parliament to overturn the discrimination that had been introduced.

Labor's position back in 2004 has received further scrutiny over the years. In 2010, Mark Latham did an interview with the *Kyle and Jackie O Show* program on 2DayFM, saying that he regretted not supporting marriage equality when he was the leader of the Opposition in 2004, blaming the influence of religious groups over both the major political parties. Later, he reverted to his previous position, becoming a prominent campaigner against marriage equality during the postal survey in 2017. In 2012, Nicola Roxon came out in support of marriage equality.

Once Labor had announced it would support defining marriage as between a man and a woman, it was inevitable that the changes would pass through parliament. At 5:45 p.m. on Friday 13 August 2004, the *Marriage Amendment Act* passed through the Australian Senate. There were thirty-eight 'ayes' and six 'nos'. The Greens and the Democrats had driven the 'nos'. In fact, the Australian Christian Lobby issued a press release emphasising that 'the Democrats and Greens Senators expressed disgust and outrage at the Bill' and that Democrat Senators Brian Grieg and Andrew Bartlett, along with Greens Senators Bob Brown and Kerry Nettle, were 'highly vocal' on the afternoon of the Bill's passage.[13] Penny Sharpe, a member of the Labor Party who would join the New South Wales Legislative Council the following year in 2005 and would become one of the strongest advocates for marriage equality within her party, remembers seeing the proposed law change and recognising 'it required a lot of work to undo'.

At the time, the media reported that the Opposition, led by Mark Latham, had been scared of being wedged by the Howard Government on this issue. Certainly, an election was two months away and support for marriage equality in Australia at this time was estimated to be at around 38 per cent.

The Greens labelled the changes as discriminatory against the LGBTIQ community and condemned both the government and the Labor Party for their actions in passing it. Bob Brown remembers, 'The whole world was moving towards equal marriage and I knew it would be undone but I knew we were also seeing in that legislative action by the combined parties a big delay which would cause a lot of suffering and heartache and it did'. He was absolutely correct.

It would take thirteen years and twenty-two attempts before the legislation was undone and marriage equality became the law of the land. The first attempt to introduce marriage equality was in May 2004, when New South Wales Greens MP Michael Organ attempted to introduce the Same Sex Relationships (Enduring Equality) Bill. This vote did not proceed beyond the first reading.

The Democrats also viewed the 2004 changes to the *Marriage Act 1961* as discriminatory and unnecessary and voted against them. Natasha Stott Despoja said, 'This has been a shocker of a week, an embarrassing, shameful, disgraceful week. In fact, it's one of the most embarrassing weeks in this parliament'.[14] Andrew Bartlett spoke beautifully in support of the LGBTIQ community. In a quirk of fate, in 2017, the upheaval caused by the changes in the Senate composition due to dual citizenship issues saw Bartlett, who had been a Queensland Democrat in the Senate in 2004, return to the Senate, this time as a Green. Once again, he expressed his support for marriage equality and was able to cast a vote in support of the LGBTIQ community and undo the legislation that had passed in 2004.

Luke Gahan still recalls the 13 August 2004 passage of the legislation well:

I got home, I rushed in, turned the radio on and the ban went through. And I have this memory. Maybe it's dramatic and it's my memory. I remember it being dark in Sydney that day. And I remember my partner who was not very political. But anyway, I remember that night … he walked in that front door and was crying. And I was shocked. I thought, 'Oh, if it's affecting him, this is huge'.

In Brisbane, Geraldine listened to the passage of the legislation on the radio at home on the couch in the dark, entwined with her partner, Beck. She remembers thinking that, now that the legislation had passed, 'this is going to be really hard to get out of'. She felt 'outraged. Like it was unacceptable'.

Alex was only just becoming comfortable with his sexuality as the same-sex marriage ban passed. 'It certainly didn't help me to have the parliament say, "Come out and you're less equal". At the time, I was running my family's recruitment business with my parents, who were divorcing. I remember being really angered by Howard's move, but not having the personal and emotional strength to do anything about it. I was impressed by the bravery of those who were able to stand up then and advocate for what was right – community campaigners, a handful of politicians and even some journalists.'

Shirleene was not yet publicly out about her sexuality either in 2004. 'Writing this book has made me reflect on this. Growing up in Brisbane in the 1980s with a mother who immigrated from Fiji, I had always been aware of the destructiveness of racism. At university, I had focused on unearthing the history of Aboriginal people who had experienced a legacy of horrifying treatment and yet had given so much, only to be written out of the nation's story.

The ramifications of Australia's dark past were overwhelming and contending with my sexuality as well felt like yet another overwhelming battle. The very week that John Howard passed the amendments, I was starting my first academic job at a university on the Gold Coast. On the one hand, I was being told that I had succeeded, I had a PhD, I had a contribution to make to society. Yet on the other hand, I was receiving an unmistakable message of prejudice that was only too easy to absorb.' In 2018, when Shirleene met both Luke and Geraldine, 'I was struck by the strength they had both showed in 2004. Both did the most difficult tasks we can ask of anyone – they spoke up and told the country who they were and who they loved. They believed that change could and eventually would come'.

When the ban passed, there was a community reaction, with the first protest against such a ban in Australia. In Sydney, around 400 people gathered together to protest the passage of the legislation and demand that it be repealed. The rally had been organised by Community Action Against Homophobia, a group convened by a coalition of socialists, members of the Greens and grassroots activists under the leadership of Rachel Evans and Simon Margan.

Democrats Senator Brian Greig told the assembled crowd, 'I think most Australians believe Australia is a decent and tolerant place and we believe in a fair go for all. This is not decent, it's not tolerant and it's not fair at all'.[13] Clover Moore, the Lord Mayor of Sydney and then State Member for Bligh, also addressed the rally, speaking out in support of equal marriage rights and condemning the way legislation had been quickly pushed through Federal Parliament.

In Victoria, in the aftermath of the legislation passing, Equal Love began as a campaign by the Victorian Gay and Lesbian

Rights Lobby but eventually became an independent group. Equal Love pushed for marriage equality and an end to discrimination against LGBTIQ people by applying pressure to the government through protest and other actions. They would continue to be a major force in organising protest events across Australia until marriage equality was achieved.

Luke remembers media interest in the cause significantly picked up in the aftermath of the passage of the 2004 legislation. 'That's when the phone started ringing, that's when suddenly our press release made sense. And the mainstream media did pick up on it then.' At this time, Luke also found his relationship thrust into the public eye in a way he had not anticipated.

While the *Marriage Act* changes were receiving media attention, it was still difficult to convince many members of the LGBTIQ community that marriage was worth fighting for, let alone the broader community. Some LGBTIQ organisations were outright hostile to the cause. Many did not believe that marriage should be a priority when a range of other forms of discrimination still existed, while others thought of it as an outdated construct. Luke remembers 'going to bars in Sydney and talking to people, just casually, it wasn't a deliberate move. And people would laugh at you or tell you that you were stupid. "Why are you doing this for?" That was the general reaction'.

As Geraldine remembers, she and others in AME, including Rodney, held the view that the journey to marriage equality would also see other significant gains for the LGBTIQ community on the way. When others in the LGBTIQ community asked her, 'Why would you go for crumbs?' given that there was still a distance to be traversed on issues such as the equal age of consent, parental rights, health care and a whole suite of other issues,

Geraldine 'understood that'. However, 'we had been at that for years with little change. I knew that if you went for the top, which was marriage equality, some of those things would emerge'. The challenge that lay ahead for advocates was convincing others to take up the cause and to increase support amongst the main-stream community.

Building support

Between 2005 and 2007, the marriage equality movement increased its support amongst the Australian public and it did so spectacularly. A Galaxy poll commissioned by progressive non-profit organisation GetUp!, and published in *The Age* in June 2007, found support had leapt from 38 per cent in 2004 to 57 per cent in 2007. A twenty-point jump in three years was remarkable and those who were centrally involved in the cause during these years fought hard for it. Despite the growth in public support, the Howard Government remained fiercely resistant to marriage equality throughout this period.

The first task marriage equality advocates had to confront was to convince the LGBTIQ community that the reform mattered. The second was to increase support across the wider community. The third was to increase political backing. They achieved these tasks through public actions and meetings, through couples in same-sex relationships increasing their visibility, and by advocates having a range of conversations with different supporters from right across the country and the community. Such conversations emphasised that at its heart, marriage equality was an issue that affected people across all communities and was about their right to be treated fairly and equally. A growing international movement was also influential.

Luke Gahan remembers the national launch of Australian Marriage Equality (AME) in 2005. Back then, there was very little interest even from within the LGBTIQ community. The launch was held at the Erskineville Town Hall in Sydney. Kerryn Phelps and Jackie Stricker-Phelps agreed to speak on a panel. Luke arranged for some music and the hire of a small room. 'I had this idea that if you have a small room, it looks busy and it looks full.' The gay press didn't come to the meeting. A few others did, though. 'We talked, that was it and they left.'

Geraldine Donoghue found that some from the feminist community were perplexed that she, as a woman and a lesbian, was taking up the issue of marriage. They saw it as a patriarchal institution responsible for oppressing women. She recalls doing an early radio interview with a Melbourne station where she was interrogated about why she would want to engage with an institution that had not served women well historically.

Geraldine pointed out that for her, it was about having the option. 'If we eventually win, that doesn't mean lesbians will have to get married or gay men will or that difference or diversity is going to drain out. It's still about the importance of choice.' Geraldine credits her 'incredibly supportive workplace' from this time, who let her do interviews at work and after work, using their telephones in an era when mobile phone usage was still not widespread. She remembers there 'was not a single person in the workplace who wasn't supportive. That was tremendous'.

Rodney Croome took the weight of the pressure in doing media interviews. This was at a time when opponents of marriage equality openly used hateful language and homosexuality was often cruelly and wrongly equated with pedophilia. Opponents were well funded and received media traction. Misdirection and callousness would be an ongoing strategy for their campaign. By 2017, transgender and gender diverse people would be the primary targets of misleading and damaging statements.

As the campaign was trying to increase support in these early years, logic completely disappeared from many opponents' arguments. Supporters of marriage equality were accused of promoting a movement that would see people wanting to marry inanimate objects and even animals. During this era, the children's television show *Play School* was criticised by federal politicians for 'indoctrinating' children by showing a family with two mums in one episode. Geraldine credits Rodney with always being 'calm and reasonable' under difficult conditions.

The difficulty in building broader support for the issue in Queensland was that it seemed 'nobody cared'. Geraldine felt that even the LGBTIQ community shut down attempts to advance the issue. Her efforts to involve the Queer Collective at her university were met with requests to 'stop spamming us. We have no interest in marriage equality. We think you are so far removed from what we need as a community'.

Geraldine understood that there were historical reasons why many in Queensland were reluctant to push for LGBTIQ reforms. Queensland had been the last state on the mainland to decriminalise homosexuality and it was evident that a range of other reforms were still needed. Luke in Sydney encountered a similar sentiment. 'We were not only up against a hesitant mainstream society, but we were also up against a stale gay leadership who fuelled anger towards same-sex marriage in our own community.'[1]

In New South Wales, advocates were able to gain some visibility for same-sex couples who wished to commit to each other through a scheme offered by the City of Sydney. The former South

Sydney Council had offered a Partnership Register and Sydney Lord Mayor Clover Moore arranged to rename it as the City of Sydney Relationship Register after the South Sydney Council was disbanded. As part of this system, couples were able to have a ceremony and the images that came from these ceremonies showed happy same-sex couples making commitments.

In May of 2005, though, an event in Sydney showed that the LGBTIQ community was far from united on the issue. In April of that year, constitutional law expert Professor George Williams from the University of New South Wales had suggested that state marriage laws for marriage equality could provide a path forward as they would be constitutional so long as they did not overlap with federal legislation. For much of the marriage equality campaign, the introduction of state- and territory-based Bills would continue to be an important means of keeping marriage equality on the political and social agenda. In 2013, these efforts halted when the High Court of Australia overturned a successful ACT marriage Bill.

After Professor Williams' advice, in May of 2005, Tasmanian Greens MP Nick McKim introduced a bill to recognise same-sex marriages into that state's parliament. After the first stage of the debate, it was sent to an inquiry. Lee Rhiannon, who at that stage was a New South Wales state MP for the Greens, followed this by introducing a private members Bill for marriage equality into the New South Wales Upper House in May.

Due to this legislative action, advocates decided to hold a community forum in May 2005 at the Newtown Hotel. At this event, tensions between supporters of marriage equality and others in the LGBTIQ community erupted spectacularly. Speaking at the forum in support of marriage equality were Rodney Croome,

Luke Gahan, Nick McKim, Lee Rhiannon and Farida Iqbal from Community Action Against Homophobia. Ray Goodlass, convenor of the New South Wales Greens LGBTI Working Group, moderated. Both AME and Community Action Against Homophobia accepted that state-based legislation could provide an important way to move the issue forward in the absence of federal recognition.

The other speakers, David Scamell, co-convenor of the New South Wales Gay and Lesbian Rights Lobby; Stevie Clayton from ACON (a NSW organisation for HIV prevention) with other board members from ACON; and some Labor Party members associated with Rainbow Labor, maintained that they were not outright opposed to marriage equality but did not believe there had been enough community consultation to proceed with any legislation. Scamell also issued a press release, asserting that marriage equality should only be pursued on a federal level.

Supporters of marriage equality in the audience believed that the lobby was not ready to embrace the issue at this time and were more intent on removing marriage equality as an issue that might affect the Labor vote. Luke believes 'supporters of Rainbow Labor had very carefully stacked the room in true Labor fashion'.

This was the climate when Malcolm McPherson became engaged with marriage equality – a cause he would stay committed to from 2005 until 2017, when the reform was finally achieved. Malcolm was, at this time, still married to his wife of twenty-four years but came out as a gay man around June 2004. Malcolm believed firmly that the option of marriage should be available to those in the LGBTIQ community as well, believing 'committed loving same-sex relationships to be equally valid and valuable'. Throughout the marriage equality campaign, he was a constant and steady presence. Self-deprecatingly, he says, 'I kept turning up. I am indebted to Trevor Khan for that life wisdom – that life is about turning up'. Malcolm's calm and thoughtful personality, inner strength and firmly inclusive nature won him deep respect from all who got to know him.

After coming out, Malcolm signed up to volunteer with the New South Wales Gay and Lesbian Rights Lobby. He wrote a letter to his local paper, the *Northern District Times*, on the topic of marriage equality. He found that the Gay and Lesbian Rights Lobby seemed not interested in pursuing marriage equality as a cause. As a result, he reached out and became involved with AME.

Malcolm remembers about thirty people being in the audience at the May 2005 forum and an aggressive reaction from the New South Wales Gay and Lesbian Rights Lobby, who were at that time dominated by LGBTIQ Labor members. He recalls that 'it was the most disturbing meeting I have ever attended. The level of unexpressed aggression was huge'.

Luke Gahan was spat on by someone as he was leaving. 'They were angry. They were furious.' It had not been a good day for Luke, who had been personally accused by a member of the Christian right on national radio of being a 'moral terrorist' for advocating for marriage equality. He was being attacked on all fronts. Luke remembers some ALP members telling him as he left the forum that his activism would result in Labor losing the seats of Sydney and Grayndler to the Greens. Some of those Rainbow Labor activists have since reflected that to us: for better or worse, marriage just wasn't a priority for them at this time. They were focused on shorter term issues and healthcare concerns, which they believed had more immediate importance.

While this was a particularly dramatic forum, other events helped to gradually build support. Luke remembers initially 'people were very aggressive but we slowly started to get people on our side'. He acknowledges that paradoxically, Howard's actions in ramming through the legislation in such a quick and cynical way to wedge the Labor Party probably helped to motivate the LGBTIQ community to get behind the issue. Luke feels the sentiment amongst the LGBTIQ community was moving towards 'how dare you take marriage equality from us, even though there [had been] no marriage equality, you know. How dare you say we can't!'

Building support amongst the broader community also took enormous energy and effort from those involved. One of the key reasons the movement was able to build success was its positive tone. From the very start, advocates emphasised that marriage was simply about enabling two people who loved each other to make a legal commitment to each other. They focused their messages on marriage equality being about real people who should be able to have the same aspirations in life as everyone else. They also emphasised that it would be something positive, not only for those immediately affected but for their family and friends and for society as a whole.

As the first-year anniversary of the 2004 amendment to the *Marriage Act 1961* approached on 13 August 2005, rallies in major cities were organised to mark the passage of the discriminatory legislation and to draw public attention to the issue. Malcolm with Peter Furness of AME helped organise the Sydney rally with Rachel Evans, Simon Margan and other members of Community Action Against Homophobia.

He remembers trying 'valiantly' to convince the New South Wales Gay and Lesbian Rights Lobby, New Mardi Gras and

ACON to come on board but it proved 'fruitless', even though he was on the committee of the New South Wales Gay and Lesbian Rights Lobby at the time. To provide some atmosphere for the Sydney rally, Malcolm 'bought 300 helium-filled pink balloons and handed them out to marchers on the route'. He remembers around 800 people turning up to the Sydney rally. Participants marched from Taylor Square on Oxford Street to New South Wales State Parliament.

In Brisbane, Geraldine Donoghue encountered both a lack of interest and a level of hostility when she organised the rally in that city for August 2005. Her initial approach to Brisbane City Council about using King George Square for a rally received a positive response. However, once she mentioned that the rally was for marriage equality, she found that King George Square had suddenly become unavailable for 'technical reasons, governmental reasons'. Instead, she was offered the use of a small park near Roma Street train station.

Geraldine approached Democrat Senator Andrew Bartlett to speak, which he agreed to do, 'absolutely without a doubt' and he also provided crucial assistance. Geraldine, who had not organised a rally before, relied on him to help source a microphone and a speaker for the day. She emailed contacts including the Queer Collective at QUT and other LGBTIQ groups. She was quickly told: 'We are not interested and do not want to be a part of this. We are not attending and if we do, we will be protesting'.

Undeterred, she pressed on. Geraldine and her partner Beck made up around ten cardboard signs and a long fabric sign. On the day of the rally, it became clear that not many were going to attend. She feels that there was a sense amongst the community that 'You don't rock the boat too much, especially in Queensland'.

Andrew Bartlett told her, 'Don't worry, just plough on'. Somewhere between six and ten people ended up attending. There were not even enough people to carry all the signs the two women had made. Andrew Bartlett continued regardless and 'spoke beautifully'. While some from the Queer Collective had turned up, they were quiet. They later used the small attendance to argue that no-one cared about marriage equality and that the issue was dead.

For Geraldine though, it only served to reinforce that every movement had to start somewhere. She remembers thinking, 'This will grow. It's okay'. At one point, a teenage boy, who had clearly been intending to attend the rally, had looked over, seen the small crowd numbers and turned away. Geraldine thought, 'I could see it was just so confronting and he stopped and just sort of turned away and walked away. And I thought, that's okay, one day you'll come back. Now's not your time, that's okay. We'll get there'. In one of the most beautiful interview moments imaginable, Geraldine told Shirleene that and she and Beck had been in the crowded Queens Park in the centre of Brisbane, waiting for the results of the postal survey in November 2017. In fact, Geraldine had not missed a Brisbane rally since 2005. In Queens Park, on that day in 2017, she saw that, just as she had always known would happen, Australia had indeed gotten there.

Creating broader public awareness about the issue was also important, and one of the ways to do this was to draw attention to the commitment and love that existed amongst LGBTIQ people in the community. One such opportunity to increase awareness came from unlikely quarters. Geoff Field, a newsreader who was working on the *Kyle and Jackie O Show*, had been open about his relationship with his partner Jason since 2004. He would often discuss his weekends or the two men's shared life with the two radio hosts. The radio show had very high ratings at this time, reaching over a million people each day.

While Geoff, Kyle and Jackie saw their discussions about their lives and their partners as quite normal, it was still quite unusual for a newsreader to openly discuss a same-sex relationship on air. This was confirmed when a tabloid newspaper published a Sunday newspaper article about 'Sydney's gay newsreader, Geoff Field'. While Geoff remembers the amendments to marriage law being passed in 2004, he doesn't remember it as a major story across commercial news. He also recalls a fairly muted response from the LGBTIQ community about the changes.

One October morning in 2005, Jackie O and Kyle arranged for Jason to come to the studio and deliver a surprise proposal to Geoff, live on air. Geoff accepted but insisted later that the wedding be labelled 'The illegal gay wedding' to emphasise that same-sex couples were not able to marry in Australia.

Geoff remembers that the couple were overwhelmed with support when their ceremony on 25 November 2005 was broadcast on the show and was then replayed across the Austereo network. A Metropolitan Community Church minister had presided. Geoff remembers, 'I'll never forget walking up that aisle with my mum and Jason's grandmother, God rest her soul, she would have been about ninety and she was there'. It was later broadcast live on Seven's *Sunrise*, replayed on the television news that night, and was covered in *New Idea* and the Sunday papers. The two men received more than 20 000 emails of support, which Geoff has kept.

Millions of people listened to Geoff and Jason's wedding on the radio. One of those was Alex, who sat in his office in the Sydney

CBD alone, closed his door, let the phone ring, and listened to every word of the wedding. He remembers thinking, 'these two brave men are sharing this personal moment with the nation and putting themselves out there to make it easier for others'. It was a watershed moment for Alex: while his parents were divorcing, two men in love were 'illegally' getting married. He remembers saying to himself, 'This shouldn't be illegal, I'm going to do something about this'.

During this era, there were shifts in the team at AME. Luke Gahan stepped down as co-convenor after moving to Canada, though he later returned to Australia. Around the end of 2005 or beginning of 2006, Geraldine also stepped down as co-convenor due to health problems. She stayed involved with AME, contributing where she could, for a couple more years and supported the cause by attending rallies. Peter Furness, who had been a founding member of AME, took over the role of national convenor.

In April 2006, Peter Furness married his partner, Theo, in Canada. He let *60 Minutes* film their journey, in a story that was aired on 25 June 2006, allowing more Australians to understand the importance of the reform. The story featured Jim Wallace from the Australian Christian Lobby asserting, 'I think it's very hard to argue that a homosexual lifestyle is not unhealthy and unnatural. It is both'.

While Jim Wallace espoused cruel language, Peter and Theo stood up as everyday Australians who were affected by the lack of marriage equality. Peter pointed out that 'until we have that right, clearly we can't say we're equal Australian citizens'. Luke Gahan, living in Canada at the time, also appeared on the programme to point out the significance of the reform. Once they had returned to Australia, Peter and his husband Theo staged a sit-in at the

Australian Bureau of Statistics (ABS) to draw attention to the fact the census excluded same-sex couples who had married overseas. From 2011, the ABS did count the number of Australians in same-sex relationships who had married overseas.

By August 2006, two years after the Howard ban, public support had grown enough to see the size of rallies increase. The largest attendance reported was in Melbourne, where over 2000 people turned up and fifty-five people took part in a mass commitment ceremony. In Sydney, 1500 people gathered together and around twenty people took part in a mass commitment ceremony. The Perth rally attracted 300 attendees, while 150 people were present at the Adelaide rally. In Hobart and Lismore, around forty people gathered together and Sharon Dane, who would become the third National Convenor of AME, organised a seven-car cavalcade to drive through Brisbane. Participants in the Blue Mountains also staged an action involving commitment ceremonies.

People in positions of leadership in religious organisations were having conversations amongst themselves and were speaking out, explaining that marriage equality was not inconsistent with their faith. The Metropolitan Community Church continued to conduct ceremonies between same-sex partners, though they were not officially recognised as marriages. In December 2005, the Anglican Dean of Perth, John Shepherd, was reported as strongly supporting marriage equality and gay clergy.

A number of other religious leaders were working hard within their faiths to advance the issue. Rabbi Jacqueline Ninio, from the Emanuel Synagogue in Woollahra, was working within Progressive Judaism, advocating to recognise same-sex marriages. In April 2007, the Religious Society of Friends, otherwise known as the Quakers, conducted a same-sex marriage between

Evan Gallagher and David Mills in one of their Canberra meeting houses. While the ceremony was not legally recognised in Australia, the two men were thereafter considered married by Quakers around the world.

In May 2007, the Council of Progressive Rabbis of Asia, Australia and New Zealand made a decision to allow its rabbis to officiate at same-sex commitment ceremonies. LGBTIQ people of faith and their family and friends were also having conversations within their religious communities that helped move marriage equality forward.

Political lobbying in the initial years was very challenging. The federal election of 2004, which John Howard won by a clear majority, made it seem as though marriage equality was off the political agenda. In the early stages of the campaign, it was very difficult to even secure meetings with politicians. Luke remembers, 'I did try but we got a lot of hang-ups'. Geraldine remembers Rodney as being the person who drove political lobbying, remembering he was 'bipartisan' and would have conversations with anyone required to advance the issue.

In December 2005, some supporters of the LGBTIQ community from within Federal Parliament, including Judi Moylan, Mal Washer and Leichhardt Liberal MP Warren Entsch, suggested that civil unions could provide some level of recognition for same-sex couples. Warren Entsch had earlier broken ranks with the Liberal Party in the election campaign of 2004 to oppose the ban on recognising same-sex marriages. In 2006, he appeared on the episode of *60 Minutes* that featured Peter Furness, declaring, 'I see a minority of individuals that are being treated as second-class citizens and I don't think it's fair'. Entsch was not a member of Federal Parliament between 2007 and 2010 but on his return, he continued to advocate for marriage equality until it was finally achieved in 2017.

Advocates within the Labor Party also encountered considerable difficulties in working for change. At the forty-fourth National Labor Conference, held in April 2007, Louise Pratt, at that time a Labor member of the Western Australian Legislative Assembly and a very strong advocate for LGBTIQ rights, raised the issue with then Opposition Leader Kevin Rudd. Louise had already achieved numerous important state wins in Western Australia. Brave, intelligent and deeply connected to the sentiment of the LGBTIQ community she was part of, Louise had been endorsed as a Federal Senate candidate for the forthcoming election. She was friends with Graham and Damien Douglas-Meyer, the couple who had married in Canada and were on the founding phone call that started AME. She had attended a Perth ceremony the two men had shared and supported marriage equality right from the start.

When Louise courageously raised the issue of marriage equality with Kevin Rudd, 'he just shut it, shut it down. But, you know, it was very clear that marriage equality had risen in the popularity polls and it was becoming more viable to do it and that frankly I think our platform should have had room for it at that time'. Penny Sharpe also remembers this stance of Rudd's at the 2007 National Conference and the disappointing outcome being the 'vaguest of nods that we may be able to do civil unions'.

In 2007 though, the party's platform was modified to note that Labor supported the 'development of nationally consistent, state-based relationship recognition legislation' for same-sex couples in line with the scheme that had existed in Tasmania since 2004 but that it would not 'create schemes that mimic marriage or undermine existing laws that define marriage as being between a man and a woman'.[2] Joe de Bruyn, head of the Shop, Distributive and Allied Employees Association, a union with more than 200 000 members, was behind the push for this addition.

A number of crucial voices within the Labor Party, such as Penny Wong, Louise Pratt, grassroots advocates such as Jamie Gardiner, Kate Deverall from Canberra and New South Wales Legislative Councillor Penny Sharpe, worked tirelessly within the party during these very early years to build support and emphasise the significance of marriage equality to the community. Joseph Scales, who would later become a pivotal advocate within the Labor movement himself, notes that Penny Sharpe's long advocacy is often not fully appreciated. She is 'a humble activist, which is a funny way to describe an elected member of parliament. Her public achievements for the LGBTIQ community are well known, but her work behind the scenes within Labor and in fact within other parties, and various parliaments, to progress the issue of marriage equality has been integral'.

As personally difficult as Federal Senator Penny Wong had found Labor's support for discrimination in 2004, she chose to stay and fight for change from within. She later stated, 'I had a choice at that time. I could go out in a blaze of publicity, take a public stand against my party and become an outsider in a pretty dramatic way. I decided to fight this discrimination from within the political system and I chose to stay and accept the solidarity to which I had signed up as a member of a collective political party'.[3]

Growing awareness within Australia about the international movement also helped to build support. Advocates within AME were able to use this to help their cause. In 2005, Canada introduced marriage equality across the entire country, not just in certain provinces. Spain also introduced marriage equality in 2005 and South Africa's parliament legislated same-sex marriage in 2006. As international laws changed, advocates in Australia were able to point out the benefits that flowed from marriage equality.

Civil partnerships also reinforced images of committed and loving LGBTIQ couples, although advocates continued to stress that civil unions were not the same thing as marriage. In 2004, the UK passed the *Civil Partnership Act 2004*, which allowed same-sex couples to obtain the legal benefits that came with marriage. Many Australians with British citizenship took advantage of the opportunity to have their relationships recognised. Importantly, British consulates within Australia allowed couples where one partner was British to have civil ceremonies on their premises. The visibility of these ceremonies on Australian shores only served to reinforce the lack of national recognition available to Australian couples.

In February of 2006, Barbara Yapp and Laraine Jones were reported to be the first couple to undertake such a civil partnership ceremony at the British Consulate in Sydney.[4] In May 2006, Sharon Dane from AME entered a civil partnership with Elaine Crump. When asked by the ABC what she thought of the Federal Government's current attitude, Sharon replied, 'Not much. I guess that's the way to say it without being rude. I'm hoping that it's just a matter of time'.[5]

Between 2004 and 2007, Australians began to think more and more about marriage equality. By entrenching discrimination, John Howard had laid the foundations for a movement that would endure for thirteen more years. The hard work of advocates, the conversations that were happening in families and across communities, increased visibility and international trends all played a part. By 2007, the Australian community had gone on a journey. The difficult challenge would be convincing politicians to reflect the will of the Australian people.

Breaking through

In 2007, quite a few Australians were daring to dream that marriage equality was on the horizon. Political change had come after eleven years and Australia ushered in a new prime minister, Labor's Kevin Rudd. The John Howard era had come to an end. A growing number of Australians were starting to notice the injustice that had been done to the LGBTIQ community and were ready to work hard for change. The Rudd years that followed would continue to present political challenges but the grassroots advocacy never wavered and public support was climbing. On the marriage equality front in that year, political figures who would go on to play long-term roles in the movement also emerged with higher profiles. The Greens' Sarah Hanson-Young and Labor's Louise Pratt were elected to the Australian Senate and both became tireless advocates. Alex joined Australian Marriage Equality (AME) in this year. Tim Wilson, who would later become friends with Alex and go on to win a seat for the Liberals in the House of Representatives, also became a more vocal advocate for marriage equality around this time. Ten years later, Sarah, Louise and Tim were all able to cast their votes in parliament to support the successful marriage equality legislation.

Back in 2005, Alex had been very moved by the publicly broadcast wedding of Geoff Field and Jason Kerr. He says, 'I had thought about the issue of marriage equality long before this, though, even before I came out as a gay man. In 1996, I had been significantly affected when then Prime Minister Paul Keating, whom I admired greatly, said that "two blokes and a cocker-spaniel don't make a family"'. Alex emphasises, 'I had always respected and valued the institution of marriage and to hear the prime minister say that if I was gay, I couldn't marry, kept me in the closet for many years. It wasn't until other countries started to change their laws in the early 2000s to allow marriage equality that I thought something could happen in Australia too'.

Alex remembers 'disliking the fact that there was a law that said people could not do something simply because of their sexuality'. He says, 'the injustice embedded in the 2004 *Marriage Act* motivated me – and I decided in 2007 that I was prepared to take on an active role to fix this'. On a very personal level, Alex remembers, 'I had just started a relationship with Victor Hoeld, the man I would later marry, and my parents had recently finalised their divorce. I remember the many happy times my family had growing up, and feeling a loss of connection to that with my parents' divorce. This made me keen to one day have a long-lasting, happy marriage. Having met the man of my dreams, the only thing that stood in my way was the law'.

As he became more comfortable in his own sexuality, Alex was excited by starting to see media reports about AME's work in the mainstream press. He recognised the name of the national convener, Peter Furness, whose South Sydney Council election campaign he had worked on a few years earlier. Alex reached out to Peter and they had a beer together at the Clock Hotel in Surry Hills. From there, he signed up as a member and worked hard within AME as a volunteer. Shortly after, he assumed a leadership role as the national secretary. Malcolm McPherson, who had been active with AME since 2005, remembers Alex joining as a turning point in the movement:

> I think that Alex's appearance made a dramatic change to AME and how we operated and that certainly gave me hope at that time because I could see that he ... brought something to this that was special.

Alex says, 'I had no idea that I would be there right up until the end but what has sustained me was the people I shared the journey with and the hope that it provided'.

Up in Brisbane in 2007, Shirleene was also starting to pay more and more attention to the issue of marriage equality, though quite separately from the AME group. She remembers, 'I had become more open about my sexuality and was acutely aware that much greater reform was needed on that front and thought perhaps I could play a role. The way I usually advocate for change is through research, so I began a project exploring homophobia in Australia's past. I also became a regular attendee at Equal Love rallies'. They were the most visible group campaigning for marriage equality in Brisbane at this time and were a volunteer initiative, led by Jessica Payne. The group organised regular rallies as a means of drawing attention to the issue. The rallies were crucial to building capacity in these earlier years of the movement – connecting people and allowing them to share ideas and plan actions.

During this period members of the AME team continued to be active – including Sharon Dane, who served as national convenor of the organisation, and her partner and soon to be wife under Canadian law, Elaine Crump. Shirleene had not believed that any change to the 2004 amendments to the *Marriage Act* was likely to happen while John Howard was in power but had paid close attention to the election campaign between Kevin Rudd and John Howard, which began on 14 October 2007.

Shirleene did not realise at that time there was a dedicated group of people working extremely hard within the Labor Party trying to change its position on marriage, including Senator Penny Wong and Senator Louise Pratt in Federal Parliament and Penny Sharpe in the NSW Legislative Council, alongside a number of other critical voices, but that they were not meeting with success. Rudd made the view he had expressed at the 2007 Australian Labor Party (ALP) National Conference public on 23 October, during the course of a radio interview on the *Kyle and Jackie O Show*, when Geoff Field asked him his view on marriage equality. Kevin Rudd declared that marriage 'is between a man and a woman and that's just been our traditional, continuing view'.

Shirleene watched the election results come in on the night of 24 November 2007 with Sarah Midgley, who at that stage she had been dating for around a month and would later marry. Sarah was originally from the Hawkesbury in NSW and had moved to Queensland to pursue her PhD in physics. Both Shirleene and Sarah knew, even in the early stages of dating, that their relationship was something special. Both were big enough fans of politics that a date night spent glued to a federal election special with Antony Green commentating seemed perfect. Despite his disappointing views on marriage equality, Shirleene and Sarah were both hoping that Rudd would win. They believed very strongly that Indigenous Australians were owed an apology for what had happened to them in the past. They were aware of the continuing present disadvantage that had flowed on from this and were impressed that Kevin Rudd had campaigned strongly on the rights of Indigenous Australians. On 13 February 2008, Rudd did deliver an apology to Indigenous Australians, a powerful, long-overdue moment in our nation's history that few will forget. From his comments during the campaign, though, it seemed clear that Rudd was not going to move on the issue of marriage equality.

Shirleene simply could not grasp why Kevin Rudd would not pursue marriage equality. As a result, she and Sarah made efforts to become more connected to LGBTIQ advocates and kept attending rallies together. Shirleene also penned a letter to her federal MP, the Member for Moreton, Labor's Graham Perrett. Graham was very kind in his response and wrote back, arranging to meet Shirleene, Sarah and some marriage equality supporters at a local cafe in Moorooka. When Shirleene and Graham talked in 2018, Graham reflected back on that initial meeting:

> I remember meeting you and that group in the cafe and it's like, yeah, these are just everyday people that I've walked past in the street who are saying, 'What are you doing about this?' If we can take any message from the whole marriage equality campaign, it's don't ever think that those little conversations don't change the world. You know, taking the time to write is what makes changes. That is what changes the world. So thanks for taking the time to write to me.

From that initial contact and realising that Graham was a man of great integrity and decency, Shirleene, Sarah and Graham ended up with a genuine and meaningful friendship that has endured for over a decade.

Shirleene and Sarah did not realise it at the time, but this initial outreach to their local federal MP was the beginning of their shared journey into grassroots community organising. Like many marriage equality activists, they felt drawn to the cause as a way to achieve positive change for the LGBTIQ community in a range of areas but did not anticipate the complex twists and turns that would occur along the journey.

In Sydney, Alex was working hard with the AME team, while also continuing his job in human resources and recruitment. One of the first projects he would pitch to the national organising committee was to reach out to corporate Australia. The aim was to help them to recognise the marriages of LGBTIQ staff who had married overseas. Alex remembers some trepidation from the committee about this idea, with some doubting corporate Australia would care. Alex's experience in working with major banks meant he was convinced that support was out there and could be directed towards tangible goals on the path to full equality.

After much going back and forth with contacts, Alex secured the support of Westpac, the Commonwealth Bank, IBM, Seek and Air Canada. Earlier, Peter Furness, who worked at Qantas, had successfully secured the airline's support. To show Canberra that corporate Australia was coming on board, AME placed a story with the *Sydney Morning Herald* in April of 2008. They ran the headline, 'Big business joins push for same-sex marriage'.

Alex would tell the *Sydney Morning Herald* that: 'These businesses choose to treat all their employees and customers with the same dignity and respect, regardless of their sexuality or gender. As the number of countries which provide same-sex marriage grows, along with the number of Australians entering same-sex marriages, such recognition becomes a valuable tool in attracting employees. What we're really hoping is that the government can see this as a really good sign of the extent of the acceptance out there'. Alex was pleasantly surprised that corporates were also happy to be quoted in the story, especially at a time when it was rare for businesses to comment on controversial political topics. Seek would say, 'We strongly believe that everyone should be treated equally and when we heard about this initiative we were happy for Seek to be involved'. A spokesman for the Commonwealth Bank said, 'The bank does not condone discrimination, harassment or bullying of any sort'.[1] AME's Jay Allen would later continue this work and from 2015, AME's co-chair, Janine Middleton, would increase this list of supporters to nearly 3000.

Meanwhile, over in Adelaide, 25-year-old Sarah Hanson-Young was running as the Greens' lead Senate candidate for South Australia. She had always believed in marriage and her Christian upbringing taught her the importance of treating everyone fairly and lovingly. She tells us:

> I've always had a very strong social justice passion and ever since I was a kid I've always believed that people should be treated equally. I remember going to high school and having gay friends, and just thinking why are these kids being treated differently? Why are they being picked on, they don't deserve to be picked on.

She also saw racism against Aboriginal people, which horrified her and confirmed her passion for change. 'So, I think, I grew up in a small country town and went to a small country high school and it taught me a lot about difference and tolerance.'

Sarah could see that there was a void in political campaigning for marriage equality in the 2007 federal election. With Adelaide's famous 'Feast Festival' coming up, she saw an opportunity to bring attention to the issue. She issued a press release saying, 'Australia has always prided itself on treating people fairly and equally. It's time we made this a reality for all people, regardless of the gender of the person they love. It is disappointing that in 2007, neither of the major political parties support the rights of marriage for same-sex couples'.[2]

Sarah was successfully elected to the Senate in 2007, becoming a senator in 2008. Founder of the Greens Bob Brown told us that at her very first Greens party-room meeting, 'Sarah was specifically wanting to campaign on marriage equality. She was quite specifically pursuing a policy of the Greens being out there on it, not just responding to what was happening but being in front and it made a very big difference and she was relentless on it'. Though neither Bob or Sarah would realise it at the time, Sarah would go on to introduce and sponsor more marriage equality Bills than any member of Australian parliament ever. She was there in the Senate on that day in December 2017 to cast her vote once more, making marriage equality a reality.

Change was also afoot in Western Australia. Louise Pratt, who had earlier raised the issue of marriage equality with Rudd, was elected to the Senate. In her first speech as a senator, she would decisively state that: 'I look forward to a time when we will have removed at a federal level all discrimination on the grounds of gender identity and sexuality'.[3] This was a significant and brave statement from a new senator and over the course of her career, Louise has continued to work hard and courageously to remove discrimination at all levels.

Also in 2007, Tim Wilson would begin taking action advocating for marriage equality. A member of the Liberal Party and consultant for the think tank the Institute of Public Affairs, Tim took his advocacy to the very top, to Prime Minister John Howard, before his defeat by Kevin Rudd. At a Liberal Party function held at the Sofitel in Melbourne he went up to John Howard and said:

> Your government has got the debate on marriage wrong. This is a big deal and actually needs to be supported because it will actually be a good political thing for you to do. And it's also the right thing to do. But, politically, the community has moved and the government is out of step with it.

Tim remembers Howard being very polite and putting forward his arguments for opposing it. Halfway through the conversation, the prime minister's wife, Janette Howard, came over and was more forceful in her opposition. They spoke for about fifteen minutes, with the party faithful waiting for photos and chats with Howard, but this didn't faze Tim, who from that point would spend much of the next decade advocating for marriage equality, particularly within his own party, bringing many from his side of politics with him.

That same year, the Australian Human Rights Commission released a report, *Same Sex: Same Entitlements*, along with an audit of Commonwealth legislation that discriminated against same-sex couples and their families. In 2009, the Rudd Government addressed this and amended eighty-five Commonwealth laws in order to end this discrimination. While this was certainly a significant step forward, unfortunately, marriage rights were not part of this reform.

In 2008, Tim Wilson appeared on the top-rating *Q&A* show alongside Penny Wong and Malcolm Turnbull, when a questioner raised the issue of marriage equality. Tim looks back at this appearance with great pride, reflecting his belief that it was important for a gay man from the Liberal Party to discuss this issue. Tim thought, 'I've just gone way further than most of them are comfortable with, particularly on this issue'.

Importantly, LGBTIQ members of the Liberal Party and their allies could see someone who was out and paving the way for them to take a stand. Tim would get a great deal of feedback from this cohort:

> There was a lot of people who were gay and on the Liberal side
> of politics, that had never seen – and again this is something I
> didn't appreciate at the time – they'd never seen somebody on
> the centre right being publicly out. Now that doesn't mean there
> weren't people, but they'd never seen it, and so comfortable
> with it … I got this huge group of, particularly, younger gay
> men – and some lesbians as well – who were involved in some
> way in politics and they suddenly felt like they had somebody
> they could talk to.

Back in Parliament, following a meeting with Rodney and LGBTIQ advocate Corey Irlam in Canberra, Sarah Hanson-Young would start work on legislation to achieve marriage equality. The following year the 'Marriage Equality Amendment Bill 2009' would be referred to the Senate's legal and constitutional affairs committee. AME would start a campaign encouraging people to share their personal stories and support for marriage equality with the Senate in the hope of encouraging a good outcome. Personal stories included in the AME submission, which was authored by the AME team, included voices from all sections of society. One mother wrote:

> I am a heterosexual woman who is almost 30. I have two
> children who are pre-school aged. I would hope that whether
> they grow up to be homosexual or heterosexual their
> relationships would be seen as equal regardless of the sex or
> gender of their chosen partner. I couldn't look my child in the
> face and tell her that her love was not legitimate.[4]

The importance of family shone through in many submissions. A person who was raised by two mothers wrote:

> I lived with my mum and her same-sex partner from the age
> of ten. I could not have had a better set of parents. They are
> my role models when it comes to how a long-term relationship
> should look, and I hope my husband and I are as happy as they
> when we have been together for 20 years. Yet these women, who
> I love dearly, are denied the opportunity to legally marry. They
> came to my wedding and celebrated with me – yet I cannot
> celebrate the same happy occasion with them. Their union
> is like a marriage in every sense, so why are they denied that
> legitimacy? Why was I denied the legitimacy of my parents
> being married? It is time to end this discrimination.[5]

The call to action for submissions helped AME to interact with more marriage equality supporters than ever before; the membership list swelled to around 700 people in 2009 – a 50 per cent increase on the previous year. There was representation from all states and territories, including metropolitan and regional areas, and around 5000 people subscribed to the group's newsletter. Well-resourced opponents of marriage equality leveraged established networks to also run a campaign to encourage submissions. A number of prominent people and organisations engaged at this time, with South Australian Labor MP Ian Hunter writing in support of Sarah Hanson-Young's Bill, along with Sydney Lord Mayor Clover Moore. Cardinal George Pell would write a submission opposing the Bill. All up the committee would receive 28 000 submissions, with 17 000 opposing the Bill and 11 000 supporting it.[6]

At the same time, support for marriage equality was growing within the Labor Party, ahead of their 2009 National Conference. The issue would be on the agenda thanks to the Tasmanian Labor Party Conference endorsing a motion, but there was also support from Victorian Labor minister Bronwyn Pike, the ACT Labor Government, and Young Labor. In response to the Tasmanian victory, Rodney Croome would say, 'This decision will send a strong message to the upcoming ALP National Conference and the Rudd government to support equality in marriage for same-sex partners. Clearly, the grassroots of the Labor party has heard the message that a majority of Australians support marriage equality for same-sex couples, even if the party's federal leadership is lagging behind'.

Rainbow Labor would work with AME to encourage them to get their supporters to contact conference delegates and urge them to back the motion to support a change in party platform. Rainbow Labor had been agitating behind the scenes, but the Australian Christian Lobby managed to get hold of a copy of the delegate list and started a targeted lobbying effort. AME was then provided with a list of delegates, their names and their phone numbers, and sent this to the LGBTIQ press and their growing supporter list with an urgent call to action. It was a tense and busy period for all. On the ground, a national day of action was held with Equal Love rallies planned across Australian capital cities to coincide with the conference. At the conference venue in Sydney's Darling Harbour, a mass wedding of around eighty couples even took place.[7]

Unfortunately, despite the valiant efforts of Rainbow Labor, their motion would not get up to change the party platform. It had strong opponents, including the former prime minister, Kevin Rudd, who told reporters ahead of the conference that: 'We went to the last election being very clear-cut about our position on marriage under the *Marriage Act* being between a man and a woman'.[8]

Rainbow Labor, however, was encouraged by the words of Anthony Albanese, who said, 'I believe that the issue of equality for all is something that is unstoppable'. Rainbow Labor knew that at the next National Conference they would need to be more organised than ever before and they did this in a way that was outstanding.

In November that year, the multi-partisan committee looking at Sarah Hanson-Young's Bill handed down their report. It recommended that the Bill not be passed, with Sarah being the only member of the committee to write a dissenting report in support of marriage equality. Sarah was unfazed; she knew she was on the right side of history and that supporting marriage equality was the right thing to do. Two days after the report was handed down, Sarah and Alex would finally meet, on 28 November (Alex's birthday) at a marriage equality rally in

Sydney at which they were both speaking. In a testament to the ability to laugh that has sustained advocates over the years of marriage equality activism, Sarah tells Alex she remembers he was wearing very short shorts and that she thought he was very cute. Alex fondly remembers Sarah's smile, tenaciousness and energy. The two would soon cement a very close friendship that endures to this day.

By this point, Alex had taken over from Peter Furness as national convenor of AME. Alex and Sarah would meet to discuss the next moves for marriage equality – the Labor Party motion had been defeated, the inquiry into her Bill had a negative impact, but public support was high with polls indicating around 60 per cent of Australians now supported reform. Alex, with the support of the AME team, and Sarah decided to turn the pressure up. A growing number of MPs said they supported marriage equality but very few were doing anything publicly or declaring how they would vote on a Bill. Legislation had never come to a vote on a marriage equality Bill and Alex and Sarah agreed that it was important to show that it wasn't good enough just to say you supported marriage equality. What mattered was whether you would vote for it. As Sarah said, 'the majority of Australians who supported marriage equality deserved to know where their senators stood'. So Sarah convinced the Greens party room to use the limited time they were allocated for Bills to push for marriage equality.

Alex and Rodney joined a small handful of marriage equality supporters for the debate and the vote, although the Bill didn't pass, with both major parties having binding positions against marriage equality. The result of the vote was five 'yes' votes (all Greens) and forty-five 'no' votes, but the fascinating part was that twenty-six senators abstained including Labor senators Penny Wong and Louise Pratt, and strong LGBTIQ allies in the Liberal Party, Sue Boyce and Simon Birmingham. Alex took this to mean that a number of senators couldn't vote for marriage equality because of their party's position, but didn't want to vote against it. Alex would tell journalists at the time, 'the fact that twenty-six senators were absent from today's debate is an indication that there is dissent in the ranks of the major parties, dissent which we believe will only grow'.[9]

After the vote, the supporters joined Sarah in her office to celebrate the first time the parliament had voted on marriage equality and debrief on what had happened. Sarah was very happy that the number of abstentions gave us something to work with, but she was even more chuffed by comments she received from then Shadow Attorney-General George Brandis. In his capacity as the opposition portfolio holder responsible for this legislation, Senator Brandis would provide a very robust, yet technical, speech in opposition to it. Once he finished it, though, he came over to Sarah. She remembers him thanking her for introducing the Bill and encouraging her to keep going with the cause of marriage equality. Senator Brandis was also one of the twenty-six abstentions, and like Senator Birmingham and Senator Boyce, would never vote against marriage equality.

Despite the Labor Party conference, the Senate report and the Senate vote not supporting marriage equality, the always-positive Alex was satisfied that support was growing. The LGBTIQ community and supporters had definitely started to embrace the issue more actively and were starting to lobby their MPs. Ahead of the next challenges they now needed more money to combat the campaigning of the Australian Christian Lobby, who had greater access and influence in Canberra as well as more funds to spend on campaigns.

On the community front, Mardi Gras floated the idea of a fundraiser for AME as part of their 2010 festival. The dinner was held at Taronga Zoo and attracted members of all major political parties, including the Liberals' Shayne Mallard and Labor's Meredith Burgmann (herself a 78er who attended the first Mardi Gras. Interestingly, her son, Patrick Batchelor, a respected campaigner in his own right, would later be the YES campaign's National Field Director during the 2017 postal survey). International DJ Corey Craig and drag queen Shequida Hall would perform. Alex remembers the vibe of the night as positive, with people feeling hopeful, and that the LGBTIQ community was prepared to get behind and propel marriage equality.

During the course of the evening on 3 March 2009, news was coming through that in the United States, Washington DC had begun issuing marriage licences to same-sex couples, adding to the feeling of possibility in the room. Sarah Hanson-Young attended the event, and it was the first time Alex met Kerryn Phelps and Jackie Stricker-Phelps. A solid friendship between them and the campaign also formed that night. Kerryn would deliver the keynote speech and urged those in attendance to own what opponents were throwing at us and 'be a threat to society as we know it. Because things need to change. It is called standing up for what is fair and just and right. I am asking you now … are you prepared to stand up for your right to choose?' Everyone in the room stood up and delivered a massive round of applause.

For the AME team, this evening was a breakthrough moment. It showed that despite the setbacks of the Labor Party conference, the Senate report and the Senate vote, the resolve of people from across politics, the business community, and LGBTIQ community could not be diminished. It was growing and people were coming together to not only support the work of AME, but also fork out much-needed money to help fund their campaigning. The event raised $10 000 – the most any fundraiser for marriage equality had ever raised by this point. Alex was hopeful that AME would soon stop losing to the ACL and the funds, community support, and momentum would soon help AME become more active, especially ahead of the next federal election.

The power of marriage

From 2009 onwards, Alex became increasingly motivated by what a founder of the global marriage equality movement, Evan Wolfson, called 'the power of marriage'. This was the way the campaign encouraged greater visibility than ever before for LGBTIQ people in the media and popular culture. People could see that same-sex relationships should not be stigmatised and that their love was equal. Marriage was a concept people understood, and one that they would back to support their LGBTIQ friends, family members, workmates and neighbours. The flow-on effects from marriage equality meant that LGBTIQ people would experience a range of benefits and sense of social inclusion far beyond the legal certainty provided by a marriage licence.

The positive momentum that had been building buoyed Australian Marriage Equality (AME), but the group still needed to prove its political relevance. A federal election was expected sometime in 2010, and thanks to the work of Sarah Hanson-Young, the Greens made their position on marriage equality a major point of differentiation in both the Senate and inner-city lower house seats.

Alex, Rodney, and Peter Furness agreed it was time to turn the pressure up on Labor. They argued that AME needed to prove that, unless Labor moved on the issue, they would lose votes and maybe even seats to the Greens. While Liberal seats at this time appeared immune to a Greens challenge, there were definitely target Labor seats that could be vulnerable to an electoral-based campaign focused on marriage equality. With the funds raised from the recent dinner at Taronga Zoo, the team designed and printed pre-election flyers with a photo of Kevin Rudd for distribution in inner-city Labor seats saying:

> Labor politicians will not deliver marriage equality until the electorate forces them to. At this year's election, we need your support to achieve full legal equality for gay and lesbian Australians. Labor doesn't support equality, don't support them.[1]

Peter and Alex each led a small group of volunteers to distribute the flyers across Sydney. Alex was joined by his close friend Elaine Czulkowski, who became a critical part of the campaign till the very end. Elaine was extremely loyal to AME and was motivated by seeing the impacts of inequality while growing up in the United Kingdom and by having many LGBTIQ friends who couldn't marry. At the time, she didn't release the true extent of what she was putting her hand up for. She told us, 'Alex asked me to help out – distribute a few flyers one day – and next thing I know I am organising nationally broadcast events and helping to raise ten million dollars for the YES campaign. When Alex asks for help, be careful!'

The flyers had an immediate impact. The Canberra press gallery could see we weren't just talking, we were taking action. It became clear that Labor was getting nervous. Peter had made sure that flyers were in the mailboxes of people he knew were

ALP members. AME also conducted polling to show it would be a vote-winner for Labor to support marriage equality, but Labor was not happy with the targeting. In response, Peter told journalists, 'Senior Labor figures have told us they will only take marriage equality seriously when they see constituents taking it seriously enough to change their vote. We are now following that advice'.[2]

This was the first time that AME had engaged in any significant field activity. It was small but very targeted and effective. The group was also planning to letterbox the seats of Melbourne and Grayndler but suddenly needed to change the flyers. This wasn't because of the content. It was because the prime minister of the country was about to change.

In June 2010, Julia Gillard mounted a successful leadership challenge against Kevin Rudd and became Australia's first female prime minister. This gave the campaign hope. Gillard was an atheist and had a strong background in social justice. The campaign halted the letterboxing and sought a meeting with Gillard to discuss a way forward for marriage equality. Alex told journalists:

> Although Julia Gillard has previously opposed marriage
> equality, we want an opportunity to appeal to her stated values
> of inclusion, fairness and equality. If Prime Minister Gillard
> can show Labor is open to allowing same-sex couples to marry,
> there is less need for our campaign.[3]

Gillard would follow in Kevin Rudd's footsteps and address the issue in an interview on the *Kyle and Jackie O Show* soon after becoming prime minister. Again, it was gay newsreader Geoff Field who asked the question about her position on marriage equality. On a sad day for LGBTIQ people, their friends, families and supporters, Geoff remembers Australia's first female prime minister telling 2DayFM's million-plus listeners that, 'I have nothing against gay and lesbian people. Some of them are my best friends. But I'm a traditionalist'. Geoff responded with a 'Really?' Gillard continued, 'We believe the *Marriage Act* is appropriate in its current form, that is recognising that marriage is between a man and a woman. But we have as a government taken steps to equalise treatment for gay couples'. Geoff also remembers the response to Gillard's stance being much greater than the public response to Rudd's. The station was inundated with calls in support of marriage equality.

AME responded quickly, saying, 'The sixty per cent of Australians who support same-sex marriage will be deeply disappointed by Julia Gillard's failure to grasp that full equality means marriage equality. But we are still hopeful her position will evolve and remain keen to meet her and put our case for ending discrimination'.[4] Gillard's opposition came as Iceland's prime minister, a lesbian woman, Jóhanna Sigurðardóttir, married her wife. Alex wrote directly to the Icelandic prime minister, asking her to lobby Gillard directly.

Penny Wong remembers of this time, 'Julia's elected and has the position she has. You know, a lot of people had a go at me about that and that was hard'. It is difficult to comprehend how emotionally strenuous this period must have been for Penny Wong, who had spent years working within the internal structures of the Labor Party with others to bring about change. As a minister in the Gillard government, she would have faced expulsion from the party, and lost any political opportunity she had to bring about marriage equality, had she publicly challenged what was then Labor policy. Yet, within the internal structures of the ALP, she was working closely with others to move many to support the issue. The complexities of this were not always apparent to some in the broader community and she had to deal with public blame for the prime minister's stance. Working within for change not seen by the wider community could be hard. She reflects, 'It didn't get me that many friends at times. It's a longer play. It's a longer strategy'. Ultimately, it would be a very important one.

Notwithstanding opposition from Julia Gillard, LGBTIQ activists within the Labor movement and their allies, led by Rainbow Labor, continued to organise within local branches and unions to build support for marriage equality – groundwork which later proved crucial at the 2011 ALP National Conference. They kept in touch with AME about their internal efforts.

AME continued its election campaign and worked closely with News Ltd journalist Claire Connelly, who wrote an article with the headline, 'Gay rights group plan anti-Labor campaign'. The article noted that campaigners were aiming to reach 120 000 homes across the electorates of Grayndler, Sydney and Melbourne.[5] This further frustrated Labor, who were facing a tough battle in the seat of Melbourne against the Greens' Adam Bandt.

Alex remembers receiving 'pissed off' phone calls from people he believed were in the Labor Party, warning him off the campaign. AME found out that Labor had made an official complaint against the flyers to the Australian Electoral Commission.

The campaign and the media attention it attracted worked. There were swings against Labor and to the Greens in all three seats and the Greens won the seat of Melbourne, with analysts attributing marriage equality as a major factor that helped them to pick up that seat.[6] This small, targeted campaign, powered only by a handful of volunteers and a couple of thousand dollars for printing flyers, had proven that people were voting on this issue and that Labor's blanket opposition was a politically untenable position. It showed the power of marriage.

Reflecting on Labor's evolving relationship with marriage equality, Alex and Shirleene hope that history shows that it was the determination and sacrifice of grassroots ALP members and people like Penny Wong, Louise Pratt and Penny Sharpe, who changed their party's position, which would ultimately deliver the bulk of the parliamentary votes for marriage equality.

It wasn't just Gillard's opposition that got attention during the campaign. The position of the Liberal Party was also receiving attention. On an episode of *Q&A*, Opposition Leader Tony Abbott was confronted by a Vietnam War veteran and western Sydney plumber, Geoff Thomas. Geoff's question was:

> I am a Vietnam veteran, I have operated a plumbing
> business for 37 years and I support a liberal philosophy.
> I have a gay son who is a very hard working and decent
> person that I am very proud of. I easily overcame my
> ignorance regarding gay marriage once I gave it a small
> amount of consideration. When will you and the Liberal
> party overcome your ignorance and start treating gay
> people with the respect and dignity that they, like all other
> Australian citizens, deserve?[7]

While Abbott's response wasn't a surprise, as he restated his well-known opposition, the internet and other media went into overdrive, impressed with Geoff's conviction and love for his son. AME's own online presence, which was steadily increasing, covered this, as did Equal Marriage Rights Australia's Facebook group and mainstream media sources. Geoff later joined AME and Parents, Family and Friends of Lesbians and Gays (PFLAG) in directly lobbying MPs and speaking at public forums. He continued to advocate relentlessly for the rights of LGBTIQ people right through until the postal survey and beyond.

Julia Gillard won the election of 21 August 2010, but with Labor as a minority government, requiring the support of the Greens and the Independents. Bob Brown tells us that he did try to include marriage equality as a condition of support, but says that Gillard's opposition to marriage equality was as strong as Abbott's and she wouldn't budge. However, the Greens were able to secure time for debate on marriage equality legislation and Labor would support Adam Bandt's motion calling for MPs to gauge their community's support on marriage equality.

Bandt's motion at the end of 2010 was critical in providing AME the platform it needed to really engage on the ground in key electorates to demonstrate support. Along with Queensland mother and PFLAG leader Shelley Argent, Rodney Croome, Daniel Witthaus, and on occasion Geoff Thomas, Alex travelled the country running forums and workshops on how to lobby your MP and share your personal story.

This campaigning led to a number of MPs and senators canvassing support and ultimately declaring their hand. Labor Senator Doug Cameron was one of the first to publicly back marriage equality and urge the Labor Party to take a stronger stance to 'allow Labor to reconnect with progressive Australians'.[8] He also argued that party discipline should be loosened to allow greater debate. He was soon followed by Senator Mark Arbib from Labor's right faction who said, 'If I was the parent of a gay son or daughter I don't know how I could tell them they didn't have the same rights as I did'.[9] Bill Shorten declared his support on *Q&A*. Queensland Premier Anna Bligh then became the first Australian premier to declare her support, saying, 'If people love each other and they build lives together and they want that recognised, I think that's perfectly reasonable'.[10] Support was also growing on the Coalition side with Senator Simon Birmingham and Mal Washer also backing reform in 2010. Long-time advocate Warren Entsch continued to emphasise his support.[11]

In response, the Catholic Church started aggressively campaigning against marriage equality, with the Sydney Archdiocese writing to all parishioners warning that 'the Greens continue their assault on the culture of life ... every Catholic should let federal legislators know that marriage and family, the cornerstone of society, must be protected at all costs'.[12]

Member for Wentworth Malcom Turnbull surveyed his electorate in early 2011 and found that nearly 72 per cent of the 4000 constituents he canvassed supported marriage equality. Despite having powerful opponents, AME was breaking through to both major parties and supporters were becoming very experienced and organised in their lobbying efforts, both in Canberra and their local communities.

Also in 2011, after lobbying from AME, the Australian Bureau of Statistics counted same-sex married couples in the national census for the first time. This basic recognition had not been easily obtained. Peter Furness and Alex had lobbied the ABS to include it, and even threatened an LGBTIQ boycott of the census if they didn't, arguing, 'If you want the LGBTI community to fully engage in the process, you need to fully recognise their relationship status in your statistics'.[13] AME ran a very successful campaign called

'Be Counted', encouraging and showing same-sex couples who had married overseas how to ensure their relationship status was counted. The statistics would come out at a critical time two years later, showing at least 1300 people had married overseas.

The LGBTIQ community was galvanising behind the marriage equality campaign, and AME, despite being solely volunteer-led and run, was punching well above its weight, becoming a nationally significant organisation. In early 2011, the work of AME was gaining attention. Geoff Field remembers being relieved by seeing a campaign that was very organised: 'Things really started to happen, there were fundraising dinners, lots of lobbying of MPs, a strong media profile and I felt like wow. There's something going on here. Change is really happening and people are really determined to see change'. Sarah Hanson-Young could also see the pressure mounting, telling us, 'Australian Marriage Equality was everywhere they needed to be, building relationships and getting things done'.

Alex would soon meet Tim Wilson for the first time at the SameSame '25 most influential LGBTI Australians' event. Both had observed and respected each other's work and that evening developed the foundations of a strong friendship that helped them get through some extremely tough times in the campaign together. Tim travelled all the way to Argentina to attend Alex's wedding to Victor Hoeld in 2012, and Alex was Tim's witness and signatory on his marriage certificate to Ryan Bolger in 2018. Tim was criticised by the LGBTIQ community at various times but Alex notes that he has always respected his honesty and consistency: 'People didn't always like what Tim had to say, but he was always honest, direct, and accurate when talking about advancing marriage equality in the Liberal Party'.

GetUp! had also decided to enter the marriage equality campaign in a big way. They had previously released the first poll that showed majority support for marriage equality in 2007 and consistently encouraged their members to lobby MPs on the issue, but now, with a lot of momentum building, their national director Simon Sheikh was keen to have a bigger impact. He had built a strong working relationship with AME, and on Valentine's Day 2011 both groups launched a national television campaign featuring twins David and Paul, one gay and one straight, to show the unfairness of the discrimination in the *Marriage Act* and how it was affecting families.

At the launch of the advertisement, Simon told journalists, 'During the federal election, it became evident that marriage equality was an issue Australians cared about despite the major parties' failure to address it. Our politicians are elected to lead, but are far behind the public on this – it's time they step up to the plate and support equality and fairness for all couples'.[14] Alex added, 'David and Paul remind us that gay and straight Australians lead the same lives, form the same loving relationships, belong to the same families and communities – that sexual orientation is the least important difference between us. It's time for our politicians to recognise this fact by removing the discrimination and exclusion entrenched in the *Marriage Act*. It's time to reinforce the values of love and commitment that underlie marriage by allowing all loving, committed couples to marry'.[15] GetUp! continued to be a significant ally throughout the marriage equality movement, appointing a permanent marriage equality campaigner in Sally Rugg for the final few years of the campaign.

Alex remembers the first half of 2011 as one of the most exciting and rewarding times of his involvement with AME. The team was down in Canberra every sitting week bringing delegations of parents, priests, and psychologists to meet with MPs and senators and could see the numbers growing in support. AME had developed a strong media profile. There were marriage equality television ads, and the LGBTIQ community was celebrating the progress at events across the country and through social media.

The biggest celebration was the 2011 Mardi Gras Parade, in which AME entered their first ever Mardi Gras parade float. Elaine spearheaded organising the float and remembers her brother-in-law and a small team of volunteers dressing a truck in the loading dock of her apartment building: 'It was a lot of work, but worth it when you saw the amazingly warm response we would receive the whole way down Oxford Street, and seeing the joy in the couples and families who had travelled from all over the country to join our parade entry'. Senator Sarah Hanson-Young, Geoff Field, and Geoff Thomas with Kerryn Phelps and Jackie Stricker-Phelps joined the AME float. The tradition of marching in the parade continued until after marriage equality was achieved, with advocates, couples and supportive politicians from across Australia being part of it over the years.

Another big celebration would happen a few months later in Federal Parliament, at the annual Midwinter Ball, held by the Federal Parliamentary Press Gallery as a charity event bringing together politicians, journalists and business leaders. Simon from GetUp! called Alex and suggested that they bid for 'Dinner for six with the prime minister', an item at the ball's auction. The funds raised would go to charities that helped children and cancer patients. The PM had not met with LGBTIQ advocates at this stage and had been avoiding the issue of marriage equality when it was increasingly becoming a hot political and community issue. GetUp! and AME needed a couple to be the face of the campaign to bid for the dinner. Alex had met two mums who would be perfect, Sandy Miller and Louise Bucke, at a marriage equality workshop in Newtown. They really impressed him as 'passionate, articulate, and they had the smartest and nicest kids I had ever met'. Sandy quoted her youngest son:

> Our youngest often asks us, 'Mummies are you going to be engaged forever? Why don't you get married?' It has been hard trying to explain that our government won't let us get married and he doesn't understand why everyone else can get married and become a family legally and we can't.[16]

GetUP! and AME pushed hard for crowdfunding through their respective databases and social media platforms. The LGBTIQ community was very keen to win the dinner and the LGBTIQ press backed the campaign. In addition, AME also bid on dinner with the three Independents who held the balance of power.

The Labor Party was getting concerned. It wasn't a good look that an NGO which had the majority of Australians on its side had to bid at an auction to meet the prime minister. Alex received a call from someone believed to be close to the prime minister telling him to drop out. He remembers, 'I was told it was embarrassing the prime minister and wouldn't end well for us, I was also told that we weren't going to win the dinner so we were wasting our time and our supporters' money. Interestingly, the person who called thought it was a great idea we were bidding for dinner with the Independents'. Alex's immediate reaction was to call Simon and suggest that they increase the amount they were prepared to bid to secure their dinner date.

They were ahead of the bidding with an hour to go at $20 000, and Simon and Alex had agreed to go up to a $32 000 reserve; using eBay's automated bidding tool, this meant they would automatically outbid anyone who bid under that number. With ten seconds to go in the bidding process, someone else made a bid for $30 000, but the automated bidding tool ensured we bettered that. AME had a dinner date! Or two, as we would also secure dinner with the Independents.

Alex was never sure whether the prime minister was aware of the call he received, but he remembers that, although it was frustrating, it strengthened their resolve to win the bid. He notes, 'When people tell you not to do something because it's embarrassing to them, it usually means what you are doing is actually working. This call was an own-goal tip-off that helped us ensure we would win the dinner'.

Gillard delayed, avoiding the dinner for another six months. When the dinner was finally held, she would indicate her belief that marriage equality was inevitable. Alex reflects on this. 'She was essentially saying, "It's going to happen but not on my watch".'

Gillard could not avoid the issue indefinitely though, with Labor's National conference happening later that year and Rainbow Labor getting more active and organised than ever before to pursue the issue internally. A three-way battle was flagged at the conference, with the potential options being: no change to the platform, a change to the platform with a conscience vote, or a change to bind federal members in support.

The stakes were high. If Labor did bind in support (as they did on most issues) there was a chance marriage equality could be delivered under the Gillard Government. With Rob Oakeshott likely to support and Andrew Wilkie prepared to co-sponsor a

Bill, only one vote from the Liberal Party was required to offset Tony Windsor's opposition. To secure that vote in case Labor did bind, Alex did what he had been urging all marriage equality supporters to do, and met with his local member, Malcolm Turnbull.

Over green tea in Turnbull's Edgecliff electoral office, Alex took him through the various scenarios and possible outcomes of the Labor conference, including that one vote might potentially be needed from the Coalition to secure victory. Alex remembers Turnbull telling him that he would seriously consider crossing the floor if that scenario presented itself, but given the risk, could only ever do so if that vote was what it took to get marriage through.

Gillard was feeling the pressure of a growing internal Labor campaign and external AME campaign. We again joined forces with GetUp! for a video to highlight the growing support for marriage equality. Produced by much-loved Sydney DJ Dan Murphy, the video shot in Sydney's Town Hall had people from the community, and well-known personalities, representing the various demographics of majority support for marriage equality.

The ad starred Jason Kerr and Geoff Field, journalist Mia Freedman representing parents with young children, Julie McCrossin representing Christians, YouTube star Natalie Tran representing young Australians, gay farmer Dave Graham of *Big Brother* fame representing rural and regional supporters, and also featured Carl Katter, the gay brother of Bob Katter, and Geoff Thomas with his son Nathan. The video was a beautiful representation of the growing support for marriage equality across all walks of life and was viewed hundreds of thousands of times online and broadcast on national television shows.[17]

Alex and Rodney remained a regular fixture in Federal Parliament, often working out of Sarah Hanson-Young's office.

They continued to build strong relationships of trust across the parliament, including amongst Labor MPs and senators who were keen for a binding vote on marriage equality. They had been tipped off that Gillard was about to pre-empt the conference outcome by saying she would support a conscience vote on the matter. Concerned that this would stymie the progress towards a binding position, the person who tipped them off was prepared to share this information anonymously with media, and LGBTIQ publication the *Star Observer* reported:

> A senior Federal ALP source has told the *Star Observer* that Prime Minister Julia Gillard is planning to announce she will allow a conscience vote on same-sex marriage in an effort to short-circuit debate at the ALP National Conference in Sydney in December.[18]

The debate would still occur but the source said Gillard believed that pre-empting the outcome would take the wind out of the sails of any decision made by the conference.

The source said Gillard knew she didn't have the votes at the conference to prevent marriage equality from being added to the ALP national platform, which would put her at odds with her own party on the issue. The source was also concerned that having an issue like same-sex marriage decided by a conscience vote would set a bad political precedent, as conscience votes were usually reserved for life or death issues like abortion or therapeutic cloning, whereas marriage equality was an issue of policy. The story was then picked up by national media, with respected columnist Peter van Onselen writing: 'If any advocates within Labor think a conscience vote on gay marriage is a win on this issue they have got another thing coming. If the Liberal Party impose party discipline to block a parliamentary motion, that's the end of it'.[19]

Not soon after the information was leaked, Gillard did indeed come out saying there should be a conscience vote. Her office called Alex to give him the heads-up and ask him to 'welcome' the good news and suggest it showed progress, as she had previously opposed a free vote. Alex remembers responding with 'This isn't good news, but will only further motivate those in Labor who want a binding vote in support of marriage equality'. Alex wrote an opinion piece for News Ltd with the headline 'Gillard giving in on gay marriage'. He wrote:

> For the Prime Minister to make such a conscience vote announcement before the ALP National Conference in December would be the best indication yet that the adoption of a policy in favour of marriage equality at that Conference is a not only possible but likely. By laying out the conscience vote option now, and by associating it with her opposition to equality, the PM will give marriage equality supporters the time and ammunition they need to shoot down a conscience vote and focus Labor on what really needs to be debated in December, a binding marriage equality policy. Since I started marriage equality campaigning I have never seen the kind of strong resolve within the Labor Party to deliver marriage equality as there is now.[20]

That resolve was about to be put to the test on the floor of the ALP conference.

Rainbow warriors

In 2011, the opportunity to change the national platform of the Australian Labor Party (ALP) to include marriage equality and to address the issue of either allowing members a conscience vote or binding to vote as a bloc in favour of marriage equality were both on the agenda. Advocates within the party had been working hard since 2009 – and even earlier – to address this. In the last chapter, we set out the challenges marriage equality advocates encountered when Julia Gillard was prime minister. But it is also important to acknowledge those within the ALP and the union movement who helped move the party to a position where marriage equality became part of the ALP platform. From the moment this happened, marriage equality became much more achievable. Without the efforts of rainbow warriors and their allies, the 2017 victory would not have been possible.

The challenges of 2011 were many. There were members within the ALP who were opposed to the change – most notably right-wing powerbroker Joe de Bruyn of the Shop, Distributive and Allied Employees Association (SDA) and Prime Minister Julia Gillard, who had publicly reaffirmed her opposition to changing Howard's 2004 amendments to the *Marriage Act*. There were also activists from outside the party who put those within Rainbow Labor under enormous pressure to achieve both a change to the national platform and a binding vote. While Rainbow Labor would have loved this, the chances of this kind of win were not promising.

Labor MP Terri Butler, who had always supported the marriage equality movement within the ALP and in 2016 would become the Shadow Minister for Equality, remembers, 'You could see that the groundswell of opinion was shifting towards marriage equality, even though it did seem at the 2009 National Conference so out of reach'. She adds, 'so when we had the movement towards 2011, that was a really big deal. It wasn't easy'.

It was clear that change was afoot. Rainbow Labor had been organising energetically ever since the last National Conference. Sean Leader, a grassroots member from Queensland, and the Australian Services Union's Joseph Scales from South Australia were both going to the National Conference in Sydney in 2011, hoping to make history. They would both continue their commitment to and involvement in the marriage equality campaign. Sean remained dedicated to advancing it within Queensland, winning the admiration of many from his party and community. Joseph Scales, only twenty-two years old in 2011, also continued his advocacy. In 2017, he brought that experience with him when he volunteered at the Sydney postal survey headquarters, becoming a senior and vital element of the campaign's success.

In 2011, Rainbow Labor went in fully prepared, determined and organised as never before. They were also organised across right and left factions. Some politicians were unstinting in their support. There was Louise Pratt, who had courageously mentioned the removal of discrimination on the grounds of gender and sexuality as a goal in her maiden speech in the Senate back in 2008. She opened up her office and made it 'Rainbow Labor Central'.

Other experienced political leaders, including Ian Hunter, Penny Wong and Andrew Barr, also gave their time and energy – and political capital. Joseph Scales acknowledges the respect that federal parliamentarians such as Louise Pratt and Penny Wong have engendered through their efforts over many years. 'Penny Wong and Louise Pratt are celebrated by Labor and by many in the LGBTIQ community because they have been champions and they've put themselves on the line and they've worked within.'

Penny Sharpe, member of the NSW Legislative Council, who had been advocating and organising for so long, was also in attendance. Joseph Scales points that out her lengthy and critical role deserves recognition:

> The LGBTIQ community will never know the depths to
> which Penny Sharpe has gone for us. Whether it is young,
> closeted staffers who slip into her parliamentary office for some
> advice on coming out to their boss; or a community leader who
> needs help to understand how to lobby effectively any number
> of political parties; or navigating through the complex web of
> Labor's decision making, she was always there, at the end of the
> phone, not inserting herself but doing whatever she could to
> make sure that LGBTIQ rights prevailed.

In the lead-up to the conference, Penny Sharpe remembers, 'We really worked on the basis we are going to have to go full tilt and change the platform in favour of marriage equality. And so that was a huge campaign in the lead-up to that conference, which was incredibly successful'.

It is also important to acknowledge people from the union, staffer and grassroots levels who have moved change. Sean

Leader and Joseph Scales have shared their journeys with us here. But they are both quick to point out the roles of so many others, including Sally McManus, who later became the first female ACTU secretary; Kate Deverall; Feyi Akindoyeni; Steve Michelson; Steve Staikos; Stephen Dawson; Robbie Moore; Nick Thompson; Jamie Gardiner; Matt Loader; and Thomas Mooney, who have made immense contributions.

Sean Leader remembers that advocates within Rainbow Labor made sure that they called up every delegate and proxy delegate they knew was attending the National Conference and sent out a series of postcards and information packs. No delegate would go to the National Conference unaware of why marriage equality mattered. He describes 'going and talking to people and getting every vote, one at a time'. Rainbow Labor kept a meticulous spreadsheet of delegate positions and it was updated right up to the National Conference, and even while the conference was occurring in December 2011.

As mentioned earlier, momentum for change within Labor was enhanced not only by activity from Rainbow Labor but also by voices within parliament and from unions who spoke out in favour of marriage equality. What was truly impressive was that the issue cut across the left and right factions. Members of the right such as staffer Steve Michelson; Neil Pharaoh, national co-convenor of Rainbow Labor with Sean Leader; Gillard's former chief of staff Amanda Lampe; and Steve Staikos, founding co-convenor of Rainbow Labor Victoria, were critical in moving parts of that half of the party onside in 2011. Having the support of the ALP's national president, Anna Bligh, also the premier of Queensland, made a powerful statement. The trade union movement also showed that it was prepared to back the change, with many voices on the left, as well as powerful voices from the right such as Paul Howes from the Australian Workers Union and Tony Sheldon from the Transport Workers Union, declaring support.

Crucially, over the past year, as the National Conference approached, state Labor conferences were passing motions endorsing marriage equality in South Australia, Queensland, Victoria, Western Australia, Tasmania, the Northern Territory and the ACT. At the New South Wales conference, delegates voted to refer the matter to the National Conference. Penny Sharpe remembers, 'We ran what I consider to be a really good campaign where we passed motions through state conferences. All of our state groups basically lobbied and got change. We came together and got a form of words [that could be moved as motions through the various state conferences]'. Sean Leader knew that the country was paying attention when the New South Wales decision was reported in the media as being out of step with the momentum built across the other states and territories. New South Wales had actually not even said no to changing the national platform, they had just deferred the question onwards to the National Conference.

The 2010 South Australian state conference was significant for a number of reasons. First, the conference endorsed changing the platform to include marriage equality and that resolution formed the basis for motions in conferences across the country.

Secondly, the person who seconded the motion to include marriage equality had not been on the draft running sheet. However, after advocate Matt Loader moved it, it was delegate Penny Wong who stood up, on 27 November 2010, to speak in favour of a motion calling on the ALP National Conference to support the legal rights of all couples to be married, regardless of their gender.

In her powerful speech, Penny Wong told delegates she had been pushing for Labor to change its platform. She asserted:

> I believe the ALP National Conference should change our
> platform and I will be advocating with many people for that
> change. I will be advocating for our party to support equality
> including in relation to marriage for same-sex couples. And
> I do so because I have a deeply held commitment to equality
> as many in this room do too. A principle in which our party
> believes, and a principle on which our party has delivered.
>
> Delegates, I came to this country in the 1970s and like many in
> this room I do know what it's like to be the subject of prejudice.
> Like many in this room, my personal politics have been cast
> by the experience of discrimination and a deep belief in the
> principle of fairness.

She ended her speech by stating:

> Delegates, there are some who say this Convention should
> not express a view. Well I say this: this branch, this state was
> the first state in this nation to decriminalise homosexuality.
> Why would we now resile from expressing our view, our
> support for the principle of equality here today? I commend
> the motion to the floor.[1]

Joseph Scales remembers this speech as truly remarkable and feels enormously privileged that he was there to see it. 'I try and not be

emotional thinking about it, it was such an amazing moment.'
He continues:

> Suddenly there was no more talking in the room because
> up until this point Penny had never spoken publicly about
> her support for marriage equality, because she'd always said,
> 'I support the Party position and if I have anything to say
> about that, I'll do that through the Party', and so she did.
> And she stood up and gave an extraordinary speech.

While momentum was increasing, Sean Leader and the other
co-convenor of Rainbow Labor, Neil Pharaoh, were finding it difficult to meet with Julia Gillard to discuss marriage equality, even
though they had spent twelve months trying. As the National
Conference grew closer, finally they received a telephone call and
were offered the opportunity to meet. Sean remembers Rainbow
Labor decided it would be most effective to send in two advocates
from within the parliamentary system. Penny Wong from Labor's
left and Andrew Barr from Labor's right would be ideal. After
this pairing was suggested though, Rainbow Labor struggled to
secure a meeting date from Gillard's office.

In the lead-up to the National Conference, just about the entire
Rainbow Labor national leadership met in Andrew Barr's office.
He was deputy chief minister for the ACT at the time. Louise Pratt
was also there, as were Ian Hunter, Penny Sharpe and a number
of other LGBTIQ parliamentarians – themselves a reflection of
Rainbow Labor's success in building support for the community
in the ALP, including through preselection. Grassroots rainbow
activists, young and old, were also there, keen to be involved and
to contribute. There were probably about a dozen committed

advocates there together. Sean Leader's determined advocacy was conducted under extremely difficult personal circumstances. On the cusp of the conference he had found out that his father had stage four cancer. But, after his father, who understood just what it meant to him, told him, 'I love you. I'll still be here. Go and do this', Sean prepared to go to the conference.

On 2 December 2011, journalist Lenore Taylor reported that as delegates arrived in Sydney on Thursday night for the National Conference, Julia Gillard was meeting with Joe de Bruyn, who was fiercely opposed to any platform change. One insider tells us that Gillard did not know the numbers were there for the platform change until the night before, Wednesday. In her meeting with de Bruyn on Thursday, she told him she would allow a free vote on changing the platform. It was less clear if the numbers were there to move to a binding vote on marriage equality. Sean emphasises, 'We were looking at binding' but advocates did not know the exact numbers from either New South Wales or from Victoria. Lenore Taylor paid tribute to the incredible efforts of those within Rainbow Labor and their allies for the outstanding work they had done to bring the issue this far. She reported that while a platform change would succeed, a conscience vote was the likely outcome.

That did not stop determined advocates from working hard to get every vote they could. They were joined by some unexpected allies. Sean Leader pays tribute to Tony McGrady, the former Queensland state member for Mt Isa, who for a long time had not appreciated Labor's outreach efforts to the LGBTIQ community. Yet, on the night before the marriage issue was going to come to a vote, Tony went to the hotel where Rainbow Labor was holding a social function. He told the group he supported them and that he was going to speak with the Australian Workers Union delegates in the National Right caucus room, where he was going to try and get every vote he possibly could for them. This reinforced to Sean that 'there is no one we can't talk to in the end'.

In her report, the day before the vote, Lenore Taylor noted that some would be bitterly disappointed with a conscience vote, rather than a binding vote. Yet advocates had succeeded in changing the party platform and they had opened up the space for Labor advocates to vote in support of marriage equality in parliament. Lenore Taylor wrote that Rainbow Labor and others within the party:

> spent two years talking and arguing and meeting and persuading. And it worked. The lesson from the conference is that people do mobilise behind issues they care about and they do get involved when they can have a say. And for the party and its established power structures, that can take a bit of getting used to.[2]

As was reported, Andrew Barr and Penny Wong moved a motion the next day, referred to forever after as the 'Barr-Wong Amendment', that said, 'Labor will amend the *Marriage Act* to ensure equal access to marriage under statute for all adult couples irrespective of sex who have a mutual commitment to a shared life'. Further, it added that the amendment should ensure nothing in the *Marriage Act* would impose an obligation on a minister of religion to solemnise any marriage, quoting Section 47 of the *Marriage Act*. The vote to the party platform was carried on the voices (that is, clear support meant there was no need to count the numbers). Penny Wong remembers 'being quite emotional' at this major and hard-fought achievement. She points out that 'it's a big thing to take on the prime minister, a sitting Labor prime minister, and a lot of activists don't understand historically how big a thing that is, for a Labor conference to not do what the Labor prime minister wants'.

The conscience vote issue, which had the backing of Julia Gillard, passed 208 to 184 votes. This was closer than many had anticipated. On reflection, there are many within the Labor Party and union movements who believe that the ALP only avoided a binding vote because the leadership of the prime minister was so tightly associated with the conscience vote issue. Amending the party platform was an enormous achievement and it is one that deserves to be celebrated. Penny Sharpe points out the broader importance of this change:

> My view very much is that the timing for marriage equality in
> Australia accelerated the minute the Labor Party signed up to
> this. The minute that a major party that could form government
> did, it was a huge win. And it was a massive campaign. And it
> was one of the best things I have ever worked on in terms of
> just working with really great people with shared values and
> fighting a really hard fight but winning and winning well and
> knowing that change has made a real difference to what you're
> trying to win. So it was really, really good.

Joseph Scales reflects on being there to see this historic achievement:

> It was a very special day. That wouldn't have happened without
> sub-branches who are the rank and file of the Labor Party

and more progressive than the parliamentary caucus. Many of them aren't factionalised, they're just good Labor people and this is what they fought for over a long time and now the Party reflected it.

In her speech in 2017, when the Act that would finally bring about marriage equality was being debated, Terri Butler paid special tribute to Rainbow Labor, grassroots members of the party and to Sean Leader:

> I remember, just over six years ago, our National Conference, where Sean, despite having some terrible things going at home with family members' health, still made it all the way to the conference, went to Sydney and argued for us to change our platform. It's because of the work of people like him, hundreds of rank and file members of the Labor Party, and the leadership of members of parliament that the platform was duly changed.[3]

For Penny Wong, who had worked so hard since 2004 within the internal structures of the ALP to bring about change, often while being publicly criticised by some in the community who did not see the difficult work that she was doing, it was liberating to finally be able to publicly advocate for marriage equality and to vote for it in parliament. She emphasises, 'It was a bloody relief'. She adds:

> because, you know, it's a ridiculous position we were all being put in. It was just ridiculous. Not just me personally voting for your own discrimination, but most people didn't agree with the position. It was the wrong thing for the party and it was personally corrosive to continue to have to argue that position,

so it was a relief when we changed. And I suspect a lot of
Labor people might say that because I think a lot of people had
shifted before the party shifted formally.

In the immediate wash up of the vote, advocates got to work on
deciding on how a Bill might proceed. They decided it would be
best coming from someone from the regions, someone heterosexual and someone who was a person of faith. Stephen Jones,
Member for Throsby in the Illawarra region, was willing to do
this and put forward the 2012 Bill.

In the aftermath of the conference, in the biggest rally to take
place outside an ALP conference, around 10 000 marriage equality
supporters from across the community marched from Hyde Park
North to the Sydney Convention and Exhibition Centre in Darling
Harbour. At Hyde Park, Aboriginal academic Larissa Behrendt
provided an acknowledgment of country, while a range of other
speakers, including Sydney's lord mayor, Clover Moore; activist
Norrie May-Welby; and Peter Urmson, the chair of Sydney's Gay
and Lesbian Mardi Gras, made it clear the nation was watching
the ALP conference and hoping for a favourable outcome.

At Darling Harbour, Ali Hogg from Equal Love in Melbourne,
Kerryn Phelps, Shelley Argent and Alex all spoke. From the
union movement, Sally McManus from the ASU spoke, as did
Labor's Mark Butler and Louise Pratt. Cat Rose and Ben Cooper
from Community Action Against Homophobia closed the event.
Louise Pratt remembers being struck by the size of the crowd. 'So
we came out and celebrated the great win we'd had in winning
the change in platform ... there's no doubt what a turning point
that conference decision was in terms of setting us on the path of
getting it done.'

Weddings on Australian soil

Marriage equality supporters entered 2012 feeling there was some momentum behind them. Advocates within the ALP had achieved a significant win when the party adopted the issue within the national platform at the end of 2011. While a conscience vote was not the outcome some had hoped for, it still meant that federal Labor politicians were, for the first time, free to vote and advocate for marriage equality.

Australian Marriage Equality (AME) started the year intending to keep public attention on the issue. In 2012, with GetUp!, the group sent 3000 red roses to parliament for Valentine's Day. Alex, along with GetUp!'s Simon Sheikh, would push a trolley full of roses to Prime Minister Julia Gillard's office. Later that morning in an office filled with roses, Alex told the prime minister's advisors that Magda Szubanski was planning to come out later that day, and that she was doing this to support marriage equality. Alex remembers the moment well. 'By the looks on their faces, they knew this was going to have a massive impact.' Alex also told Greens leader Bob Brown, who said, 'Tell Magda, welcome to the club!'

In 2012, various Bills for marriage equality were drafted with votes likely in the House and Senate towards the end of the year. One of those Bills was from Sarah Hanson-Young, who knew more work needed to be done and more voices needed to be heard before any votes went ahead. Alex and Sarah devised a plan where Sarah's Bill would be referred to another committee, one with a membership that supported marriage equality, and AME would campaign to make sure this time they had more submissions, both in terms of quantity and quality, than their opponents. Alex remembers the only problem was that Labor wasn't keen on the idea, as they were determined to deal with the matter inhouse. This meant Sarah needed the support of the Coalition to establish an inquiry, which the resourceful young senator succeeded in securing, thanks to senator Simon Birmingham. On the first sitting day of 2012, the Bill was referred to the Senate's Legal and Constitutional Affairs committee.[1]

The Senate Inquiry was critical for two reasons. First, it showed that supporters of marriage equality were turning their support into political action and breaking records: the inquiry received an unprecedented number of submissions, totalling approximately 79 200. A majority of approximately 46 400 submissions supported the Bill, and approximately 32 800 submissions were opposed.[2] Secondly, it provided Liberal senators Simon Birmingham and Sue Boyce with a platform to support marriage equality, and deliver a majority report doing so.[3]

A second inquiry would be conducted by the House of Representatives Standing Committee on Social Policy and Legal Affairs, which tabled its advisory report on 18 June. It received a record-breaking number of submissions and a majority were in favour, just as they had been for the Senate Inquiry. The House of Representatives Inquiry received 276 000 responses. Rodney and Alex gave evidence to the inquiry. The committee chair, Labor's Graham Perrett, told the *Sydney Morning Herald* that, 'Australians have been ahead of the world in removing many forms of discrimination. It's indefensible and unjust that two people who love each other are unable to marry each other because of their sexual orientation'.[4] In an act of kindness, he sent a copy of the report to Shirleene and Sarah, always keeping his commitment to update them on progress for marriage equality.

Both the positive Senate and House of Representatives reports were significant. They showed that in just three years after the issue lost a vote and had negative inquiry reports, AME with its small team of volunteers had outplayed the Australian Christian Lobby by raising the volume of supporters' voices to a level that parliament could no longer ignore.

There were also a number of important victories in states and territories during this time. The Tasmanian Lower House passed a motion in support of marriage equality, along with the Australian Capital Territory (ACT) Assembly, and in the New South Wales Parliament, a motion from the Greens' Cate Faehrmann passed, with the support of members of the Liberal and National parties. This was the first time Coalition MPs had voted for marriage equality in an Australian parliament. The Nationals' Upper House MP, Trevor Khan, would write for the *Australian* newspaper, urging the Coalition to embrace marriage equality, saying, 'The conservative course is not to banish gay people from such commitments. It is to expect that they make such commitments'.[5]

Another important voice from the conservative side of politics emerged in April 2012, when the *Australian* newspaper revealed that Christine Forster, the sister of Tony Abbott, had fallen in love with another woman and the two had been together for the past four years.[6] Alex remembers this well. 'Christine and her now wife Virginia really put themselves out there, and proved this was an issue that affected every family in Australia. Their contribution to the marriage equality movement was immeasurable, and would have been extremely tough at times.'

International developments at this time helped to keep hope alive. On 9 May 2012, then United States President Barack Obama spoke out publicly in support of marriage equality. New Zealand Prime Minister John Key, who had initially been opposed to marriage equality, soon followed and expressed his support. New Zealand has a system where MPs can lodge a proposed Bill through a ballot system. Numbered tokens are drawn from a container, with one token drawn for each available place.

On 14 May 2012, Louisa Wall, an openly lesbian New Zealand Labour Party MP, stated she would introduce a private member's Bill to allow couples of any sex to marry. On 26 July 2012, a ballot draw of five members' Bills saw her Marriage (Definition of Marriage) Amendment Bill drawn and introduced. It passed its third reading seventy-seven votes to forty-four. In the immediate aftermath of this, the gallery applauded, cheered, and then started singing, 'Pokarekare Ana', a beautiful Māori love song. The touching moment was beamed around the world, moving so many.

The Bill received Royal Assent on 19 April 2013 and the law took effect on 19 August 2013. In his valedictory speech, John Key identified the same-sex marriage Bill as one he was particularly pleased he had supported. Alex, who was born in New Zealand, attended the vote. His pride in New Zealand achieving marriage equality was equally matched with frustration that things were taking so long in Australia.

Alex married his husband Victor in Argentina in May 2012 with a small group of friends and family present. They were ready to get married and didn't want to wait. They picked Argentina as it was equally inconvenient for all their German, American and Australian guests. They were the first foreign same-sex couple to marry in Buenos Aires. Until very recently, the city had limited marriage to residents but Sarah Hanson-Young wrote to its mayor, Mauricio Macri, to ask him to waive that requirement on compassionate grounds for same-sex couples. Sarah had planned to attend Alex's wedding, but a change in Greens leadership meant she had to stay in Australia.

However, Tim Wilson was able to make the wedding after a marathon flight and Alex and Tim sat at the bar at Alex's hotel the night before the wedding. With glasses of Malbec and gin and tonics in hand, they talked about the importance of marriage and their determination to see the law change in Australia. Alex's mother Carolyn and Victor's mother Claudia walked the grooms down the aisle, and Elaine Czulkowski narrowly grabbed the bouquet thrown by Alex and Vic – then, suddenly realising she didn't want to get married again, passed it on to the person she had pushed in front of to catch it. Nick Smith, the recipient, would later have his New York wedding to Joe Murphy feature in 2017 advertisements for the YES campaign. After Alex and Victor's wedding, local activists agreed to get Argentina's president, Cristina Fernández de Kirchner, to write to Julia Gillard to ask her to support marriage equality, making headlines in Australia.[7]

Federally, in response to the Greens introducing legislation in the House and the Senate, the ALP decided they would introduce their own separate legislation. This move concerned AME. We would have favoured everyone signing on to a joint Bill, but also had no control over when these Bills, under the influence of an adversarial prime minister, would be brought forward for a debate. To heighten the pressure, Lyle Shelton, who was then chief of staff at the Australian Christian Lobby and became managing director from 2013 to 2018, had been pushing for a vote to see it voted down while momentum was still building. The Australian Christian Lobby, an extremely well-funded group who had lobbied John Howard to change the *Marriage Act* to prevent marriage equality back in 2004, were far from representative of mainstream religious thought. Alex says, 'Lyle would often make cowardly attacks on the most vulnerable in the LGBTIQ community, including the children of LGBTIQ parents and the trans and gender diverse community'. Appallingly, he said that the children of same-sex couples could be considered another stolen generation.[8] While Lyle Shelton wanted to see the Bill introduced quickly, Sarah Hanson-Young and Alex had a contrasting approach, holding off to build support and wait for the right moment.[9]

On 19 September 2012, Alex said many people thought that 'Prime Minister Gillard granted Lyle Shelton his wish'. The Marriage Amendment Bill, which was introduced into the House of Representatives by Labor's Stephen Throsby, was defeated. While Labor had a conscience vote, the Coalition did not. News Limited reported, 'Julia Gillard and Tony Abbott help defeat same sex marriage bill 98–42'.[10] Former prime minister Kevin Rudd also voted against the legislation, though he would later come to support marriage equality.

The next day, on 20 September, the Senate voted down the Marriage Amendment Bill (No. 2) 2012, which was introduced by Labor senators Trish Crossin, Carol Brown, Louise Pratt and Gavin Marshall. The Coalition again voted as a bloc against it. Liberal Senator Sue Boyce spoke in favour of the reform and did not vote in the Chamber. In a very moving speech, Labor's Louise Pratt told the Senate:

> I ask senators in this chamber to remember, when they
> are deciding how to vote, we exist, we already exist, our
> relationships exist, our children exist, our families exist,
> our marriages exist and our love exists. All we ask is that
> you stop pretending that we don't. Stop pretending that our
> relationships are not as real as yours, our love not as true,
> our children not as cherished, our families not as precious
> – because they are. Removing this last vestige of legal
> discrimination against gay, lesbian, bisexual, transgender
> and intersex Australians from federal law now has the
> support of the majority of the Australian community. It is
> my sincere hope that it also has the support of the majority
> of senators in this place.[11]

The vote failed, twenty-six votes to forty-one.

Alex told the media that 'now the Federal Parliament has effectively brushed the wishes of a majority of Australians aside, the states and territories will take the lead'.[12] He was proven correct. While it looked as though progress in Federal Parliament was extremely unlikely, with the Coalition prevented from having a conscience vote and Prime Minister Gillard making it clear she did not support this, it was important to keep building on the community support that was already out there to let politicians know that this issue was not going to go away. While many were disappointed with the outcome, and the way the vote was rushed to fail, the campaign was only set to strengthen and build momentum further.

The active team at AME was much smaller at this time than people might have imagined, though there was a lot of support from people out in the community. Rodney, Alex, Malcolm McPherson, Jay Allen, Elaine Czulkowski, Ivan Hinton-Teoh, John Kloprogge, and Carol Burger were the core team, with others contributing where they could. As the team was spread across the country, we held regular phone meetings where people could discuss ideas and what was happening and make plans.

Malcolm McPherson believes that Jay Allen had brought with him a range of talents that really enhanced the group. He says, 'He had his own business, so he knew how to run a business and had all of that technical expertise. So he brought a huge amount of skills and organisational ability to Australian Marriage Equality at that point and that was really important'. Prior to joining AME, Jay had reached out to advocate Shelley Argent, who had become a very public face working for marriage equality on behalf of her gay son, but also other LGBTIQ people. Jay offered her assistance with social media and Shelley encouraged Jay to reach out to Rodney Croome and AME.

Jay, who had not previously conducted any sort of lobbying, thought, 'Why don't I go to the US and have a crash course in training with the organisations that are there. So I organised catch-ups with the Human Rights Campaign and with Evan Wolfson from Freedom to Marry'. Jay remembers that Evan Wolfson was 'amazing' and introduced him to people who showed him how to produce memes on Facebook, 'One of the things we brought back to both Australian Marriage Equality and to Equal Marriage Rights Australia'.

Evan Wolfson also introduced Jay to John Berry, who later became the United States Ambassador to Australia. One meeting Jay remembers well was with a previous executive director of the United States LGBTIQ organisation the Human Rights Campaign, Elizabeth Birch. Jay remembers Elizabeth taking his AME business card, looking at the logo, which 'was basically two men next to each other', and saying, 'Oh honey, we need to rebrand you!' Jay took this on board and the group arranged a new logo, 'hands making a heart shape with an equal sign in the middle of it'.

Jay also made connections with the ice cream company Ben and Jerry's in the United States. In 1985, when this company first offered national stock, it had issued a three-part mission statement, which included aiming to 'make the world a better place.' Amongst other social justice issues, Ben and Jerry's had supported the US marriage equality campaign. The support of Ben and Jerry's in Australia helped AME run a significant campaign in the lead-up to the 2013 election.

The AME team at this time was not only spread across Australia, but team members were also in some unexpected locations. Carol Burger, a married straight woman with three young children, had joined the group from a small farming town in rural Victoria with a population of under 300 people. Carol had not known any out LGBTIQ people while growing up but in 2011, she had watched a clip made by American filmmaker Shane Bitney Crone. In this clip, he shared his experiences of being prevented from attending the funeral of the man who had been his partner, Tom Bridegroom, as Bridegroom's family did not approve of the relationship, which was not legally recognised as it would have been had the two men been married. Shane Bitney Crone was also omitted from the obituary and was denied hospital visitation rights when Tom was alive.

Carol was deeply affected by the story and the 'injustice and unfairness of it all'. While she had previously worked for a local employment network, she now had young children and had not been able to stay on. She saw an advertisement on Facebook, asking for a voluntary administration officer for AME, and thought 'it was something that I thought I could contribute my time to'. Very quickly, AME's national secretary Jay Allen taught Carol how to create memes, use MailChimp and send out newsletters. She also learned how to use the accounting system and began setting up appointments with politicians for Rodney. Over the years, as a result of her support for marriage equality, Carol received anonymous hate mail and her husband even received a call from a woman demanding he make Carol stop her involvement with AME. Needless to say, neither she nor her husband listened! Carol did not waver in her commitment to the cause and never gave up. She was never paid for any of the work she did. Unsung but indispensible heroes such as Carol have been essential to the success of the marriage equality movement in this country.

AME continued to hold marriage equality workshops to keep up community motivation and build support. In 2012, there were marriage equality forums held in Sydney, Melbourne, Adelaide and Perth. International experts such as Evan Wolfson offered help when they could. Evan travelled to Australia to speak at a function co-hosted by AME and the University of New South Wales in August 2012.

In September 2012, Alex was endorsed by Clover Moore to run for the seat of Sydney in New South Wales Parliament. Clover, who had held the seat and was also the lord mayor of Sydney, had been forced to resign from parliament after the introduction of laws popularly termed 'the get Clover law', which made it impossible for a state member of parliament to also serve on local government. At the end of 2012, Alex won the election and entered the New South Wales Parliament. He was the first person in a same-sex marriage to become a member of an Australian parliament. Rodney Croome took on the role of national convenor while Alex kept up his involvement with AME.

This was the group that Shirleene and her then fiancé Sarah Midgley joined. Shirleene had moved to Sydney from Brisbane for work in the middle of 2011 and Sarah joined her in 2012 after a short stint working in London. Both started attending marriage equality and LGBTIQ events, including hearing a speech on the issue given by Senator Penny Wong and attending a dinner held by AME for people who wanted to become more involved in the marriage equality movement. Shirleene remembers meeting Evelyn Gray, the mother of two daughters, one straight and one gay, who was one of the movement's strongest and most dedicated allies, during these initial stages.

Shirleene says, 'Sarah and I joined AME because we both saw the discrimination against LGBTIQ people that had been written in the 2004 Amendments as something that sent a terrible message to younger LGBTIQ people about the status of their relationships, as well as denying older couples recognition many desperately wanted. We thought the law needed to be changed. And we thought that we should offer to do something to work towards that'.

Gradually, we got to know the team, particularly Malcolm McPherson at first. We also got to know Alex and Elaine much better after Steph Sands, a wonderful advocate for LGBTIQ rights in Sydney and former co-chair of Mardi Gras, sat us together at an event. She and her partner Fran Bowron have both given an enormous amount of time and energy to movements for LGBTIQ and women's rights. After Shirleene and Sarah had spent some time getting to know the organisation, Malcolm, who was the New South Wales convenor, asked the pair if they would like to join him as New South Wales co-convenors. Malcolm had always strongly supported diversity and including women and saw that this would enhance AME capacity. Rodney was also very supportive.

Reflecting on asking Shirleene and Sarah to join him as co-convenors, Malcolm tells us, 'It was my pleasure because Shirleene and Sarah contributed an enormous amount to the organisation. And it was important as Australian Marriage Equality really did have a problem with being mostly male, mostly Sydney-based and it needed to have better gender inclusion and a greater geographical coverage. I couldn't do much about the geographical coverage, but I thought you were the right people who would be able to contribute to this in a way that I, and a lot of others, couldn't'. As the three co-convenors, we formed an enduring friendship and shared a great many experiences over the years. Shirleene says, 'Malcolm is an extremely kind and unassuming person. His presence and steady encouragement and advice was very important in sustaining so many of us through what was a rollercoaster journey at many times'.

Alex was also grateful and relieved that Sarah and Shirleene joined the team. 'Suddenly we were joined by these two giving and positive women. They were willing to help in any way they could, from stuffing envelopes to fronting national media. They were both brave and determined, two of the key attributes needed to survive the marriage equality movement. And they stuck it out until the end!'

Shirleene reflects, 'I was – and am – a lot shyer than people realise. But I pushed myself because I truly believed this would change the experience of being an LGBTIQ person in this country and make Australia better for everyone really'. Sarah remembers, 'Our marriage equality experience was a joint one. So many moments were unbelievably tough. They were for so many people. But we kept going because we believed our community deserved to have their rights respected and we knew Australia would get there'.

Shirleene and Sarah made the decision to become involved together (which is not always common amongst advocates – perhaps sensibly!) because they both thought they could contribute different things to the group and support each other. Perhaps more importantly, they thought that if they were going to be doing voluntary work outside of normal work hours, they might as well do it as a couple so that they could see each other. Reflecting back, Shirleene says, 'I am glad that we shared this together. It ended up becoming a really big part of our lives for a long time'. Sarah Midgley remembers, 'We found the AME team was small but in close contact very often. We had weekly phone meetings and held regular events or actions and were able to put forward ideas and contribute. I was in awe of the tireless commitment of the team, including Rodney and Alex.'[13] Tim Peppard came on board as the Victorian director in 2013, bringing a very important perspective. He had a strong appreciation for marriage after living through the HIV and AIDS epidemic and losing loved ones.

Shirleene says:

As Sarah and I were based in Sydney, we saw close up the scale of work that Alex was doing. I don't think people are aware of just how much he did over such a long time. He had a lot of pressure on him to think strategically, work with politicians from all sides and to reassure the community, all while trying to move support and action for marriage equality along. What I think really made us all respect him so much is that he never asked anything of the team that he wasn't prepared to do himself. If we needed to be somewhere at six in the morning for a grassroots action, then Alex would already be there, assembling a table, sticking up flyers and getting to work.

In 2018, Shirleene interviewed Trevor Evans, federal MP for Brisbane. Trevor told her, 'Alex was so genuine, so representative, that he was able to work with people right across the political spectrum and it's that ability to work with people right across the political spectrum that actually achieves reform. And so, from that point of view his involvement, his role, was invaluable and I'm not sure that the [marriage equality] reform could have been achieved without people able to speak to people right across the parliament and across the political spectrum'. Shirleene says, 'When Trevor said this, it really reflected back to me what I had witnessed over so many years, that Alex was prepared to work with everyone, no matter their views or background, and that he really did play a critical role'.

Back in 2013 though, international developments were providing advocates with inspiration. The issue of marriage equality returned to Federal Parliament in 2013. The fact that Australian couples could take a flight to New Zealand or so many other culturally comparable countries and get married really served to emphasise that Australia was increasingly out of alignment with a world that was becoming more inclusive. On 16 May 2013, a

Marriage Act Amendment (Recognition of Foreign Marriages for Same-Sex Couples) Bill was introduced into the Senate. The intention of this Bill was to recognise same-sex marriages that had been solemnised in a foreign country. Sarah Hanson-Young told the media that:

> We have thousands of couples now living in Australia who've gone overseas and gotten married ... and they arrive back home at Sydney International Airport and all of a sudden they have to check their marriage at the customs gate.[14]

Louise Pratt told the Senate that the current law imposed 'unnecessary hurt and hardship on couples' by rejecting their marriages when they arrived home after marrying overseas. She emphasised that 'As an LGBTI Australian myself and as a member of this place I am not going to stop fighting until our equal rights are achieved'.[15]

Senator Sue Boyce played a historic role when she became the first federal Liberal parliamentarian to vote in support of marriage equality. This required a great deal of bravery and garnered her a lot of respect from across the community. In 2012, Sue had spoken in favour of marriage equality when the Labor Bill had been put up. Her colleague, senator Dean Smith, had come in to listen to her speak and she was particularly pleased about this.

In her 2012 positioning speech, Sue had referred to a couple of married mothers she had known in Melbourne in the 1980s with children who attended the same school as hers. Gradually, over a number of years, the two women had fallen in love with each other. One had three sons and the other had two. Sue witnessed first-hand the disapproval and prejudice they had to endure to be together. She was struck:

> [by the] enormous courage on their parts – in the face of opposition, even antipathy, from their families, their church and most of their community – to leave their heterosexual marriages and set up home together within that same community with their five sons. I cannot begin to imagine the depth of their love for each other that they managed to establish and maintain a stable relationship in the face of the disapproval they experienced.[16]

In 2013, when the Marriage Act Amendment (Recognition of Foreign Marriages for Same-Sex Couples) Bill was introduced into the Senate, Sue made the courageous decision to cross the floor. This made her the first and last Liberal to vote for marriage equality until 2017, after the postal survey. Sue tells us that she crossed the floor for two reasons:

> Firstly, it seemed completely unreasonable to me that we would not recognise the validity of marriages performed in the country with which we have such close cultural and social ties [New Zealand]. Secondly, supporting the validity of overseas marriages was an important, but lesser, step than outright support on the floor of the Senate for marriage equality in Australia – an option which was then opposed by the Liberal Party room.

Sue phoned Tony Abbott to tell him that she intended to vote 'yes' on the Bill. His reply was to politely affirm the right of all back-benchers to a free vote on any topic. Sue says, 'I'm not sure what the party's view would have been had the Bill been likely to pass'. It took a few days for Sue to realise just how much of an impact the image of her crossing the floor to become the first Liberal to support marriage equality in Federal Parliament had. She says, 'A couple of days later, one of my staff told me I was a meme and I didn't know what a meme was!' By taking those powerful strides, Sue showed the country that marriage equality did not belong to any one party. It mattered to the entire country.

Sue retired from the Senate in 2014 'and was very disappointed that we didn't get it done before I left'. She campaigned actively with the Libs and Nats for YES during the postal survey in 2017 and tells us that she cried when the postal survey results came in, though she had always believed in Queensland and thought her state would support this. She just possessed the foresight to appreciate this earlier than her Coalition colleagues.

On 27 June 2013, Australians had a change of prime minister when Kevin Rudd successfully challenged Julia Gillard for the leadership of the Labor Party and was sworn in once again. A month earlier, he had announced that he had come to support marriage equality. For the first time, Australia had a prime minister who supported marriage equality, although the numbers were not there for any movement on that front. As part of his election campaign, Rudd promised that if he was elected, Labor would introduce marriage equality within its first hundred days of government. However, this was not to be.

In July 2013, international movement was afoot. Legislation to allow same-sex marriage in England and Wales was passed by the United Kingdom's parliament and came into force on 13 March 2014. At the time the legislation passed, the Conservative prime minister of Great Britain, David Cameron, said:

> Conservatives believe in the ties that bind us; that
> society is stronger when we make vows to each other and
> support each other. So I don't support gay marriage despite
> being a Conservative. I support gay marriage because I'm
> a Conservative.[17]

The first same-sex marriages in the United Kingdom took place on 29 March 2014.

While the United Kingdom developments looked positive, AME kept working to build community support and support inside parliament. Jay remembers developing the concept for a Vote4Love website, with financial support from Ben and Jerry's, in the lead-up to the federal election. The website was set up so that people across Australia could type in their electorate and see each political candidate and their stance on marriage equality. Carol, who did an immense amount of work on this website from her home in regional Victoria, remembers how much work was involved in Vote4Love. She says, '2013 was the first time I ever did it and it was huge. And I think I lost about five kilograms working on it!' Jen Allen, Jay's mother, also offered some assistance.

Carol remembers she had to 'spend hours and hours and hours on websites trying to find who was running for each electorate and put them into a spreadsheet. That was hard work in itself'. And making the work more difficult, politicians twice threatened to sue Carol, as the project's point of contact, for not putting their views on the website. She points out it was not possible for her to add their views if they had not yet made them clear.

On 15 August 2013, the Vote4Love website was launched. Senators Louise Pratt and Sarah Hanson-Young joined members of the team, including Alex, Malcolm, Ivan and Shirleene, in Sydney to help promote it. In all the interactions we had with the community, we could see that there was enormous support for marriage equality. In the last week of August and first week of September 2013, with the election around the corner, we continued our efforts.

Malcolm and Shirleene headed out to the Campbelltown Show at the end of August, where, for the first time, AME held a stall over the weekend. In a statement issued at the time, Malcolm said that 'there are many supporters of marriage equality in western Sydney and our stall is a way for them to find out how they can "vote for love" on September 7th'. We both remember this as a very positive experience as we had lots of people sign up to our database and indicate their support for the reform. It was very clear to us both that marriage equality was not just an 'inner-city' issue, as we were being told by certain politicians, but something that reached right across Australia, affecting many.

Nathan Thomas, from Tony Abbott's electorate of Warringah, also held a rally at the Manly Corso on Saturday 30 August 2013. On the Sunday, Ben and Jerry's arranged to transport a giant rainbow wedding cake to Manly to reinforce the message, along with a supply of free ice cream. The enormous cake had been a huge hit earlier in the week when it was displayed in the Pitt Street Mall. A rally was also held at Sydney's Town Hall on Sunday 31 August 2013.

On election day, 7 September 2013, as part of the Vote4Love campaign, team members handed out leaflets at targeted electorates, urging people to vote for candidates who supported marriage equality. Regardless of what happened at that election, we could try and bring in as many supporters of marriage equality to parliament as possible. Shirleene and Sarah handed out the Vote4Love cards in Joe Hockey's North Sydney electorate, a seat that would later be won in a by-election by the first openly gay man in the House of Representatives, Trent Zimmerman. Malcolm McPherson remembers stints handing out cards at North Sydney and Crows Nest.

Kevin Rudd would lose the 2013 election to Tony Abbott, although more supporters of marriage equality were elected than in the last parliament thanks to the Vote4Love campaign.[18] Despite more supporters joining the new parliament, advocates knew they would struggle to achieve marriage equality with Abbott as prime minister. Therefore, the focus had to be on advancing the issue in state and territory parliaments.

Surprisingly, the first same-sex couples to marry on Australian soil were married when Tony Abbott was prime minister. The marriages, which took place in the ACT after it attempted to pass marriage equality legislation, were soon ruled invalid but the visual images of joyful couples and their family and friends marrying and celebrating in this country undoubtedly opened the hearts of many.

There were numerous attempts to legalise same-sex marriage on a state or territory level after 2004, but only the ACT's attempt was successful, briefly. The state's *Marriage Equality (Same Sex) Act* passed into law on 19 September 2013. The first marriages took place on 7 December before the High Court unanimously ruled on 12 December that the ACT law was inconsistent with the federal *Marriage Act* and therefore no part of the ACT legislation could operate. The marriages that had occurred were declared void, a cruel blow to those who had undertaken ceremonies.

Ever since the 2004 Howard Amendments, many had wondered if it might be possible to introduce state or territory marriage laws dealing only with same-sex couples as the federal marriage legislation specifically precluded them. There had even been some steps towards this and the ACT's move came on the back of the Tasmanian Lower House passing a same-sex marriage Bill, one that their upper house would later vote down.

In 2013, Anna Brown, who was by then based at the Human Rights Law Centre in Victoria and was well respected for leading major LGBTIQ law reform across the country, had conversations with Rodney around the prospects of state-based law reform:

> So I worked with AME and we briefed Bret Walker, Chris
> Young and Perry Young, three barristers, and worked on some
> legal options that analysed the constitutionality of the state-
> based instruments that had been drafted in the Tasmanian
> Parliament and also the New South Wales Parliament.

Anna remembers, 'the ACT surged ahead of everyone and developed its legislation as well. We hadn't seen that legislation before they released it and it was all moving very quickly'.

It was critical that the ACT legislation not replicate the *Marriage Act* because, under the Constitution, federal law would negate anything states or territories did if they covered the same terrain. Anna feels that the ACT legislation could have been strengthened by the ACT government in this respect by drawing out the distinction but the ACT government went ahead and passed the legislation. In the six days before the High Court of Australia overruled the ACT legislation, thirty-one Canberra couples married. Western Australia Upper House Labor MP

Stephen Dawson and his partner of ten years, Dennis Liddelow, were the first to do so when they married on the lawns of parliament after midnight on Saturday 7 December. Stephen told the media that:

> We chose to do it here for symbolic reasons I guess. Everybody knows that parliaments make laws in this country. This place has been slow in making laws, particularly on the issue of same-sex marriage.[19]

When the Commonwealth announced it would challenge the constitutional validity of the ACT legislation, AME had the option of intervening as a friend of the court – an opportunity to argue why the legislation should survive. Anna thought, 'It was really important for the marriage equality movement that the voice of the movement was heard in this proceeding'.

While the battle in the ACT was happening, advocates were working closely with New South Wales (NSW) parliamentarians, who had previously formed a cross-party working group to advance state-based marriage equality. Until 1961, marriage had come under the jurisdiction of state and territory laws and the feeling was that if a state or territory passed legislation for marriage equality, it would start a precedent. It was also important that supporters saw that people were still pushing for change at a time when it appeared there was Federal inertia and hostility towards the issue. The NSW cross-party working group consisted of the Nationals' Trevor Khan, Labor's Penny Sharpe, Liberal MP Bruce Notley-Smith, and the Greens' Mehreen Faruqi, and Alex as an Independent MP. Following an inquiry and detailed consultation process, the group was confident they could deliver the strongest possible state-based same-sex marriage Bill. When Penny Sharpe introduced it, she described it as 'the best Bill that has been put forward across Australia'. They got within one vote of the Bill passing; a major factor in the loss was the confusion caused by the ACT's Bill and the Commonwealth's challenge, and the question of whether legislation on marriage was solely up to the federal government or whether states and territories had their own ability to progress legislation. An angry Trevor Khan would tell journalists, 'I find it difficult to accept that people are being asked to wait at the back of the bus for a little longer because somebody's saying there's going to be a Mercedes bus coming down the road in another five or ten years' time'.[20]

Although the High Court did strike down the ACT's legislation, Anna feels a critical outcome of the case was that 'we raised a question that wasn't before the court' in asking 'whether Federal Parliament had the power under the Australian Constitution to legislate for marriage equality'. Alex remembers that politicians would raise this issue when the team lobbied them. But, as Anna points out, 'in the end, the High Court answered this question and it said, unanimously, that the Federal Parliament did have the power to legislate for marriage equality'. This unequivocally showed that there would not be a need for a referendum on the issue. Given the defeats in NSW, Tasmania, and in the High Court, it was very clear that the path ahead for marriage equality across Australia was through a vote in Federal Parliament.

Communities and corporates

The true strength of the marriage equality campaign always depended on the countless people across the country who came forward and gave a great deal of themselves. There would not have been a marriage equality movement without growing numbers of people having conversations and being out about who they loved, even when it required considerable bravery. Our group, Australian Marriage Equality (AME), depended entirely on volunteers and donations, and many people who were doing it hard financially themselves gave what they could because they truly believed in this issue. More and more local champions emerged over time, people who were powerful advocates in their own communities and knew how best to drive change in their own regions. From 2014 onwards, AME had a goal of building support in fifty key electorates so that we would have a majority of supportive MPs in parliament. We also ramped up our efforts to create links with corporate supporters to try and build the pressure for a free vote in parliament.

In February 2014, AME launched the 'We're Waiting' campaign, designed by Brendan Spencer, in Sydney. Alex, Rodney, Malcolm and Shirleene, and senators Sarah Hanson-Young and Louise Pratt were present with a representative from Ben and Jerry's. At this point, we knew we needed to convince around twenty-five more members of the House of Representatives to support marriage equality and the best way to do that was to have locals from their electorate share their personal stories.

To keep the issue fresh in the minds of politicians, just as we had done in years past, on Valentine's Day 2014, AME sent deliveries of roses to fifty MPs from across the country. Wayne Swan even received bunches of flowers from two separate constituents. He later came out in support of marriage equality, although we are fairly certain we can't attribute it to our roses! Wallaby David Pocock and his partner Emma threw their support behind the campaign. They had previously declared that they would wait to marry until all loving couples had the same right.

The electoral visits of 2014 kicked off across four states. We would often do the events with at least two or three of the team but sometimes just one, depending on who was available. We think that most of us look back on them as a highlight of campaigning. More and more local champions were emerging across the country. Rallies, often organised by groups such as Equal Love and Community Action Against Homophobia, sometimes in conjunction with AME, continued to form a large visual presence on the streets of the capital cities and the regions alike.

In April 2014, marriage equality campaigners suffered a blow when one of the most prominent and longest-serving advocates for marriage equality within parliament left the Senate. Labor's Louise Pratt had been placed below Joe Bullock in the Western Australian Senate ticket. Bullock had not gained as many votes as expected and had made homophobic comments on the campaign trail. In her valedictory speech, Louise Pratt reaffirmed that:

I support the end of discrimination in the *Marriage Act* – not
because it affects me, although it does affect me, but because
equal rights for all Australians has always been a touchstone
for me in all aspects of my political involvement. I can assure
you that this will remain the case in the future. More than
65 per cent of Australians agree with me. If this parliament
truly reflected the views of those who elect us marriage equality
would be a reality.[1]

While no one could have foreseen it then, Louise would return
to the Senate again in 2017, casting her vote supporting the legislation that finally undid the discrimination embedded in 2004.

Outside of parliament, grassroots advocates were working
hard and bringing about real change. Sharyn Faulkner, former
mayor of the city of Colac and the mother of two sons, one gay
and one straight, was one powerful and very dedicated champion
to emerge in 2014. When one of her sons married, she was filled
with happiness but also saddened to think that her other son
could not legally do the same. As a result, she made contact with
Rodney Croome, founded Geelong for Marriage Equality and as
an initial action, arranged a meeting of twelve people. From that
meeting, forty letters in support of marriage equality were delivered to the federal member for Corangamite, Sarah Henderson.
The *Colac Herald* and the *Geelong Advertiser* both published articles about marriage equality as a result. Rodney Croome, Ivan
Hinton-Teoh, Shelley Argent, Daniel Witthaus and Tim Peppard
also came to Geelong to meet the community.

Sarah Henderson visited a stall Sharyn had set up at the popular
Belmont Markets in Geelong, where nearly 200 postcards were
signed. Sharyn later arranged for a further 500 postcards to be

delivered. The *Geelong Advertiser* ran a follow-up piece. Rodney, Ivan, Shelley and Tim returned to Geelong's Waterfront Market, where the team managed to get 700 postcards signed. Tim Wilson, then the Human Rights Commissioner, came to Geelong and opened the 2014 *Case Against 8* film about the Supreme Court overturning California's Proposition 8 ban on same-sex marriage. The screening sold 116 tickets and saw a further fifty letters signed and delivered. Another seventy letters were delivered to Sarah Henderson's Ocean Grove mobile office. Geelong for Marriage Equality also set up and ran a popular Facebook page.

Not satisfied with these impressive achievements, Sharyn also managed to get the Geelong Football Club to write an open letter in support of marriage equality. She also wrote a letter to the AFL, asking it to declare its support. Gillon McLachlan, CEO of the AFL, replied saying that football was no place for homophobia, and gave his personal commitment to 'continue to speak out in this area whenever I can'. This was a major turning point. In 2015, Sarah Henderson publicly announced her support for marriage equality.

A range of councils also responded to Sharyn's efforts. The City of Greater Geelong Council, led by Cr Jan Farrell, announced its support for marriage equality, as did Surf Coast Shire Council, led by Mayor Cr Rose Hodge. Colac-Otway Shire Mayor Cr Lyn Russell also declared her support for marriage equality in the *Colac Herald*. Mayor Cr Darren Lyons of the City of Greater Geelong was also supportive, appearing on Channel 10's *Studio 10* programme and promoting *The Case Against 8*. Jan Farrell from Geelong Council took on a leadership role herself in moving a great many councils to support marriage equality. In fact, the *Sydney Morning Herald* would call her 'marriage equality's secret weapon' for her ability to bring so many councils onside.[2]

The Australian movement also got a further boost in 2014 when same-sex couples started marrying in this country. At the 2011 ALP National Conference, the requirement for a Certificate of Non-Impediment had been waived. Then, in 2013, when the United Kingdom (UK) passed legislation for marriage equality, the Australian Coalition Government agreed that UK consulates in Australia could marry same-sex couples where at least one person had UK citizenship. This meant that legally recognised same-sex marriages could take place in Australia, although they would not be recognised once couples stepped outside of the consulate.

On 27 June 2014, Gordon Stevenson and Peter Fraser, who had been together for nineteen years, were the first same-sex couple to be married in Australia under British laws when they exchanged vows at the British Consulate in Sydney. Shirleene, Sarah, Ivan, Rodney and Alex were lucky enough to be able to celebrate after the wedding with the truly lovely husbands, Gordon and Peter, who very generously let them tag along.

In 2014, in his role as AME's national director, Rodney Croome stated, 'It is hopeful that the Australian government has allowed Australians to marry in UK consulates. The majority of Australians who support marriage equality will be asking, "If this can happen in a UK consulate then why not everywhere else in Australia?"' When marriage equality legislation was finally passed in Australia's Federal Parliament in December 2017, UK consulates were no longer legally able to marry same-sex couples based in Australia as those weddings now had to take place under Australian law. But between 2014 and 2017, 469 of these marriages had been performed within UK consulates across

Australia. On 7 March 2018, Shirleene, Sarah and Alex attended a beautiful celebration that the British Consulate held in Sydney to commemorate those marriages. The British Consulate staff told us that they were thrilled that marriage equality was now a reality for all Australians and emphasised what a privilege it had been for them to see such joy in all those weddings.

One of those marriages had been between Sarah and Shirleene on a beautiful September day in 2014. The following day they had another ceremony – one that was legally unrecognised – on Balmoral Beach, where many friends and family members joined them. Shirleene says:

> We were not sure what response to expect from the members
> of the public who also happened to be at the beach and park
> at the same time but it was extremely positive. A group of
> teenagers saw us and said, 'A gay wedding! Cool!' Although
> the marriage was not legally recognised in Australia, it was a
> beautiful and meaningful moment in both our lives.

Sarah remembers:

> What really surprised us, in the best possible way, was how our
> family and friends came together to support us and to make
> sure the day was perfect for us. We had guests come from as far
> away as Cambodia, Japan and England as well as from interstate.
> There was love, joy, so much laughter and – if I'm honest – some
> stressing over planning two days of ceremonies. But the memory
> of both our mums and dads walking us down the aisle will be
> something we cherish forever. Marriage is about love between two
> people, but it is also about expressing that love and celebrating it

with the people who mean the most to you. The experience also renewed our energy to keep up our work for equality.[3]

In the middle of 2014, swimming legend Ian Thorpe, Australia's most successful Olympian, publicly came out as gay. Watching this on television in Mosman, Janine Middleton, a Liberal-voting Catholic and married heterosexual woman, was deeply moved by the pain of his journey. At this time, she was recovering from a serious illness. On the surface, Janine, who had twenty-five years' experience in banking and was a former managing director of JPMorgan Chase & Co in London, was not the most obvious supporter of marriage equality but she had seen and tried to address homophobia within the corporate world and had witnessed the pain of individuals having to hide who they were at work. She had also seen a dying friend feel that she had to hide her relationship with her female partner. Within months of Ian Thorpe coming out, Janine would become deeply involved in the cause, refusing to stop until marriage equality was achieved.

In August 2014, advocates were buoyed when political polling firm Crosby Textor released polling that showed that 72 per cent of Australians supported same-sex marriage.[4] This was a major boost to advocates as it reinforced what all the other polls had been saying. The Australian community was way ahead of federal politicians and they needed to listen to what the community wanted.

In September 2014, Janine Middleton met up with Jay Allen after sending through an email that said, 'I'm straight, married, Catholic, and a Liberal voter. I live in Mosman. I'm an ex-investment banker and I never leave the house without my pearls on'. Having described herself this way, Janine added, 'If there's a role for me, I'd really like to join'. Not really being sure what to anticipate,

Janine arrived at the meeting wearing a suit, expecting to hear about a large-scale organisation. 'I remember thinking I could do Fridays … I thought that it was a big organisation and he had an office and I'd work in the office stuffing envelopes or something. I couldn't have been more wrong on every level.' She soon found out that AME did not have a physical home, that it was entirely volunteer-run and that it consisted of fewer than fifteen active people.

Jay introduced Janine to Alex at the bar in New South Wales Parliament, where he convinced her to take on a major role in AME over a few bottles of wine and a very frank conversation. Alex was open about the challenges of a small organisation dealing with growing public support for reform, while politicians were trying to kill off the issue. Janine and Alex immediately saw that she could add value, structure and an important new voice to a growing organisation. Alex was impressed by the kindness that motivated her to volunteer her time and expertise, and her 'no bullshit' approach to politics internally and externally. At the end of their meeting, Alex asked if Janine would join as the co-chair of AME.

Janine hesitated, asking, 'Quite frankly, shouldn't the co-chair be a lesbian?' But Alex insisted that Janine was perfect for the role with her background and skills and convinced her to agree. She said, 'If I'm going to do this, I won't quit. I will never quit and I will be with you in this role until marriage equality is achieved'. She stood by her words and remained with AME until the reform was achieved in December 2017. Her immediate tasks were governance, including setting up a board, examining the accounts and ensuring we had an up-to-date and legal constitution. Both early risers, Alex and Janine would have morning calls at the crack of dawn for the next few years to deal with internal and external challenges.

Magda Szubanski, who met Janine in 2016, was seriously impressed with her commitment to the cause. She says, 'I spoke to her before I met her. Alex put me in touch with her and we spoke on the phone for nearly two hours. I loved the fact that she is everything I am not: a North Shore, twin-set and pearls wearing, straight-lady banker. But we found we had so much in common. There was no reason for her to fight this fight other than common decency. And boy did she put her shoulder to the wheel. These are the kinds of allies that help win campaigns – indefatigable, unlikely, hilarious, hardworking, super smart and just plain dogged'.

In January 2015, we again announced that we were continuing with the policy of targeting key electorates to build support for marriage equality before the next election due in 2016.[5] Shirleene and Sarah remember this announcement quite well because the *Sydney Morning Herald* did a photo shoot with them early on the morning of 1 January when they were both still feeling a little sorry for themselves from their New Year's Eve celebrations the night before! So many different people in different states undertook electorate visits that it is difficult to capture the spirit of all of them. Needless to say, we all met a lot of dedicated Australians who just wanted to see a simple law change happen soon.

Generally, the AME team did electoral visits in the states in which we were based, though people such as Rodney travelled more extensively. Shirleene was also keen to visit Queensland electorates when it was possible. She remembers a 2015 visit to Rockhampton in the Capricornia electorate fondly, where Shelley Argent also spoke and around fifty overwhelmingly supportive people turned up. One of the forum organisers, Christie

Green-Williams from Parents, Family and Friends of Lesbians and Gays (PFLAG) Central Queensland, gave Shirleene a stuffed toy bull to commemorate the visit, as Rockhampton is Australia's beef capital. It still sits on Shirleene's desk.

In Victoria, AME board member Tim Peppard would travel the state to help local LGBTIQ organisations and marriage equality supporters. He says, 'Over the years, we saw people go from passive to interested to actively supportive – it was hard work but inspiring to be a part of'.

In February 2015, Ben and Jerry's helped us with an #EqualityCalling campaign. Jay Allen had worked very closely with the group to make this campaign a success. It allowed people from all over Australia to dial one phone number, leave their postcode and then leave a voice message that would be sent onwards to their MP. The campaign was promoted with an old-school telephone booth brightly painted in rainbow colours which we took to the Mardi Gras Fair Day. Comedian and broadcaster Wendy Harmer guided people through the process of leaving their voice messages. Ben and Jerry's also showed their support by temporarily renaming their chocolate chip cookie dough ice cream 'I Dough, I Dough'.

In April 2015, we planned a memorable weekend of action in the electorate of Lindsay in New South Wales. Alex, Shirleene, Sarah and Janine all went to an Electoral Champion Building Workshop, which was held on a Saturday at the Open Door Community of Christ. We heard from Kyle Goldfinch, a young gay man who pushed himself out of his comfort zone to come along because he believed in equality for LGBTIQ people across a broad range of issues. Wayne Chilver, a person of faith with a wonderful family who came out later in life, was a fantastic organiser. Ian Matthews would also be a dedicated advocate until marriage equality was achieved. Sarah and Shirleene returned to volunteer with the team at a stall set up next to the Nepean River. We realised very quickly that the electorate of Lindsay supported marriage equality when we could not hand out postcards fast enough. In the end, the Penrith for Marriage Equality team managed to deliver 700 postcards to their MP.

In May 2015, Kristy Millers and her partner Rachelle in the bordering electorate of Macarthur would also take a public stand, sharing their story with the local press and then building community support on the ground. Community-driven campaigns were growing stronger.

From May 2015 onwards, Janine worked hard on building much closer links with the corporate sector. Malcolm McPherson believes that her efforts were absolutely critical to this. He says, 'She had skills in the corporate area and in fundraising – skills and contacts that none of us would ever have had'. On 5 May 2015, Janine arranged a corporate business event in Sydney and invited the chief executives of some of the country's biggest companies. Corporate panellists, including Ann Sherry, CEO of Carnival Australia; Lisa Annese, CEO of Diversity Council Australia; Alan Joyce, CEO of Qantas; and Michael Ebeid, managing director at SBS, spoke on the question, 'Does marriage equality matter to corporate Australia?' Janine notes that Michael Ebeid had been one of 'the first high-profile corporate leaders, also from a multicultural background, to lend his voice to the campaign'. She continues, 'His story is one of an openly gay, highly successful person from a conservative background and that resonated across all factions of the community'.

Also in May 2015, AME's capacity gained another serious boost when Liam Ryan joined as a volunteer media advisor. He brought with him a background in both politics and the media. In New Zealand, where he grew up, he had worked as the senior private secretary to the Minister for Civil Defence, Youth Affairs, Food Safety, Associate Immigration, and Associate Education in the government led by John Key. He had also worked for MTV Australia and Channel Nine. Now living in his adopted home of Sydney again, he was working for Foxtel. Liam was the proud father to three young children, being raised in a loving rainbow family. As he said, 'I believe that both mothers of my children – after eight solid years together and three healthy, happy kids – should be able to celebrate their relationship legally and legitimately in front of their nearest and dearest'.[6] In July 2015, Liam led the production of three TV commercials in Melbourne to promote marriage equality and a free vote. He also liaised with Sky News and regional media markets to get them shown.

On 23 May 2015, Ireland became the first country in the world to introduce marriage equality through a popular vote. Shirleene, who with Rodney Croome was a spokesperson for the group at this time, remembers this was the marriage equality story that received the most coverage in Australia up until the postal survey. On 24 May, the day the news broke in Australia, 'I did television interviews with ABC, SBS, Sky News, Channel 9, Channel 10 and quite a few radio interviews as well. I had never seen anything like it! The main point to reinforce was that there was no need for an expensive public vote in Australia because change would ultimately have to be made through federal parliament and that Ireland had only had a public vote because it was a requirement in their constitution'.

On Friday 29 May 2015, the country woke up to another initiative Janine had been working very hard on. It took us into new terrain. She had arranged for fifty-three companies to take out a full-page advertisement in the only nationwide newspaper, the *Australian*, showing their support for marriage equality. The companies included banks such as Westpac, St George, Bankwest, ANZ and the Commonwealth Bank; and financial companies such as PwC, EY, Boston Consulting Group, KPMG, BT Financial Group and Brilliant Money. Other corporates included Qantas, P&O Cruises, Foxtel, Gilbert and Tobin, David Jones, Dow, Fitness First, Optus, Telstra, Virgin Mobile, Virgin Money, Google and H&M.

The advertisement had been timed to coincide with Labor leader Bill Shorten introducing a private member's Bill on marriage equality the next Monday and to increase the pressure on the Coalition to allow a free vote. Without a free vote from them, this Bill could not succeed. Janine continued to build on this success. She notes, 'By the time we achieved marriage equality, we had over 2700 companies of all shapes and sizes who'd signed'.

In June 2015, another strong electoral champion emerged in the federal electorate of Hume. Tom Sebo, who lived in Goulburn, had felt annoyed for some time that politicians were not listening to the community, who he was sure supported marriage equality. In response, he and some friends decided to get active and set up a Facebook page, 'Hume Supports Marriage Equality' to build momentum. He told the *Goulburn Post*, 'You don't need to be gay to advocate for marriage equality, you just need to care. It isn't emasculating, it shows you fundamentally believe in equality; that you recognise that your sexuality doesn't define you as a person; that everybody is entitled to equal treatment in the eyes of the law; that people shouldn't be sub-categorised based upon superficial influences; that love is love. That love is a good thing, worthy of recognition and celebration'.[7]

Alex read this article and immediately picked up the phone and called Tom to see if he could offer any help. Tom arranged a public meeting in July 2015, which both Alex and Rodney attended. There were more than fifty people at the Goulburn Club. Tom says, 'The meeting was great because it energised us and got a couple of other people involved; we got a bit more of a committee kind of group'.

After reading a quote from former federal MP Albie Schultz, who said that he had received 'something like 630 letters' supporting the definition of marriage being between a man and a woman, Tom decided he could get more supporters in favour of marriage equality. 'Our team – me, Waz, Lloyd and a bunch of people went out and we hit everywhere as well as we could, trying to get signatures. We hit Cootamundra, Cowra, Crookwell, Yass, everywhere getting signatures and we ended up with 1300'. Tom was particularly impressed with the experience at Yass. 'We actually went down to the rugby fields because Goulburn was playing Yass so we went down there and we were just chatting to the rugby players.' The players looked at the petition, read it, 'and all these rugby players are like, "Oh yeah man, you got a pen?" and they're all standing there signing it, passing it around the sidelines'.

On 6 June 2015, inspired by Janine's actions with a full-page advertisement in the *Australian* in May, Lyttleton Terrace business owner Jayson Tayeh decided to run some local advertisements supporting marriage equality in the *Bendigo Advertiser*. The newspaper carried a full-page spread featuring twenty-one local businesses who declared their support. Jayson told the newspaper that 'the message I wish to convey is quite simple: I support marriage equality and so do many regional Victorian small businesses in "my world"'. He also noted that 'everyone has been very receptive, everyone has been very willing to have a conversation about it'.[8]

This in turn motivated the Hume team and Tom Sebo, who decided that they would also show that Goulburn supported marriage equality through a local business advertisement. Brian Hill, who led the project, was able to get thirty local businesses to sign up for an advertisement saying they supported marriage equality in the local newspaper. He said, 'The support, encouragement and willingness of the businesses participating was very empowering and in some cases surprising. Many of the people I spoke with told personal stories about family members who had suffered because of discrimination and the effects this had on their families – they wanted this discrimination to end'.[9] Tom told the newspaper that he 'would personally like to thank everybody involved, especially the leaders in our business community'.[10]

We were really gaining momentum. That feeling only increased on 26 June 2015, when, after hearing four consolidated cases, the United States Supreme Court ruled that marriage equality was now the law of the land. The Supreme Court had decided that marriages that were legal in one state or district should be legal in all parts of the United States. Jim Obergefell had been at the epicentre of the Supreme Court deliberations. He had married his dying partner, John Arthur, on a medical jet in Maryland and wanted that marriage recognised in his home state of Ohio. After John passed away he also wanted his name on John's death certificate as his surviving spouse.

After the Supreme Court made its decision, Jim stood on the forecourt of the Supreme Court, holding a photo of John close. On that evening, the White House was lit up in rainbow colours. In one of the best speeches that has ever been delivered about the marriage equality movement, President Obama said:

Today, we can say in no uncertain terms that we've made our union a little more perfect. That's the consequence of a decision from the Supreme Court, but more importantly, it is a consequence of the countless small acts of courage of millions of people across decades who stood up, who came out, talked to parents, parents who loved their children no matter what, folks who were willing to endure bullying and taunts, and stayed strong, and came to believe in themselves and who they were.

And slowly made an entire country realize that love is love. What an extraordinary achievement, but what a vindication of the belief that ordinary people can do extraordinary things … those countless, often anonymous heroes, they deserve our thanks. They should be very proud.[11]

On 17 July, we even had a soundtrack to celebrate the community momentum, new team members and corporate support when Janine organised the release of an album, #SayYesToLove, via iTunes. A group of prominent Australian musicians, including Jimmy Barnes and the John Butler Trio, donated their music so that all proceeds could go towards AME. This was soon followed up by a second album. Reflecting on Janine's work, Alex says, 'Janine never saw any walls stopping her, or AME, from achieving something; if a wall was put up, she would knock it down.

The drive motivated those around her, and volunteers around Australia'.

On 23 July, there was yet another boost when sixty-two businesses in Bunbury, Western Australia published a two-page advertisement in the *South Western Times*. Hamish Johnston, who had organised the advertisement, said, 'It was exciting to see the enthusiasm and support that these businesses showed when I first approached them to take part'. He added that 'they look forward to the reality of marriage equality and the added business that it will bring to the region'. Finally, on 29 July, Damien Stevens arranged for the *Shepparton Adviser* to publish an advertisement featuring twenty-nine businesses in the Murray who supported marriage equality.[12]

With such a level of activity from all sections of the community, coupled with the international movement towards marriage equality, people within AME were feeling more and more positive about the future. Yes, Tony Abbott had so far refused to allow the Coalition a conscience vote but Australia had made it clear that the issue was not going away. In fact, it was about to be brought to a head dramatically.

Lights on, hopes fade

In early August 2015, once again, it seemed that a free vote might just be possible. Opportunities had been few and far between but the pressure was mounting and there was a degree of confidence that change could be possible. In preparation for the Liberal party room meeting where the party's position would be decided, a number of the Australian Marriage Equality (AME) team members headed to Canberra, where they would be based while pushing for a vote on the Entsch-led cross-party same-sex marriage Bill. Malcolm McPherson remembers, 'I drove to Canberra on Sunday afternoon taut with anticipation. I was to be one of the "war room" team providing support to Alex and Rodney in what we thought might be the last frenzied lobbying before marriage equality was finally passed'.

Once in Canberra, the AME team in Canberra headed to the airport, but weren't flying anywhere. We were about to witness the Snow family, who own the airport, lighting it up in rainbow colours, with a giant #wecandothis sign placed on the lawns outside the airport, and banners throughout the airport calling for the passage of marriage equality. This moment was significant in many ways. MPs and senators were about to arrive in Canberra for a sitting week where the issue was expected to come to a head; it showed corporate Australia stepping up their advocacy on the issue; and it was the beginning of the Snow family's major commitment to getting reform through, led by Tom Snow and his husband Brooke Horne. The moment made international headlines, and was spread over the front pages of major newspapers. The airport would continue this practice of lighting up in rainbow colours during sitting weeks, right up until the final passage of marriage equality legislation in 2017.

This came on the back of a major push from the campaign that brought together grassroots advocates, high-profile celebrities and sporting stars, faith leaders and over 500 corporates under the slogan 'We Can Do This'. The campaign, driven by Liam Ryan, included TV and print ads with AFL players Josh Bruce and Matt Spangher, actor Hugo Weaving and television newsreader Chris Bath. The campaign wanted to empower supporters to flood MPs with calls. While advocates and supporters had been working incredibly hard, what happened over the next few days would set the campaign back years and further delay equality. It was a devastating time for many in the movement.

AME had set up the 'war room' at the Canberra office of the Boston Consulting Group. Malcolm McPherson remembers the ideal location of the space. 'The room had a view across to Capital Hill where the action for the week would be focused.' While Rodney and Ivan were up in Parliament House, Alex, Elaine, Malcolm, Liam and James Northwood were monitoring media and social media, making calls to MPs, and writing press releases. The first task was to assemble packs of letters from major corporations and CEOs to MPs calling for a free vote and marriage equality. A similar effort happened in the United States with the amicus brief (legal documents filed by non-litigants with an interest in the case) in support of the Obergefell Supreme Court case. Other activities, including a prayer breakfast with faith leaders in support of marriage equality, were being planned to complement the intense lobbying efforts that were underway. Malcolm McPherson remembers:

> The team made what preparations we could. The Coalition was to be meeting in the afternoon and we were hoping for the announcement of a free vote. We were very close to having the numbers if the free vote eventuated. There might be some who would change their minds when finally confronted with a decision. We expected more would change their minds to support what the Australian public had long indicated was their position than those would renege on their previous support. We could not be sure of winning but we were going to do our best.

As had happened in 2012 under Prime Minister Gillard, the pressure the campaign built up meant the Abbott-led government could not avoid the issue and needed to do something. Of course, the most appropriate and democratic option for the government would have been to allow a free vote on the cross-party Bill. Numbers were close, a victory wasn't guaranteed, but the public was more than ready for reform. A survey by Coalition pollster Crosby Textor had support at 72 per cent, a number of Coalition MPs were surveying their electorates and reporting strong support, and once the prospect of a free vote was live, we could increase the grassroots pressure from the powerful personal stories that were already winning over MPs and senators.

Warren Entsch's outspoken support over the years had helped many across the community. Kate Doak, a young trans woman and strong advocate for the LGBTIQ community, tells us:

When I first walked into his parliamentary office back in September 2012, I was reeling from a panic attack just a few minutes before regarding how I'd been forced back into the closet after finishing university. Upon Warren telling me during our interview about the achievements of his close friend Dr Alana Young and how she put herself through medical school after transitioning, I knew for certain that I'd finally found for the first time in my life somebody who truly got what I was going through and understood my fears, because he'd witnessed them with a person who meant (and still means) the world to him before. Hearing those words and finally talking with somebody really in depth about what I was going through truly saved my life, while also pointing it down a path where it could become a successful and happy one in its own right.

Warren believed that if the prime minister was going to let two of his MPs draft and introduce a Bill, he should let them and others vote on it. AME had shared these hopes. Sadly, logic and fairness were consistently denied when it came to same-sex marriage.

Abbott made it clear that he would prefer that Warren Entsch's Bill 'never came up' but if it was going to, gave him the green light to introduce it in the party room meeting on Tuesday 11 August 2015. What unfolded next was a staged Liberal party room meeting to catch pro-equality government MPs off-guard and, controversially, invite the more conservative Nationals to attend. Government minister Christopher Pyne referred to this as 'branch-stacking' at the time. The meeting lasted six hours, with government MPs split multiple ways: some wanted a free vote, some wanted a referendum, some a plebiscite, some no change, and others wanted to stop talking about it.

Much has been written about this party room meeting, but very little about what was happening from AME's perspective. Here we share it for the first time. Rodney and Alex were on the phones to MPs and their influencers trying to get a good outcome, providing research, arguments, pathways and emotional support as it was a tough meeting. We had a direct line to some in the room, but there was no clear insight into the outcome and no idea what process it would follow: would there be a formal count or a ballot? One senior government advisor told us, 'Don't worry, there is no way we are settling on a plebiscite' and one Coalition figure warned us to be 'ready for anything'. The chaos and mixed messages were extremely unsettling.

This meeting was excruciating for LGBTIQ Australians to wait through. In Sydney, Shirleene and Sarah had not been able to get away to Canberra because of prior work commitments. They watched nervously, glued to the television and their phones for updates from the AME war room team. There had been so much support and interest in marriage equality that the party room meeting was getting wide coverage. It was an incredibly tense time; the meeting dragged on and on with no clear indication of what might result from it. Our lives were being talked about without us having any involvement. We were once again pawns in a political chess game, and had to be ready for whatever was next. Rodney and Ivan headed to Parliament House for some last-minute lobbying and waited out the evening in the Fairfax offices in the press gallery. Alex stayed in the war room with Elaine, Malcolm, James and Liam.

After six hours the prime minister emerged, ready to address the media. We had been given the heads up that 'It's a public vote' but that there was little detail on what that might involve. Abbott's speech claimed to reference the 'mood of the room', but there was no vote or ballot. It was clear this was a 'captain's call' to delay reform. The outcome: a public vote without any time frame, and a commitment that this was the last term Coalition MPs and senators would be bound on the issue. Penny Wong found it astounding the lengths opponents in the Coalition would go to in order to avoid a parliamentary vote. She says, 'It is inexplicable the extent to which they fought this. I've been in a lot of political fights and I understand people with ideological difference, but the visceral nature of their opposition is extraordinary to behold. Like, they fought to *not* have a vote so we couldn't get equality for years. To *not vote!*'

Abbott's announcement was beyond devastating. Malcolm McPherson remembers:

> In the evening, we were informed that the Coalition members had opted for a plebiscite. I was horrified at the prospect. We were a very small organisation with neither the resources nor the skills to conduct the necessary campaign. The coalition parties had betrayed us in a clever piece of political manoeuvring. At this point, I was less angry than shocked. We returned to our apartment very subdued. Ivan and Rodney did not return until after midnight. They were back in Parliament House at about six to continue discussions on strategy with our allies.

Alex remembers heading into the kitchen at the Boston Consulting Group, grabbing a bottle of red wine and announcing to the team, 'We've been fucked!' He explains, 'We were put in an impossible position. We didn't want or need a public vote and the concept was imposed on us to delay, if not deny reform. There was no policy detail and we didn't know when it would happen or if we could win it. We went from riding on a high to yet again being outplayed. While I wanted to weep, I felt I had to keep appearing strong in public.' While many were deeply upset that the party that supposedly believed in freedom of conscience and reducing government interference in people's lives would instead decide to put the dignity of same-sex relations to a public vote, others also grieved about the further delay this move would cause LGBTIQ Australians who wanted to marry the person they loved in the country they loved, and at a time when the campaign was breaking through into new territory. Opposition leader Bill Shorten called and spoke to Alex, outlining his disappointment in the government's decision and his despair for LGBTIQ couples.

Malcolm McPherson remembers:

There was no point in the war room team remaining in Canberra so I drove back to Sydney. I was appreciative of the company of James Northwood on that trip as I was still in a state of shock. There have been few occasions when I felt so devastated that I was uncomfortable about driving. It appeared that our work of over a decade might have been sabotaged. We might not achieve marriage equality unless the ALP were to win a landslide victory. Until that occurred, the ALP would be likely to be dependent on support from some members of the LNP to pass the required amendment to the *Marriage Act*. We had foolishly underestimated the government's capacity for treachery.

On 17 August 2015, although Tony Abbott's intervention had meant the Bill Warren Entsch and others had been working on could not pass, Entsch became the first Coalition member to introduce a marriage equality Bill, when he brought forward a private member's Bill into the House of Representatives with cross-party support. The Bill was co-sponsored by Labor's Terri Butler and backed by Labor MP Laurie Ferguson, Liberal back-bencher Teresa Gambaro, Greens MP Adam Bandt and cross-benchers Andrew Wilkie and Cathy McGowan.

Before he introduced the Bill, Warren hugged Terri and thanked her for her support. This entire group of MPs had put individual partisan politics aside to try and make marriage equality a reality, yet their efforts had been cruelly thwarted. By still going ahead, they showed that marriage equality did not belong to any one side of politics but mattered to all. Terri said 'the Bill had support across the political divide and "broadly across the community"'.[1]

Teresa Gambaro made a courageous decision in putting her name to this legislation and one that perhaps has not been fully appreciated. Teresa said that the cross-party Bill was the result of the 'best of parliamentary processes' that transcended the political divide and that 'it would be good to be able to allow this to be debated' as 'there are a number of members of parliament who have indicated that they would like to speak to this Bill'.[2] In her speech, she said that:

> My support for same-sex marriage is based on my belief that this is what the majority of my constituents in Brisbane want and my personal view that all people, whether they be straight or gay, are entitled to make that choice for themselves.[3]

In 2017, when the postal survey results showed that the electorate of Brisbane had one of the highest levels of support for marriage equality in the country, Teresa would be proved correct. In 2015 though, Tony Abbott did not even appear in parliament for the vote. Malcolm Turnbull and Christopher Pyne from the Coalition sat in the House of Representatives when the cross-party Bill was introduced.

Sadly, we all knew that Tony Abbott would not let any legislation pass through under his government without a public vote. Lyle Shelton made it clear that the prime minister's announcement was good news for opponents of marriage equality as it would 'kick the issue into the long grass'. The government was in no rush to discuss detail and the next battle was starting: would a public vote mean a plebiscite or a referendum? Conservative forces including George Christensen and Scott Morrison were calling for a referendum; moderates including Pyne and Brandis referenced the Australian Capital Territory vs Commonwealth decision that said no change to the constitution was needed, so they argued a plebiscite was more appropriate. As bad as a plebiscite was, a referendum would have been much worse – the question would be constitutionally complicated, a majority in a majority of states would be needed, and public funds would more likely be released to the opponents of marriage equality.

AME and the majority of the LGBTIQ community were opposed to any public vote. We knew it would unleash a damaging display of prejudice from the opponents of marriage equality that would further traumatise an already marginalised community. Yet if against our wishes and advice we were to have one, AME wanted to make sure the process was fair and the question was not designed to fail. To stave off the calls for referendum and ensure any potential plebiscite wouldn't be rorted, AME called for a fair process and a carefully worded question and for this to happen quickly. AME would later work with the Greens and crossbenchers on a Bill to that end.

Many in Labor were opposed to anything that would entertain any idea of a public vote. Some community members argued we should bring on the plebiscite and win it, saying progress for the LGBTIQ community had never been easy. Others were opposed to a public vote, not because of public support, but because the campaign infrastructure to win one didn't exist. Others highlighted the distress any public vote would cause the LGBTIQ community – something AME was only too aware of. What was clear is that Tony Abbott had succeeded in creating chaos, division, and despair amongst supporters of marriage equality.

Once the Greens and Senate crossbench announced their Bill for a plebiscite with the question 'Do you support Australia allowing marriage between two people regardless of their gender?', there was a growing concern whether, if a plebiscite were to happen, we would be ready to win. A meeting of LGBTIQ organisations and community leaders was called. Don Harwin, then president of the NSW Legislative Council, and the first elected Liberal to support marriage equality, made it clear that a new purpose-built organisation and infrastructure would be needed to win. Alex remembers that these words had a major impact on him, Janine, and Tom Snow, who were all in attendance. They knew that Don had been around many successful election campaigns and knew what he was talking about.

Alex was asked to dinner by Labor NSW MP Penny Sharpe and Nationals NSW MP Trevor Khan at the Midnight Shift on Sydney's Oxford Street. They urged him and AME to slow things down on plebiscite talk and kill off any support for a public vote. Alex raised the idea of a Senate Inquiry into the Greens and cross-bench Bill with a membership that would highlight its flaws. Both Penny and Trevor saw merit in the idea. Alex then shopped the idea around and the various political groups saw the value in it and a motion to establish an inquiry passed.

Throughout the inquiry many leading LGBTIQ groups and community leaders were consistent in their opposition to a plebiscite and urged the Senate to reject the prospect. In addition, many made suggestions on questions, process, and legislation. The result of the inquiry was a recommendation that the Senate should reject the plebiscite, and the report outlined the damage that one would cause to the LGBTIQ community and whether it was a waste of money for something that was the parliament's job to resolve. That didn't mean it was over, but everyone had time to take a deep breath and plan for the various outcomes that could follow.

Early days of preparing for a plebiscite

Prime Minister Abbott's party-room manoeuvre for a public vote continued to cause enormous upset and unrest, not only for community advocates, many of whom saw it as further game-playing and yet another delaying tactic, but also among Abbott's own Liberal Party colleagues. Tim Wilson recalls the impact of this policy on him: 'I was so distraught and angry and upset, and I remember calling somebody and saying, "I need a liberalism counselling session because this is so illiberal"'. Ryan Bolger, now Tim's husband, and a former political staffer, teacher, and Liberal Party member, told us it was the only time he considered quitting the party.

One of those leading the charge against the plebiscite policy internally was the communications minister at the time, Malcolm Turnbull, who reached out to influential radio broadcaster Alan Jones to intervene. Jones recalls Turnbull declaring the public vote was another 'captain's call' by Abbott and needed to be stopped. Jones remembers Turnbull telling him: '"He wants to have a plebiscite on same-sex marriage. I mean, this is ridiculous. The matter's got to go to the parliament. The parliament's got to decide". And I said, "Malcolm, if that's what you believe, go into the parliament, argue in the party room and win the debate'". Alex would work with Alan Jones, who would oppose the plebiscite, including covering a PricewaterhouseCoopers (PwC) report on his 2GB radio program that said the total cost of the plebiscite could exceed $500 million.

Ultimately, the Abbott Government's handling of marriage equality was one of the reasons for its downfall. The leadership of the Liberal Party, and therefore the prime minister of the country, was about to change. Malcolm Turnbull seized on the fact that the Coalition had had thirty bad polls and mounted a successful challenge against Tony Abbott. The change of prime minister initially gave marriage equality advocates some sense of new possibility. Was this the opportunity we needed? Would Turnbull overturn the Abbott directive? After all, he had advocated publicly for marriage equality and made it clear he supported a free vote.

Australian Marriage Equality (AME) issued a challenge to the new prime minister: deliver marriage equality through a parliamentary vote, a policy and pathway he had said he supported. But it was not to be. In his first day as prime minister he answered a question from the federal Member for Sydney, Tanya Plibersek, and made it clear he would not deliver marriage equality through a free vote in parliament. Instead, he declared his support for a public vote. This was a clear backflip on his previously stated view. Penny Wong says, 'Add this to the list of things on which he's changed position'. Turnbull decreed that the vote would take place after the next election.

The hopes of so many Australians passionate about this issue had been crushed by personal political compromises and a failure of leadership time and time again. As had occurred when Julia Gillard became prime minister, Turnbull failed to seize the chance to lead and to champion a reform the majority of Australians wanted to see. Instead, yet another prime minister opted to allow a minority of right-wing voices in their party to constrain him. The delay Australia now faced would have serious consequences for the lives of LGBTIQ Australians and their families and friends. It would mean the grief of families would be increased when partners died before being able to marry, that couples would face obstacles when trying to visit their sick partners in hospital, and that parents or grandparents lost their chance to see LGBTIQ family members celebrate their commitment and love through marriage. People died waiting. This should not be forgotten.

Political setbacks like this had hit AME before. Despite the campaign's incredible success in opening hearts and minds across Australia, flipping the script from minority to majority support in just a short few years, campaigners were used to politicians being out of step with the public on this issue. But this time, something was different. The marriage equality movement was about to face one of the greatest challenges it would ever experience – internal struggle and heightened uncertainty.

At this stage, AME was a proudly volunteer-led organisation that had punched well above its weight, with limited resources and a modest network of core volunteers across Australia. The organisation had its beginnings before the social media age and unashamedly rode the online activism wave to organise and engage with supporters of marriage equality. It had successfully worked through and achieved wins along the way in increasing community awareness of and support for marriage equality, and building majority support in parliament. It did this in an increasingly volatile political environment that featured regular changes of prime minister and the growth of personality-led micro-parties.

But now the threat of the plebiscite appeared to be a real and imminent danger. A new dilemma gripped campaigners and board members of AME: where should resources and energy be focused with so little to spare? A national vote was no small feat and carried with it a great risk of a loss (which was why opponents of marriage equality were proposing it). So, should we begin preparing for a plebiscite? Or should we throw everything into a campaign against a plebiscite? Did preparing for a plebiscite mean we were consenting to it, or was it simply part of our obligation to LGBTIQ Australians to win it if it was forced on us? Was there a way we could cover all bases and do all of these things?

Wanting to avoid a plebiscite, we kept coming back to one question: if we mounted a strong electoral campaign at the next election, would this help unseat the Coalition? AME had experience in running election campaigns and had worked hard over many years to get more marriage equality supporters elected. We were experienced and comfortable in doing this. It was also becoming clear that the marriage equality community strongly opposed the concept of a public vote and that it was incumbent on AME to campaign as strongly as possible against it. So we began work on developing our election campaign strategy.

Yet, what especially haunted Alex and Janine as co-chairs of AME and the entire team was what would happen in the worst-case scenario, if the plebiscite could not be stopped? Would we be ready to campaign on the scale required to win this type of vote? AME knew more infrastructure would be required for the fight ahead. More people, more experience, and more money would be needed to deliver on the potential paths we faced.

Unfortunately, it was in this context that a fundraiser AME had previously arranged was held at New South Wales Parliament in August 2015, very soon after Abbott's public vote announcement. It still went ahead. The mood in that room that night was devastating. Shirleene and Sarah shared with each at the time that it felt like we were seeing our campaign veterans return from Canberra with much of their usual spark missing. As heartbreaking as this was, the night also featured moments of connection. American film producer and long-term supporter of AME Kirk Marcolina reached out to Alex. Kirk had married his partner, Rob, in Canada in 2003. The couple had a daughter, Sophie, in 2006 and moved to Sydney from Los Angeles in 2012 to be closer to Rob's family. Kirk told Alex he could see that this was a pivotal time for the organisation and capturing it would make a great documentary. Alex told Kirk, 'You are not filming this mess, but we do need your help'. Kirk parked the plans for the documentary and came on board as a full-time volunteer, tasked with sharing people's personal stories of why marriage equality was important to them. He would tell us later that he stayed on for the entire campaign, with all its ups and downs, knowing that he was fighting for equality for his family and for others, and because he was working alongside excellent creative partners such as producer Helen Ross-Browne.

Helen joined AME around the same time as Kirk, also offering to volunteer her expertise. She brought with her a skill set finely honed through years of experience of factual and documentary experience in Britain. A gentle and deeply thoughtful person, Helen was also a fierce believer in social justice. She had a rare ability to see the stories people were holding inside themselves and to create an open and trusting climate where they felt able to share those stories with others. Over the next few years, she brought an enormous amount of heart and depth to the creative material produced for the campaign and to the team itself. Later, in August 2016, Leah Newman joined Kirk and Helen as creative producer. Leah's unique skill set, including visual ingenuity, editing aptitude and a keen eye for advertising and branding was welcomed by Kirk, Helen and the rest of the team. Leah's relentless positive energy, kindness and dedication were also a wonderful asset. Helen and Leah's shared perspectives as lesbians and their support would be very important to Shirleene and Sarah throughout the entire campaign.

It would have been easy to get distracted by the politics of marriage equality and overwhelmed by the challenges ahead, but Kirk, Helen and Leah brought the focus back to what this reform was about – love, fairness, and equality – and did so through focusing on the experience of everyday people. This had always been something that AME had done very effectively, but Helen, Kirk and Leah's skills meant that these stories could reach a much wider audience.

We heard far too many stories over the course of the campaign involving the loss of loved ones and erasures of relationships in the legal system, further amplifying the grief felt by those bereaved. One such story was the tragic death of British honeymooner David Bulmer-Rizzi in Adelaide in January 2016, where authorities had refused to recognise David's widower Marco as his husband. This case was heartbreaking for Marco and their family and globally embarrassing for Australia, but also an important reminder of why the campaign's work was so important. Helen arranged to capture this story in a respectful and sensitive way and reinforced why marriage was so important.

Ben Jago from Hobart, whose partner Nathan had died, also courageously shared his story. After Nathan's death, the police, the coroner's office and Nathan's family had not recognised their relationship as being anything stronger than housemates. Rodney worked closely to support Ben during this difficult time. He organised for journalist Tracey Spicer to draw attention to the injustice by writing a column for Fairfax and conducting an interview which was filmed. Kirk directed the filming of Ben and his mother, who wanted people to understand the obstacles that confronted same-sex couples when a partner died without a marriage certificate. Rodney stated in the media at the time, 'As long as the *Marriage Act* says same-sex relationships don't matter, the existing legal rights of same-sex couples will be easier to disregard'.

Work on the election campaign, and to push for a parliamentary vote to achieve marriage equality, continued. AME was working with community advocates to lay the groundwork for campaigns in key electorates, including Corangamite, Farrer and Hume where outstanding equality advocates such as Sharyn Faulkner, Toni Johnson and Tom Sebo were building strong support in their communities. The business community also began raising their concerns about the plebiscite. The PwC report that Alan Jones referred to on his radio programme, which showed that the Coalition's plan would cost the economy $500 million, was cutting through and being reported widely. Despite the efforts of campaigning on the ground and within core Coalition constituencies, polling still pointed to a Coalition victory and that they would not back down from their intention to hold a plebiscite.

Alex remembers that in early 2016, community concern began to shift from 'We can't have a plebiscite' to 'What if one happens and we lose?' The implications weighed on the minds of many marriage equality advocates. Yet, as with any threat to the LGBTIQ community, the potential plebiscite also meant more and more community members and allies stepped up to help. For the first time in its twelve-year history, AME moved into a physical office and began recruiting full-time staff. The office was a shared space above a much-loved bookshop on Oxford Street in Darlinghurst, Sydney. Janine laughs as she reflects back on this first office, which another tenant had decorated with risque images. 'I used to avert my eyes as I went through … I'm a prude.' Later, the City of Sydney would provide a larger office space on Pitt Street that the team could use exclusively.

Two marriage equality supporters, husbands Tom Snow and Brooke Horne, stepped up with a generous donation that meant AME could recruit paid staff. Former GetUp! campaign director Erin McCallum came on board for a few months to establish a more robust campaign infrastructure and help build the team. Expert campaigner Dae Levine joined as stakeholder director, remaining until June 2017. Dae's commitment to marriage equality, ability to foster connections across diverse groups, and fierce intelligence quickly marked her as a huge asset to the movement. Respected trans advocate Kelly Glanney, who would work closely with Dae in stakeholder groups, remembers:

> Dae impressed me from our very first meeting as a whip-smart,
> highly skilled and experienced campaign professional, who
> fully understood the complex challenges of building the broad
> national coalition that would be required to deliver us victory
> should a plebiscite ever be foisted upon us.[1]

The relationships Dae would form, and alliances she would build between groups in support of equality, would endure for the rest of the campaign.

Adam Knobel was second on board, initially taking on the role of head of digital campaigning but soon becoming digital campaign director, joining the rest of the leadership team who would take responsibility for the overall strategy, resourcing and campaign decisions over the next few years. Just thirty years old, Adam would become vital as the campaign continued. He was an incredible asset – the team soon saw his strong work ethic, his sharp mind in action, and his willingness to implement different approaches to build a community online and offline, as well as his deep commitment to the LGBTIQ community. Adam drew out the best in staff and volunteers alike. By the time the marriage equality campaign came to a close in December 2017, seasoned campaign experts such as Tim Gartrell (campaign director for Kevin07, who would later lead the Equality Campaign for the postal survey) were calling Adam Australia's best digital campaigner.

Clint McGilvray would soon join the team as communications director. Alex had been impressed by Clint's work with former NSW police minister Michael Gallacher, and felt Clint's understanding of the conservative side of politics, rural and regional Australia, and his relationships across mainstream media outlets would be an asset as the campaign moved forward.

The team began taking stock of what AME had built, looking for new ideas we could try and things we could possibly do better together. This era of the campaign was conducted in a real start-up environment. The team were planning strategies, tactics and tools the campaign could deploy to win under the various potential pathways. They hit the phones to talk with all their contacts and skyped with campaigners around the world, including people working on the United States (US) primaries deploying the newest campaign technologies. They also ordered and built their new computers, dealt with the tax office, established staffing and administration processes, and continued supporting recruitment for new colleagues.

One innovative idea implemented during this time was the partnership between Facebook and AME. For the first time for a political or social cause in Australia, Facebook introduced a marriage equality 'frame feature'.[2] This was inspired by the viral rainbow 'filter' that social media users worldwide added to their profile pictures following the Supreme Court decision that ushered in marriage equality in the United States. The 'I heart marriage equality' banner was added to AME's profile picture – a photo of Sarah and Shirleene, arms wrapped around each other at the 2015 Mardi Gras Parade, was used as the feature image. It represented an authentic moment of happiness captured by volunteer AME photographer Hayden Brotchie. It was special for the small details – Evelyn Gray, a long-time community campaigner from whom Shirleene and Sarah had both drawn strength over several years, was in the background. A giant purple glitter transgender symbol was also there in the centre of the picture – a subtle but powerful symbol whose significance would not be lost on those to whom it mattered most.

Tom Snow and Brooke Horne were keen to start taking a more active role, seeing how they could help provide advice and connect the campaign with other donors to provide much-needed funding. Strong grassroots campaigners, like Sharyn Faulkner from Victoria's Surf Coast and Tom Sebo from Goulburn, wanted to make sure areas outside of metropolitan Sydney were not left out of the planning. They had already achieved much in their local communities and had considerable knowledge that they could share with other campaigners.

To bring everyone together for planning, a workshop in Sydney was held in February 2016. It is a meeting all involved remember distinctly and was a difficult moment for AME.

The two-day gathering brought together the entire AME board and volunteer team, rural and regional campaigners and the newly recruited campaign team. It was clear that the thirty people in attendance felt the weight of the world on their shoulders. No one wanted to have to fight a plebiscite, but no one wanted to be responsible for losing one. We were all acutely aware that a negative result in a plebiscite would likely set back not just marriage equality but broader LGBTIQ rights for a generation or more. Joining the workshop as invited guests to provide an international perspective were Ty Cobb from the Human Rights Campaign in the US, and Tiernan Brady, who was the political director of the Gay and Lesbian Equality Network in Ireland. Both had experience in public votes on marriage equality and were there to share the lessons they had learned.

It was intended to be a team-building and planning event but it turned out to be very difficult and emotional experience for everyone involved. Based on the international experience, we worked out that the potential cost to the campaign of a plebiscite would be in excess of $10 million. Hundreds more staff and thousands more volunteers would be needed, and the dirty tricks of the opponents would mean that regardless of what our polling said, we could still lose.

Participants remember this planning day as intensely traumatic and a difficult reality check. As a result of the enormous pressure people were under, some conflicts came to the surface. Shirleene remembers a mood of anxiety and uncertainty. 'There were so many people in the room who had given so much for so long. Then you also had new people starting who were trying to find their voices and roles. And despite everything that had been done, we were potentially facing a public vote on our community's equality. As the days progressed, it became apparent that things were changing and this was very, very difficult.'

Although great work was done in planning how to deal with the challenges ahead, many strong personalities were left bruised and others were left feeling confused about their place and role in the movement. Alex remembers people contacting him afterwards questioning whether they should remain involved in the movement, either because they felt overwhelmed or underappreciated, or they felt unsure of where they would fit within a growing campaign machine. This was a situation that LGBTIQ advocates should never have been placed in. It is a testament to everyone's determination to see the law changed that each one of those thirty advocates in the workshop over those two days stayed committed to the marriage equality cause in one way or another, despite the pressure and difficulty.

The imminent 2016 election helped to sharpen everyone's focus. The team at AME would continue to focus on the election campaign with a push called 'vote for equality' to get as many marriage equality supporters elected as possible to nullify the need for a plebiscite. A key component of this campaign phase was to encourage constituents to learn their MP's and senator's positions on marriage equality and vote for supportive people at the election.

At the same time, through her relationship-building work, Dae had connected with Wil Stracke, a lead campaign strategist for the Victorian Trades Hall Council (VTHC). In 2014, the VTHC mobilised 2200 Victorian union members to have over 100 000 persuasive conversations with voters in key electorates. It was a stunning campaign that led to the defeat of Premier Denis Napthine's Coalition government after only one term.

Now VTHC was getting ready to kick off its campaign for the 2016 federal election – and it added marriage equality to its agenda. Wil, who married her wife Lisa in a legally unrecognised ceremony in 2016, wanted to trial an equality field project in key Victorian seats in partnership with AME. The goal was that together we would do our best to influence the election, while also beginning to train equality campaigners in case polling was correct and the election resulted in a Coalition government and the plebiscite going ahead.

This was a crucial partnership between the AME and the Australian union movement, support that would continue to be invaluable throughout the campaign, with unions sharing expertise and resources and even seconding staff. Wil herself would join the campaign on secondment after the election to help develop the framework for a plebiscite field campaign, and would return again during the postal survey to run field operations in Victoria.

By this time (March 2016), marriage equality campaigners had established a new, purpose-built organisation called Australians for Equality (A4E) to grow campaign capacity and resources should the Coalition win and continue with its planned plebiscite. Tom Snow and human rights lawyer Anna Brown would co-chair the organisation. A4E and AME would work in partnership and later under the banner of the Equality Campaign. Anna had assisted Australian Marriage Equality previously with the earlier High Court case in the ACT and was highly respected for her intellect and her commitment to advancing the position of the LGBTIQ community. Alex sat on the boards of both organisations along with AME director Jay Allen, with Janine acting as the CEO. Early in 2017, Shirleene's wife, Sarah, would also join the second board when Jay, a strong and principled feminist, offered her his place, in part to improve gender diversity and ensure there was a voice for women and lesbians in the campaign. Alex says, 'Sarah played a leading role as a lesbian in the campaign – sitting on both boards as a volunteer while still continuing her advocacy for the community and also working full-time in a demanding job.'

A4E continued to grow in the lead-up to the election. They recruited Tiernan Brady to bring his experience from the Irish YES campaign to Australia. Brooke Horne stepped in as a volunteer to head up the fundraising effort, with long-term AME volunteer Elaine Czulkowski joining the new organisation as fundraising manager. Luisa Low also joined, bringing a background in social media channels, to the orgnisation.

Together the whole team racked up plenty of marriage equality miles during the lead-up to the election, visiting and supporting local campaigns for marriage equality in areas that would be strategic not only for the election but also if a plebiscite could not be stopped. Shirleene remembers visiting seats in South Australia, Queensland and New South Wales. Other members of the AME team including Tim Peppard in Victoria and Peter Black, who had come onboard as AME's Queensland Convenor, also travelled extensively, making sure that marginal seats knew that they had a critical role to play in achieving marriage equality. Peter, a law lecturer in Brisbane who had enormous credibility in Queensland for his volunteering amongst the LGBTIQ community, would prove to be a huge asset to the campaign. Other long-time advocates across the country proved to be powerhouses of regional campaigning.

On Saturday 18 June, Sarah, Shirleene and Alex headed up to Nowra to hold a workshop in the Gilmore electorate.[3] Although Alex was wearing a moon boot due to a fractured foot, he was still determined to make the event. Amongst a wonderful group of locals who all shared meaningful and powerful stories, we met Dawn Hawkins, who became a passionate advocate for the cause. Dawn remembers the workshop as follows:

> I was sitting in the same room with Alex and Shirleene and
> Sarah and listening to them talk about the campaign, and how
> we run the campaign and the culture of marriage equality
> with all of my background of [being a lesbian in] the 1980s and
> 1990s and marching the street and demanding what we want.
> And listening to the three of them talking ever so lovingly
> and caringly and gently how we're going to do this, I kept my
> mouth shut and I just listened. And I listened, and I listened,
> and I came to understand what they were saying and what they
> were meaning, and that we were working for love, we weren't
> fighting for love, we were working for love. And I took that up
> as my mantra too – that I was not fighting for equality, I was
> working for equality.

Dawn's drive and determination continued to astound us throughout the campaign. While we met a great group of engaged locals and a fantastic advocate in Nowra that day, we struggled to return to Sydney after ignoring the petrol gauge in the car. Fortunately, we found a remote petrol station and it all worked out!

During the final fortnight of the election, the Labor Party joined marriage equality advocates in campaigning hard against the plebiscite. They set out their alternative path – marriage equality within 100 days of being elected through a free vote in parliament. Not only did Labor oppose the policy on the grounds that it would be a traumatic experience for the LGBTIQ community, they prosecuted the case that spending millions of dollars on a non-binding plebiscite was poor economic management. They also criticised Turnbull for not delivering this through a straightforward parliamentary vote, his own stated preference. Terri Butler, Labor's Shadow Assistant Minister for Equality, remembers, 'We were confident that if we won the 2016 federal election with the members that we had and the new candidates that we had in the winnable seats, that we would overwhelmingly have the numbers to get marriage equality through the parliament'.

But as we got closer and closer to election day, polls continued to predict that a Coalition victory was likely. This caused great tension in the movement. There were some who felt we needed to accept that we would have a plebiscite – that the party which ended up in power after the election would determine the decision. Others said we needed to campaign to make sure the plebiscite was voted down in the Senate, no matter the numbers.

While some dug their heels in on their respective positions Alex, who had been around the chaos of the issue for many years, reminded everyone anything could happen, we couldn't control it other than prosecuting our case to the best of our ability and we must prepare people for the variety of outcomes.

Labor might get elected, but were the numbers there in the Senate and House of Representatives for marriage equality within 100 days? The Coalition could get elected but, depending on the numbers, the Senate could allow or reject a plebiscite. Either way, there was still no clear policy document from anyone on what a plebiscite would look like or what exemptions they would advocate for or accept in a marriage equality Bill.

Alex urged people to focus on the reform regardless of the election outcome. It was still a live issue and could come through a variety of pathways. We did know we would probably be able to celebrate the election of a whole bunch of gay and lesbian MPs in both houses of parliament, a sign of growing acceptance and also a leverage point for us in the political process.

On 30 June 2016, just days out from the election, the *Australian* newspaper published a headline that concerned and devastated many. Tiernan Brady had been quoted in an interview saying that, based on the Irish experience, a plebiscite could be a 'unifying moment' that could 'bring people together'.[4] This quote, on the front page of Australia's national newspaper, was used by people who wanted a plebiscite to argue that the experience ultimately would not be difficult for the LGBTIQ community.[5]

AME urgently released a statement reiterating that the organisation did not support a plebiscite and believed the best way to achieve marriage equality was through a free vote in parliament. Yet a number of advocates and insiders still question whether this front-page headline swung votes towards the Coalition at a critical time by diffusing the different approaches the major parties adopted towards achieving marriage equality and appearing to minimise the difficulty of a public vote on human rights.

The campaign to elect as many supporters as possible in the new parliament continued. In the final week of the election, AME's 'Vote for Equality' website received tens of thousands of visitors, allowing voters to look up their local candidates and see how they would vote on marriage equality and their preferred process for voting. Candidates who had not been forthcoming about their position started to make considerable efforts to contact us to show their support. Marriage equality was a major issue for the country. LGBTIQ Australians watched the election result very closely – the result would dictate their immediate future.

Initially, there was no clear winner, with the Labor Party doing better than polls had predicted. The results firmed however, and the Coalition pulled ahead with a one-seat majority. The make-up of the Senate was still unknown, as was whether Labor, the Greens, and cross-benchers would 'respect the government's mandate' to hold a plebiscite or vote to oppose it.

The first positive result for the marriage equality campaign was that more supportive MPs had been elected to parliament than ever before, as had more gay and lesbian MPs. However, unfortunately a plebiscite was still very much on the cards – especially with a surprisingly strong result from Pauline Hanson's One Nation – a party pushing hard for a plebiscite.

Within the marriage equality camp, the pressure of this outcome was clearly causing tension. The combined organisations would need to grow rapidly and the result made a plebiscite more likely, but not guaranteed. As a result of this tension, Rodney Croome decided to leave AME on 2 August 2016, to focus his energies solely on stopping a plebiscite. He wrote a piece published in the *Guardian* that evening, saying:

AME is the group that will have to negotiate the best possible terms for a plebiscite should one occur. Having me advocating against the government's plan for a plebiscite makes it harder for AME to engage constructively with the government.[6]

Alex thinks that many within AME had seen Rodney's decision coming, but did not expect it to happen so suddenly. Many from the community first heard the news from reading Rodney's piece in the *Guardian*. Alex was at an annual community event in his electorate when his phone started to ring with journalists wanting comment. Alex was seriously concerned that Rodney's piece implied AME wouldn't oppose a plebiscite, despite the amount of work it had done across a number of areas – from the corporate world to talks with Liberal party figures, to commentators – to get them all to join in opposing it. For Alex, this was a hugely stressful time:

> The immense pressure that was placed on Rodney and me saw
> our friendship disintegrate. I truly believe that we both wanted
> to do the right thing by the LGBTIQ community. For me, it was
> making sure we were fully prepared for any scenario, and for
> Rodney, it was killing the plebiscite at any cost. We maintained
> professionalism publicly, occasionally speaking after each
> other at the same press conferences, but our friendship never
> recovered. We went from working closely for nearly a decade
> to never speaking again after he left AME. This was one of the
> very real costs of what was imposed on us.

Shirleene remembers this as an extremely difficult time:

> For me, the most painful period in the marriage equality
> campaign was when Rodney left AME. When Sarah and I
> joined AME, Rodney had been the national director and we
> built a close relationship over those years. He trained me to feel
> confident talking on television and taking workshops, and we

spent a lot of time together. I appreciate how personally painful the decision to leave was for him. I knew that he would be a powerful campaigner against the plebiscite and I wished him the best. We went through a lot together.

Others from within AME found this a similarly challenging time.

It is to the credit of both Alex and Rodney that neither let the tensions of the time impede the work that needed to be done. Rodney continued to campaign alongside a number of other organisations until marriage equality was achieved.

Despite the turmoil, the team turned their focus to the highly volatile and evolving political dynamics that lay ahead. This included campaigning against the plebiscite, while most significantly, at the same time preparing to win one if it was imposed.

The plebiscite is voted down

The team knew they had to put all their focus on the situation ahead. The issue of whether the plebiscite could be stopped or would go ahead ultimately came down to one thing: the numbers in parliament. We had to do all we could to win the numbers to vote down the plebiscite in favour of a free vote. But if we could not achieve this, we also had to be ready to respond with a plan to win a public vote. It was a volatile situation where anything could happen.

The campaign established a political tactics group. Their challenge was to monitor events, watch numbers, and discuss approaches. Meanwhile the campaign leadership team was working to increase public support and targeted constituent action, helping to influence and improve the numbers as they were being reported by the political tactics group. The campaign team and directors were reaching out to new audiences and supporters, to build our social media and email channels and encourage action on the ground in communities. They also researched which messages had the greatest impact on the public and politicians, and began developing new creative and advertising campaigns designed to turn the heat up on the parliament.

Following the July 2016 election, we knew the numbers were there for the government's plebiscite Bill to pass the House of Representatives. We also knew One Nation, the Liberal Democrats, Jacqui Lambie and Family First would support it in the Senate.

It was initially unclear what Labor's position would be, although Penny Wong had come out strongly against a public vote in June 2016 at the 28th Annual Lionel Murphy Lecture, before the federal election was held. She remembers, 'I just said, "We shouldn't do this. We shouldn't do this to the community. We shouldn't do this to our families, and basically, if we have to wait for a Labor government so be it"'.

Once the election was over, it took several more months for the party as a whole to publicly clarify their position, as Bill Shorten, Tanya Plibersek and Terri Butler and others consulted with the LGBTIQ community. We also needed to firm up what the Greens, Derryn Hinch and the Nick Xenophon Team would do.

Once the shape of the Senate was settled, the Coalition Government had thirty senators, the Labor Party twenty-six, Pauline Hanson's One Nation four, the Greens nine, the Nick Xenophon Team three, Family First one, Jacqui Lambie one, Liberal Democrats one, and Derryn Hinch one.

This meant that the government had thirty-seven of the thirty-nine votes needed for a plebiscite to pass the Senate likely locked in. There were considerable risks before us – the Senate blocking the plebiscite or it being voted up were both live options. The two remaining votes could come from right-wingers in the ALP, the Nick Xenophon Team, or other cross-benchers. Pauline Hanson's team, who wanted a referendum, could negotiate less than optimal terms for the LGBTIQ community. A vote could happen at any time.

The campaign faced multiple challenges. On the political front, we had to watch the numbers and parliament closely and lobby for a parliamentary vote rather than a plebiscite, while continuing to engage supportive members of the government, consulting on what the fairest possible plebiscite could look like if it was forced on us against our wishes. It was better to be at the table in those moments than be served up for lunch – we needed to give our opinion on what the rules of a plebiscite should be, and the way marriage equality should look in this country, because the NO side were certainly making strong advances with their position.

Outside of the Canberra circus, we kept building support and activism for marriage equality in the community, knowing this increasing pressure would power our interventions in parliament. We also had to increase our national infrastructure and fundraise substantial amounts of money in case we were forced to face a plebiscite. We needed to keep an understandably anxious LGBTIQ community and their supporters up to date with everything that was taking place, to share the increasingly complex story of what was happening and why we had to pursue several pathways.

This was not an easy time and the uncertainty would last months more until November, taking a considerable toll on many in the campaign. Things were tough for key staff and volunteers. Not only were they stretched in competing directions, with priorities changing regularly depending on the latest information (including some that was inaccurate as we worked out the competing personal political interests of members of the new parliament), but there were also some in the LGBTIQ community who attacked them personally for spending any time at all figuring out how to win a plebiscite if one was called. Although a plebiscite was just two votes away from potentially happening, some saw any contingency plans as giving in and not fighting hard enough. No doubt strategists who opposed marriage equality, such as Lyle Shelton from the Australian Christian Lobby, had hoped that the threat of a plebiscite would open up divisions in the LGBTIQ community – dividing and conquering – and at times it felt as though they had won.

Alex remembers seeing the way vitriolic online tirades against the team hurt deeply. 'We had to deal with people not associated with the campaign making outlandish and false claims, saying that by preparing for a plebiscite, we were supporting one.' Yet this couldn't have been further from the truth. Rather, we were laying the groundwork to win a plebiscite if it could not be defeated – as well as frantically building the power we needed to win the numbers in parliament to support a free vote on marriage equality.

This was an incredible amount of pressure to place on any small team of core staff and volunteers who had to put their lives on hold to work to achieve marriage equality. Not to mention that this was taking place in a rapidly changing start-up environment. The team was quickly increasing the number of signed-up marriage equality supporters and building a powerful new campaign machine. It was also still forming a new workplace, including figuring out each other's communication and work styles.

Following the election, we moved into a new office and Tiernan began hiring more staff to work on key areas like multicultural and faith outreach. Clint and Adam were developing new messaging and refreshed branding with the support of talented researchers, copywriters and designers that aimed to engage supporters, persuade middle Australia and influence politicians.

Stakeholder director Dae Levine was racking up incredible miles flying around the country to bring supporters together, share our research and political knowledge, and form the relationships and networks we needed to not only push for a parliamentary vote, but also win a plebiscite if that strategy failed.

Adam was working late into the evenings building a new website with community campaign tools for target electorates, while Helen, Kirk and the newly hired Leah were starting to develop ideas for new advertising campaigns to help pressure the parliament into action. Brooke and Elaine were furiously meeting with potential donors who would support the campaign, working to bring in the money we needed each month to enable all this crucial work to take place. Janine's leadership at this time would give staff the support and direction needed in a rapidly evolving landscape. A full-time volunteer herself, she assumed responsibility for the budget, staffing and corporate engagement. On top of this, the campaign was heading toward its first round of departures as some who had joined the team were offered new opportunities or decided that the campaign work was not a fit for them at this stage.

It was an incredibly busy and stressful time for many, but it was particularly tough for people who had quit their jobs or put their lives on hold to jump in the deep end and build something new so we could actually win. Alex feels very strongly that 'keyboard cowards who attacked staff and volunteers during this period did untold damage to those people who would continue to campaign until marriage equality was delivered. As is often the case it's friendly fire that hurts the most'.

There were things we could have done better. We were under-resourced, working on too many things at once, and that meant we dropped some balls and missed some moments. We were also in the middle of changing how we told our story, and the political story was more and more complex every day; during this time, mistakes were made. Volunteers and grassroots supporters should have been more closely engaged across the country and within the organisation. Much of the management of volunteers fell to other volunteers. However, the lessons we learned during this period would go on to sharpen campaign decision-making processes, change the way we communicated and lead to significant improvements in the way we engaged with supporters, including those grassroots supporters and volunteers who were always at the heart of the movement.

The work against a plebiscite was there, but we hadn't packaged it and communicated it properly amidst all the chaos. While a lot of the political lobbying for a parliamentary vote happened in Canberra meetings, we also gathered together over 65 000 signatures on a petition against the plebiscite with GetUp! which we presented when parliament returned. We also collected thousands of signatures on petitions for a free vote using Victorian Trades Hall Council's Megaphone platform, and 25 000 signatures on a petition with Change.org. The marriage equality movement was building, and people were making clear to our politicians that a plebiscite was unacceptable.

Shirleene remembers speaking at forums and in the media at this time, working to make clear AME's position and build community support for a free vote: 'I hoped desperately that a plebiscite could be stopped. Whenever I had the opportunity, I was always very, very clear in outlining that. This led to some interesting conversations with people determined that one should happen, including presenter Chris Kenny on Sky News'.

The tensions that the threat of a looming plebiscite provoked continued to affect various members of the team, including Alex. They came to the surface at a large community teleconference organised by Dae Levine. This call included all leading LGBTIQ advocacy organisations across all major capital cities. It was a true testament to Dae's ability that she was able to bring together so many groups under such difficult circumstances. She remembers, 'One of the greatest pleasures I had in the campaign was being responsible for pulling together the stakeholder teleconference meetings. Although they were stressful at times, they were a critical part of the emotional development of the campaign as a collaborative tool'.

At this particular meeting, one participant started the call by saying, 'I want to know why AME supports a plebiscite'. Alex, very upset, quickly responded, 'We never did and we never will. You need to be aware of the damage you are causing by misrepresenting to MPs and stakeholders that the peak marriage equality body wants a plebiscite. If they believe you, we're all stuffed'. If politicians were under the impression that Australia's major marriage equality group supported a plebiscite, it would become all the more difficult to stop one.

While this had been a tense moment, the teleconference concluded with a number of LGBTIQ leaders telling Tom, Anna, and Alex they appreciated the very difficult work they were doing. Alex had real concerns that while the marriage equality movement was arguing about process, its opponents were getting clear air to detract from the reform. They took the opportunity to plant the seeds of doubt in people's minds about the 'consequences' of the wider reform and used their opposition to the 'Safe Schools' programme as a proxy war against marriage equality.

Communications director Clint McGilvray, an experienced crisis communication expert, was at the coalface of these attacks, dealing with right-wing commentators and their accusations on a daily basis. 'We got accused of wanting to cancel Mothers' Day and Fathers' Day, through to being compared to Nazis. They got the airtime because they were sensational, and it was more interesting to media than the process argument we were having. We had to be on guard, and stay focused, not get into fights, but always remember that we were simply working on a reform that was about fairness and equality.'

In the Sydney office, Helen, Leah and Kirk continued to produce meaningful creative content. This would remind people of what was at stake with marriage equality and why this reform mattered.

Many in the wider community, and even some within the LGBTIQ community, did not appreciate how close we were to getting a plebiscite – and one that would not be on terms in any way favourable to the LGBTIQ community. If Greens senators Scott Ludlam and Larissa Waters, and Nick Xenophon Team senator Skye Kakoschke-Moore, had disqualified themselves earlier from the Senate because of their dual nationalities, we would likely have had a plebiscite with terms negotiated by Pauline Hanson's One Nation.

During this time, not a sitting week passed without Anna, Tom, Alex, Clint and Corey walking the halls of Federal Parliament. Their presence was important in supporting those in Labor who wanted a binding position against a plebiscite. The group also had to lobby government MPs to ensure that if a plebiscite was forced on us, the YES in the question would reflect a pro-marriage equality stance, and to ensure millions of dollars in public funding was not given to the other side (or any side).

We also had to maintain strong relationships with the press gallery to ensure our messages were getting out. This team, who were later joined by Claire Dawson as the campaign's director of government affairs and Lee Carnie from the Human Rights Law Centre, became fixtures in Parliament House, working around the clock. Adam Knobel in the Pitt Street office remembers this as possibly the busiest, most stressful period of the campaign, 'a seven jobs in one' time for him.

Shirleene remembers the range of other LGBTIQ organisations and advocates from around the country who also engaged in very determined lobbying against the plebiscite at this time, and credits them for their efforts. Some collaborated closely with our campaign, while others worked independently. Placed in a situation that was not of our choosing, we all did the best we could. While many of the other advocates will have their own stories to share about their experiences and efforts, she acknowledges their contribution at this crucial time.

For example, Rainbow Families played a significant role in stopping the passage of the plebiscite through the Senate, bringing their supporters to Canberra for face-to-face lobbying meetings with politicians. LGBTIQ families were able to truly capture the impact a plebiscite would have on the community, particularly the mental health and wellbeing of their children. Felicity Marlowe, the co-convenor of the Rainbow Families Council, released a statement saying, 'Our children and families have long been the target for anti-marriage equality campaigners, so the prospect of a national, publicly funded campaign is extremely concerning for many parents and carers in rainbow families'.

It was becoming clear that efforts to stop the plebiscite were starting to work. In August, the Greens announced they would vote against the plebiscite. That same month, newly elected senator Derryn Hinch was the next to announce he would also vote against it. Many in Labor publicly opposed the plebiscite but their position and how they would deal with it in parliament (bound or free vote) remained unclear. Opposition Leader Bill Shorten continued on his tour, meeting with various LGBTIQ groups and leaders to hear their views before announcing Labor's position.

In September, Shirleene and Sarah Midgley chatted with Labor MP Terri Butler while staffing an AME stall at Brisbane Pride. They left the conversation feeling hopeful that Labor would indeed block the plebiscite. Terri emphasised that Labor had been listening very carefully to the marriage equality community and that she firmly believed it was wrong to put LGBTIQ people through an exclusionary, discriminatory and painful process like a plebiscite in order to gain equal rights.

Some conservative commentators were trying to press Labor to support a plebiscite as a method of getting marriage equality through parliament quickly, but ultimately these commentators were failing to get any wider traction as the LGBTIQ community and their allies were so united in their opposition to a public vote.

As it looked more likely that Labor would make a public statement about blocking the plebiscite, Alex became increasingly concerned about the language some advocates were adopting. False comparisons were made by some, who declared they would rather wait for marriage equality under a future government than have a plebiscite.

While AME and Alex certainly agreed that a plebiscite was unnecessary and the reform should be achieved through a free vote in parliament, no one thought LGBTIQ people should have to wait for marriage equality. Advocates had campaigned on the urgency of this reform for years and this language damaged that narrative. There was a risk it could also be adopted by opponents to say that marriage equality was not important to LGBTIQ people.

With this weighing on his mind, Alex called Evan Wolfson, one of the greatest international advocates for the marriage equality movement, who had been an advisor and confidant for many years, and asked for his advice. The forthright New Yorker loudly proclaimed, 'You NEVER say you can wait! Some people can't wait!' Evan urged Alex to do all he could to make sure that supporters of marriage equality avoided this language and instead called on politicians to do their jobs. It was time to shift attention away from the internal discussions of campaigners and back to the politicians who for years had used these distractions to avoid passing laws that would guarantee marriage equality.

While much of the attention was on the Liberal Party at this time, their Coalition partner, the Nationals, appeared to be off the hook. Kerryn Phelps and Nationals Leader Barnaby Joyce both had children at the same school, and during a parents and teachers night, Kerryn approached Barnaby and urged him to move forward with a parliamentary vote rather than a plebiscite. Barnaby responded by offering her and two other advocates the opportunity to address the Nationals. Kerryn called Alex, who said he would love to join them and suggested that Paul Ritchie come as well. Paul was a former Tony Abbott advisor and the author of the book, *Faith, Love and Australia: The Conservative Case for Marriage Equality.*[1]

At the meeting in September, Kerryn did her usual excellent job of explaining the physical and mental health benefits of marriage equality and the risks associated with a plebiscite.

Paul shared his journey to marriage equality and outlined that the appropriate and traditional way to deal with reform would be through a vote in parliament, where everyone could vote according to their conscience – something that had always been a core value of the Nationals. Alex took questions from the MPs and senators so they could understand where people were coming from.

It was clear that many in the room had not fully engaged with the reform, and Alex got the impression the plebiscite was their way of outsourcing something they found difficult to deal with themselves.

Alex and Kerryn were especially taken aback by a remark from George Christensen, in response to the concerns they raised about the mental health and wellbeing of LGBTIQ people during the proposed plebiscite. He said words to the effect of, 'What about my health and mental welfare – I was attacked, bullied and vilified for opposing Safe Schools. If I wasn't as strong a person as I was who knows what could have happened'. (In March earlier that year, Mr Christensen had linked the anti-bullying programme to pedophilia.)

Using enormous amounts of self-control, Alex and Kerryn restrained themselves from the natural instinct to scream at the man. Instead Alex asked, 'If you are concerned about the tone of the debate, why would you want to put the spotlight of a national public vote on it? Why not just resolve it in parliament swiftly?' There was no response.

The extraordinary remarks of George Christensen aside, both felt that they had a good hearing, they had built some relationships, and it was the first time in the history of the parliament that LGBTIQ advocates had been invited to address a Nationals Party room.

As pressure mounted on Labor and the Nick Xenophon Team to declare their hand, pressure also mounted on campaigners. Senior members of the government would meet with members of the Nick Xenophon Team, Labor, and marriage equality advocates, trying to see how they could make the plebiscite more palatable. Those representing the campaign held the line. They made it clear that they could not and would not support any type of plebiscite. In attempts to bring the campaign on board, we were offered a plebiscite that would have no public funding for either the YES or NO case, a 'good' question, and a part in an official plebiscite oversight body for Alex and others.

Alex remembers members of the government lobbying him personally to publicly support a plebiscite. He was told this would provide cover for crossbenchers or members of the opposition to do the same. The changing numbers in the Senate added to the air of uncertainty. Greens senator Scott Ludlam had gone on stress leave and Labor senator Lisa Singh was in the UN acting as an observer. Those two lost votes against a plebiscite were nullified when the Family First senator Bob Day quit the Senate and Senator Corey Bernardi joined Senator Singh in New York. Senator Dean Smith, who strongly opposed the plebiscite, said he would likely abstain.

At the end of August, Nick Xenophon called Alex to say he and all the Nick Xenophon Team senators would oppose the plebiscite. This meant that the plebiscite would be stopped if Labor adopted a binding position against it. The government then indicated it would move forward on the plebiscite in the October sitting weeks in order to force Labor's hand.

It was clear from Bill Shorten's language that Labor were likely to oppose the plebiscite as a bloc. Alex and Shirleene attended a consultation in Surry Hills in Sydney at the start of October where Bill Shorten and Tanya Plibersek emphasised that they were taking very seriously the concerns they were hearing from the LGBTIQ community, in particular from Rainbow Families. A range of LGBTIQ community advocates, including Lauren Foy from the New South Wales Gay and Lesbian Rights Lobby, spoke out at that consultation, stressing the increased level of vitriol that had been directed toward them since the plebiscite had been announced.

On 10 October, Labor announced it would block the plebiscite in the Senate. But the government was not prepared to give up. In a last-ditch effort to salvage it, the prime minister and attorney-general asked to meet with Tom, Alex, and Tiernan. This meeting would be held in the private jet airport hangar at Sydney airport. They put a final case forward, with the prime minister and the attorney-general saying they believed the plebiscite would be the fastest way to deliver marriage equality.

At that meeting, Alex explained the political reality to both men, saying that they didn't have the numbers for a plebiscite, that those numbers were not changing, and that Labor had won the political fight as they were seen to be listening to and representing those who the reform affected.

Alex remembers Tom putting forward one of the most compelling and personal cases against the plebiscite that he had seen. Tom said that like thousands of other LGBTIQ people with children, he didn't want them to face a taxpayer-funded hate campaign from the NO side. The meeting didn't result in any changed minds.

After this meeting, the attorney-general agreed to meet with representatives from LGBTIQ groups via a national teleconference hook-up on 16 October so we could make sure he heard their concerns first hand. We wanted to create a space where people could contribute their thoughts on what marriage equality legislation could look like. At the meeting, he would also have the opportunity to discuss the plebiscite directly with community representatives, although no one involved believed he would convince anyone to change their minds. It was also arranged for Labor's shadow attorney-general, Mark Dreyfus, to address the LGBTIQ community via a similar hook-up.

At the meeting, LGBTIQ community representatives had the opportunity to discuss their concerns. The attorney-general then put forward his case that a plebiscite would deliver marriage equality. Emotions were running high and events took a dramatic turn. Alex remembers having to quickly press the mute button at the Sydney end of the conference call when one advocate started screaming at the attorney-general. The meeting had taken place under the Chatham House rule, where information from a meeting can be revealed but not the identity of the source. Yet, as soon as this meeting ended, a number of participants went straight to journalists to attack the attorney-general. Alex contacted journalists to stress that this was the first time an attorney-general had attended such a meeting.

The media coverage was hugely frustrating to the team, because we were already strategising how we could achieve a post-plebiscite parliamentary vote and needed to maintain a working relationship with the government. For Dae Levine, the incident reinforced her concern that there were a lot of people in the movement who wanted to work together, but also 'a very small minority who were more interested in having grandstand moments with little or no outcome, or worse, sabotaging progress for their own sense of power. They didn't realise that we had the most power when we worked together, rather than tearing each other apart'.

With the writing on the wall that the plebiscite would be voted down, the campaign leadership knew it would be important to refocus minds on the substantive reform, give supporters actions to take, and send a clear message to parliament that we weren't going anywhere. With every delay, we were only going to get stronger until every Australian was able to marry the person they love.

We launched a new campaign, branding, and re-focused messaging in advance of the vote in the Senate to create the pressure needed to hold the Labor party and cross-bench firm on their commitment to vote down the plebiscite legislation. We also began laying the foundations to push politicians to do their jobs and bring about marriage equality by a parliamentary vote. Using the moniker, the 'Equality Campaign', the campaign was a joint initiative of Australians for Equality and AME.

This was where the hard work and expertise of the new team reached the surface, and for the first time was visible to the community – and also the politicians, who recognised this marked shift in power and force would make things difficult to ignore.

To refocus the media and community discussion back to just who this reform was about, the creative team had worked on a new television campaign designed to show the energy and enthusiasm of the movement. The advert, filmed in cold Balmoral streets and a local park, showed hundreds of Australians marching with purpose to create an Australia that celebrated equality, and revealed the Equality Campaign's new moniker. The band, the Birds of Tokyo, gave the campaign the use of their song 'Lanterns' for the clip. The advert featured real marriage equality supporters, including De Greer-Yindimincarlie and Kirstie Parker, a couple who wanted to marry, Ben Davison, a man who hoped to see his two mothers marry, and Thi Hy Dang, a proud Vietnamese grandmother who wanted her grandson, William Le, to have the same opportunities as the rest of her family. The creative team also began releasing videos with the personal stories of these people, showing diverse Australians for whom marriage equality was both important and urgent.

Adam would get a new website and digital campaigning toolbox in place, full of new content and stories, to encourage new supporters to sign on and empower them to take action. Along with finalising the advert, this was an enormous undertaking, and Adam and Helen worked late and on weekends to make sure it was done.

Dae would make sure all the LGBTIQ stakeholder groups felt a part of the new campaign, and Clint would sell its importance to the press gallery, many of whom felt that when the plebiscite was voted down, the issue would go the way of the republic debate. Upon the launch, the story was the number one on news.com. au – and a newly energised community began signing up to get it across the line.

For staff, the new campaign was critical for morale. With the plebiscite voted down, we were providing a pathway – everyday Australians sharing their stories and telling their MPs to do their job and vote for marriage equality. It was exciting to see Francis Voon, faith and multicultural outreach co-ordinator, build on and extend on earlier work. Francis remembers:

> Together we connected with ethnoreligious groups including supportive Buddhist, Christian, Hindu, Jewish and Muslim

leaders and communities. It is also important to acknowledge
that we engaged with LGBTIQ people of faith as well. We
also made contacts with religious and secular media. Like
with many movements of change throughout history, we
acknowledge that we stand on the shoulders of giants, and
that many individuals and groups had been doing some of
this bridge-building and networking work, sometimes quietly,
sometimes more publicly, for years, sometimes decades,
before we started, and it was because of the leadership and
passion of these elders and pioneers that we achieved as much
as we did.[2]

In the meantime, the plebiscite Bill headed to the House of Representatives, where it passed, and then the Senate, where it was
doomed to fail. The attorney-general made a last appeal to senators to support marriage equality. Importantly, the attorney-general also released a draft of the marriage equality Bill the government planned to introduce following the plebiscite. Securing
the release of this Bill was something the political tactics team,
especially Tom, had lobbied the attorney-general hard for because
people deserved to see the Bill Australians would be voting for.
The team also saw a long-term benefit in the release of this legislation if the Senate held firm and defeated the plebiscite, because it
would refocus the conversation around what the passage of marriage equality should look like in Australia.

This was a significant moment because it was the first marriage equality legislation drafted by a sitting government, but it
still wasn't quite right. Following nationwide community consultation, it would later become the basis for the much-improved
Dean Smith Bill.

On 7 November 2016, the plebiscite legislation was defeated in the Senate thirty-three votes to twenty-nine. Those who opposed it made a number of powerful speeches. Louise Pratt described the plebiscite as 'an utterly demeaning act ... No child should have their family status a subject of public debate like this'. Penny Wong told the Senate that: 'We do not want our families and our children publicly denigrated. This hate speech is not abstract. It is real, it is part of our daily life'. She later spoke to us about her feelings at this moment. 'I didn't feel jubilant. It was more, well, we've stopped something that I don't think was the right thing to do. And hopefully, protected some of our community in the process. But I would much rather it have just gone to a [parliamentary] vote. You know, we could just never get [the Coalition] to that point, could we?'

Many LGBTIQ advocates in the public gallery clapped, happy with the result. Many others watched on the news or the internet. It seemed as though a public vote on human rights had been avoided and the spectre of the plebiscite, which had haunted LGBTIQ Australians for the past fourteen months, had disappeared.

Alex sat alone in the advisor's box on the Senate floor, feeling flat. The LGBTIQ community had spoken and it looked as if the plebiscite had been stopped. But despite the final vote going down exactly as Alex's numbers had predicted, and the plebiscite being blocked, we were no closer to achieving marriage equality. And that was the political challenge that mattered.

So Alex saw that another battle was just beginning. It would involve pushing for substantive reform in an uncertain parliament with a government that had said it would no longer deal with the issue. It felt like an insurmountable challenge. Sarah

Hanson-Young, who had formed a very close friendship with Alex, saw he was feeling overwhelmed and came over to him. She gave him a hug and invited him for a drink in her office. While some were celebrating, for Sarah and Alex, the mood was sombre and the path ahead uncertain.

Uncertain future

While many in the LGBTIQ community were relieved that the plebiscite was voted down in November 2016, the campaign rollercoaster continued. Adam Knobel told us, 'We now had to prepare for every possible scenario. Like what if nothing happens and it's a complete stalemate? How do we bubble along for another twelve to eighteen months and then build up to a huge campaign with a goal of trying to change the government at the next election in order to achieve marriage equality? We had plans written for various different scenarios'.

Tim Wilson describes this as one of the most difficult times for him. He believed the defeat of the plebiscite in the Senate blocked the pathway to marriage equality. From his viewpoint, the issue within the government risked being 'dead and buried'. Pressure would soon mount on Tim and a small handful of marriage equality supporters in the government to risk their careers and cross the floor to allow a parliamentary vote.

Penny Wong and others got to work on a legislative path forward. Most on her side of politics assumed this would be in the next Labor government. Bill Shorten emphasised that Labor would legislate within the first hundred days of assuming office.

It was clear that marriage equality advocates were keeping up the pressure but supporters within the Coalition weren't sure what they could do. There was no way the government would suddenly allow a free vote. Their narrative was that Labor had killed marriage equality and they would continue to shift blame to them.

Alex knew he had to remain positive and wrote a piece for the *Huffington Post,* arguing history showed that when confronted with a challenge, the LGBTIQ community and their allies organised, spoke out and united. Now that the plebiscite had been voted down and there was some clear air, it was important to look at what had been gained, rather than stop to dance on the plebiscite's grave or emphasise the fear that marriage equality could still be a long way off.

For the first time the LGBTIQ community could see what a large-scale, professional national campaign could look like, with infrastructure built across the country in case a plebiscite was imposed on us. This in no way detracts from the significance of the previous campaign but the scale of the new one vastly exceeded its predecessor. The threat of a plebiscite had meant we needed to get more organised than ever before, which meant that a record number of people offered to help.

Interestingly, the plebiscite policy provided room for a number of Coalition members to publicly declare their support for marriage equality. These included WA Senator Linda Reynolds, Victorian National Damian Drum, and most significantly, Federal Attorney-General George Brandis.

Labor's position on marriage equality also strengthened during this time. They went from being the party who allowed a free vote on reform to a party whose leader was dedicated to delivering marriage equality. Labor had been careful to consult with the LGBTIQ community throughout and clearly understood the significance of the issue.

When the threat of an unwanted plebiscite loomed, our campaign had prepared to win. From supporting local campaigns from one side of the continent to the other, to uniting nearly ninety LGBTIQ organisations and learning from the international experience, we harnessed the incredible drive and determination that was present across the country.

Now there was an unparalleled level of organisation, infrastructure and energy in place to win a parliamentary vote. The challenge for the movement was to channel the loud and determined opposition to the plebiscite into passionate advocacy for marriage equality. Alex and the campaign leadership strongly felt it was time to use the energy and momentum that opened hearts and minds on this reform to achieve marriage equality.

There were still challenges within the campaign. Many staff and volunteers were working long hours away from friends and families in the pressure-cooker environment of a campaign that needed to cover several different directions.

One of Alex's great regrets is that women in the campaign did not receive proper recognition for their immense, vital work. The *Guardian* did a study later that year which mentioned the top names in the campaign. Alex would top that list, followed by Tiernan Brady and then Sally Rugg from GetUP! as a distant third.[1]

However, it was the women in the campaign who were largely responsible for pulling together stakeholders and keeping them up to date, ensuring we met our budgets, managing staff, writing opinion pieces and leading community forums, ensuring we maintained relationships across the parliament and told a diverse range of stories, amongst many other tasks. One insider told us, 'There was a huge amount of work that was done by lesbians in particular on the campaign – and certainly by other women too – which was completely unseen'.

Alex received this feedback from a number of male and female staff and volunteers. In response, he wrote to all the women in the campaign to thank them for the vital work they were doing and the leadership they were providing. He acknowledged how stressful, intense and tough the campaign was for them.

Anna would also write, saying, 'The number of women on this list doing fantastic things for this campaign is truly impressive. We should all feel proud of what we do and confident that the leadership of the movement has the fingerprints of some really impressive women all over it and is all the stronger for it. It is a privilege to work with you all'.

These words, although welcome, did not truly reflect the fact that we would not have achieved marriage equality, or even had a campaign vehicle to do so, without the sacrifice and dedication of the women in the campaign. It is an especially important lesson for other campaigns, especially LGBTIQ campaigns, that in getting to YES, the critical role women both LGBTIQ and straight played was never publicly celebrated or acknowledged as it should have been. Perhaps capacity was lost because of barriers experienced by women in the campaign.

Given that the government had released the Bill that would follow a plebiscite to enact marriage equality, various MPs and advocates started to think about having an inquiry into that Bill to ensure we had the best possible legislation ready to go.

One of the idea's big supporters was Terri Butler, who stopped in Sydney between flights from Brisbane to Canberra to meet with Tom and Alex at Sydney Airport. Anna Brown would join in via videoconference. Terri had cemented her reputation amongst the team as a true believer in marriage equality and someone who was prepared to work very hard to see the reform achieved. Terri believed that an inquiry would buy time, refocus minds on the legislative path, and give everyone something constructive to do. It would produce the most robust marriage equality legislation that would have the best chance of passing through parliament.

Alex and Anna, although fatigued by multiple marriage equality inquiries over the years, along with Tom, saw the merit in the plan. On 30 November 2016, the Senate would unanimously vote to establish an inquiry into the Exposure Draft of the Marriage Amendment (Same-Sex Marriage) Bill. Senator Louise Pratt, who was on this Committee, remembers:

> It was an enormous privilege to be there and to have worked
> on the drafting of it and, you know, I think without that work
> that Dean and I and Janet did, it would have been quite a
> different Bill. We went through and moved heaven and earth
> to create something that didn't compromise LGBTIQ people,
> single out LGBTIQ people for discrimination in any way, but
> named people's religious freedom so that it was something we
> could all move forward on.

The Equality Campaign would encourage supporters to share their stories on why marriage equality was important to the senators on the inquiry and would work with stakeholders across faiths, cultures, the broader community, the legal profession and human rights advocates to make sure we had both quality and quantity of submissions supporting a fair Bill to achieve marriage equality.

The campaign would continue to highlight the diverse support for marriage equality by sharing stories about its surprise heroes across social media and other platforms. Producer Helen Ross-Browne, who had an excellent reputation for finding and developing the campaign's personal stories with compassion and integrity, found one that touched many. It featured Thi Hy Dang, the proud Vietnamese grandma who had featured in the earlier Equality Campaign launch advertisement with her grandson. Her personal video with the message 'All we want is to see our families happy' would be viewed hundreds of thousands of times. These videos weren't just viral social media content. They would act as a guide for other people on how to share their story, whether it was with the Senate Inquiry or their MP, or to influence those close to them.

In the middle of this, Australian Marriage Equality (AME) received an unexpected boost to its profile when international Australian musician Sia was nominated for a number of ARIA music awards. Sia had been well aware of the hard work and effort that Janine Middleton had put into the marriage equality campaign and reached out, via her management, to ask that Janine and the campaign use any awards that she might win to direct attention toward it.

This meant that AME could nominate someone to collect the award on Sia's behalf, providing an opportunity for that person to share their story and advocacy on the national stage. Janine and communications director Clint kept this exciting news quiet while they looked for the right person. In the end, they decided to go with Angie Greene, a young, heterosexual woman from Melbourne with a gay brother. Her family were AFL royalty; her grandfather, father and both brothers were all celebrated sportsmen, so she was a good choice as a messenger in Australia's sport-loving culture. When Sia won the award and Angie accepted it, her speech had more than the desired impact – she was passionate and wanted the country she loved to treat her much-loved brother equally and fairly. Angie and her family would continue to contribute a great deal to the campaign. Liberal MP Tim Wilson ultimately dedicated his vote for the final marriage equality Bill to the Greene family a year later.

Sia's ARIA award would soon find a home in Sydney's Oxford Street. The City of Sydney had been extremely generous with their support, donating not only office space, but a shop-front for 'The Equality Shop'. Full-time volunteer Shane Lloyd, who was in charge of merchandise, ran the project to open the shop. Janine and another volunteer, Alex Zborowski, joined Shane and spent a number of days on their hands and knees scrubbing and cleaning to turn an empty restaurant space into a very cool pop-up shop.

On the shop's opening night Shirleene held up the ARIA award and spoke of how hopeful she felt about achieving marriage equality, given the growing number of allies from all parts of society doing what they could to support it. The shop would become an important community hub, providing perfect Christmas presents for 2016. It was also a very significant key to the campaign's fundraising efforts, making $250000 in profit.

Janine puts the shop's success down to Shane's dedication: 'He worked in that shop day in, day out, often by himself. There was also an amazing team of volunteers who supported him and this was a hugely successful and important part of the campaign'. One young volunteer, Lachlan Woods, a law student, would regularly commute from his Blacktown home to help out in the shop as often as he could. Sarah Midgley did the bulk of the time-consuming task of coordinating shop volunteers and commends them all for their passion in keeping the shop going. She remembers 'my soccer team, the Flying Bats, were regular helpers and that was just one example of the community spirit demonstrated all across Australia.'[2]

We started 2017 with a combination of hope and uncertainty. The campaign had some amazing team members who were working incredibly hard; the community was uniting; support in polling was strong, but we had to keep questioning whether this was cutting through to the decision makers in Canberra.

Submissions for the Senate Inquiry closed on 13 January, so Dae Levine, Sarah Midgley, Shirleene and Peter Black had to work fast to get through the thousands of submissions people had sent through the campaign website and package them together. The volume was astounding and included supportive submissions from 200 major religious and ethno-religious groups, individuals and clergy ranging from, but not restricted to, Buddhist, Anglican, Catholic, Evangelical Christian, Muslim, Jewish and Hindu representatives and celebrants from across Australia.

The inquiry would also hold hearings in Canberra, where Anna, Lee, Alex and Tom would represent the campaign. Anna and Lee were the shining stars for the committee. They knew every aspect of the proposed legislation, international comparisons, and could refute opponents' hypotheticals, such as calls for cake-makers to be able to discriminate against same-sex couples, with thoughtful and factual rebuttals.

The year also started with an intense schedule of visits to key electorates to build support for marriage equality in rural and regional centres across Australia. This project would be managed by Clint and Mike Fairbairn, a young and determined communication professional. Along with Clint and Mike, Shirleene, Peter Black, Malcolm, Tiernan, Janine, former Olympic swimming champion Daniel Kowalski, Angie Greene and Tim Peppard would share travelling to over thirty cities and towns across Australia over a six-month period. Local speakers from these regions proved to be the most compelling advocates for marriage equality.

After one forum on the Sunshine Coast in Queensland, parents Laura and Daryl talked with Shirleene about their religious faith and their love for their gay son. While they were initially shocked when he had told them he was gay, they had come to see his sexuality as a great gift, given to them by God, that had enriched their lives enormously. Their son had married his husband in New York as he was unable to in Australia and Laura and Daryl wanted to see their home country recognise his relationship and the dignity of their son's love. At a Coffs Harbour visit, we met Sam Dawson, a celebrant and mother of a gay son, who could marry heterosexual couples yet could not see her own son make this commitment. Time and time again, through hundreds of personal stories, we would hear about why this issue was significant to the country as a whole. The visits would often make front-page news in the local papers. Advocate couple Nickie Hardgrave and Penny Partridge from Redcliffe in Queensland, held a number of market stalls where they engaged so many supporters that they ran out of postcards to sign. They also held follow up actions to build momentum and engage with their MP. Whether the forums were in Tamworth, Toowoomba or any other town, the community was making it clear it wanted to see the reform achieved – and now.

With Federal Parliament heading back to work for 2017 and the Senate Inquiry expected to release their report in mid-February, and the campaign hopeful it would recommend legislation, a new, and very direct television and digital campaign would be launched. It featured doctors, lifesavers, nurses and service men and women calling on MPs to do their job and vote for marriage equality. It would include lines like, 'We can make the ultimate sacrifice but we can't make the ultimate commitment' and 'We can hold a life in our hands but we can't ask for our partner's hand'. Alex and Shirleene launched the campaign together in the Equality Shop on Oxford Street. The content was a collaborative effort between the team and advertising agency The Royals.

Alex had shown a copy of the advertisement to Tim Wilson. After watching it in Alex's office, Tim said, 'This is exactly what we need – a message about commitment, responsibility – something my colleagues can understand'. The ad would be pushed out across major television networks, in targeted digital ads in key seats, and everywhere in Canberra Airport for when MPs arrived at work.

The week of Valentine's Day 2017 would prove to be a major turning point for the campaign. The Senate Inquiry report finally came out and delivered the first ever consensus report on what marriage equality legislation should look like. The Inquiry was made up of Liberal, Labor, Nationals, Greens, and Nick Xenophon Team senators, with a mix of supporters and opponents. Together they delivered a pathway for marriage equality with suggested changes to the government's exposure draft Bill to get the balance right between allowing same-sex couples to marry and protecting the religious celebration of marriage. Anna Brown told the *Guardian* at the time that the report 'delivers cross-party consensus on key issues and sensible solutions to address concerns about religious freedom'.[3]

Penny Wong would tell the Senate this was the first time 'the clouds of partisanship had parted' on marriage equality and told *Buzzfeed* the report showed 'historic agreement on how we can move forward and achieve marriage equality. We ought to pause to consider the enormity of that achievement: in a debate so often mired in partisanship, mired in acrimony, a debate characterised by finger pointing, we have a spirit of cooperation and the agreement around this report'.[4]

Anna Brown, who had worked very hard on the inquiry with her colleague Lee Carnie at the Human Rights Law Centre, remembers this as 'a really important moment' with 'political consensus between Liberals, Labor and the Greens'. It was critical to help translate that Senate Report into legislation. Louise Pratt told the Senate the work of the committee 'demonstrated that it is not difficult to create laws that uphold freedom of religion and freedom to marry'.[5]

The outcome of the report was a credit to the hard work of the committee and the campaign team. The Canberra team, especially Tom, were determined to make sure the draft marriage equality Bill was released; the detailed submission and appearance before the inquiry made it clear we were the adults in the room. The bulk and quality of other submissions the campaign had encouraged, and Australians had provided, proved that when the plebiscite was voted down it had not killed the issue, despite the wishes of some in the government and a building narrative in the press gallery.

The consensus report provided a great deal of momentum for the movement, and saw government MPs slowly coming back to the table. The campaign was now energised to focus on further building support and new allies within the government. Work was continuing in a number of MPs' electorates. Tom, Anna, Corey Irlam and Alex would now be joined in Canberra by the very skilled and experienced Claire Dawson, who would now head up political engagement as director of government affairs. Claire had been around parliament since John Howard's time and knew everyone from the staff in the cafe to those in the prime minister's office. A straight married mother, Claire had not been personally affected by the lack of marriage equality but she genuinely understood why the issue mattered so deeply to the LGBTIQ community. She told us, 'Once you realised the impact it was having and the discriminatory nature of changing that law [in 2004], it was something you couldn't ignore any more' and she gave her role everything she had.

Alex said, 'Claire gave us a new level of confidence, energy and organisation – we were all too close to the issue and sometimes too exhausted by it to think clearly and strategically. Claire would literally say, "Sit down, calm down, eat something and we will work out what to do next"'. Claire quickly endeared herself to the team with her willingness to explain complex parliamentary procedures and her understanding of how deeply personal this issue was to so many. Shirleene says, 'Claire always appreciated that a great many of the volunteers were not political insiders who understood all the intricacies of parliamentary process'. When the campaign was finally over, Shirleene asked Claire if it had been challenging to work with volunteers not from the political world. She said, 'I wouldn't say it was challenging. I would say it was an honour ... a great honour'.

Around the time the Senate report was released, the campaign would also have a visitor, the Hon. Nick Herbert, a Conservative member of the British Parliament and one of the leading players in delivering marriage equality to Britain. Nick would join the Liberal Party's Tim Wilson and Christine Forster for a panel at Twitter's headquarters in Sydney. Supporters of marriage equality within the Liberal Party had been feeling extremely bruised by the internal divisions over the issue. They were disappointed in the party's stance on marriage equality, and while they were trying to move the issue forward internally, also felt they were being attacked by the LGBTIQ community

This event saw a number of state and federal MPs, staffers and party members come together with the campaign for a great panel on the conservative case for marriage equality and an important team-building event to get everyone together and focus on the challenge ahead. Alex's good friend Elaine Czulkowski, who had moved from being a long-time volunteer with AME to a staff member on the Equality Campaign, was friends with many of them and said this evening allowed people to vent as well as encourage each other to turn up the pressure.

Nick Herbert would also meet with a number of government members and do a series of interviews. Claire had organised a very busy meeting schedule for him and he would drive home the message, 'There is nothing to be afraid of, delivering marriage equality would be seen as a hugely significant and proud moment for a conservative government'.

The week of the Senate report and Nick's visit would culminate with the campaign hosting a BBQ in one of the courtyards in parliament. The campaign leadership, and many volunteers and staff, would join MPs and senators from every party, staffers, and journalists to hear not only from Nick, but also from the Greene family, who were in Canberra to lobby MPs for reform. A number of MPs would also make brief speeches, with each of them committing to move the reform forward.

Attending the BBQ to video MPs and senators, many staff and volunteers remember feeling more hopeful than ever that we were finally getting somewhere. They could see first-hand how effective the campaign was in the halls of parliament. After all the uncertainty and internal pressure, Kirk remembers thinking, 'this was one of the best moments for the campaign. I felt we were working to our full potential and really cutting through'.

Following this, Mardi Gras season was soon upon the campaign. Community anger at the government for not delivering marriage equality boiled over, and at a Sydney Gay and Lesbian Mardi Gras meeting a motion passed recommending Turnbull not be invited to the parade. Alex was extremely frustrated. Just as advocates were breaking back through into the Coalition, this sent the opposite message of positive engagement the campaign had been promoting. Alex said, 'We were opening doors, and this attempt to embarrass Turnbull risked closing some of them'. The withdrawal of the invitation made national news.[6] The AME board wrote to the Mardi Gras board ahead of their meeting. The letter noted that:

Mardi Gras has helped us advance marriage equality through being an inclusive and welcoming event. We believe one of Mardi Gras' strengths is the growing number of politicians who want to participate and watch the parade, providing AME and other campaigners an opportunity to showcase the growing and diverse support for marriage equality. We hope leaders from across the political spectrum, including the Prime Minister and the Leader of the Opposition, feel welcome to attend and join the hundreds of thousands of marriage equality supporters on parade day who look forward to the festivities and eagerly await the chance to celebrate achieving marriage equality together.[7]

Peter de Waal and Peter Bonsall-Boone (Bon), longstanding advocates for the LGBTIQ community who had participated in the first Mardi Gras in 1978, led the Equality Campaign's float. In October of 2016, Alex, Shirleene and Sarah had been privileged to witness one of the most beautiful and loving ceremonies imaginable when, after fifty years together, the two men spoke moving vows to each other in front of a hall packed with friends who appreciated all the two had done for the community and their deep love. In the absence of marriage equality being available, the two men wanted to celebrate their love publicly. At the time of their ceremony, Bon was sick with cancer and by the time Mardi Gras arrived in March 2017, it looked as though the two were running out of time. The courageous partication of Peter and Bon in the Equality Campaign's float and their willingness to continue to advocate for marriage equality, even while Bon dealt with very serious health challenges, moved many.

Peter and Bon reinforced the message that marriage equality was not something that could be pushed to the side or delayed. There were people who needed this reform to happen and urgently. Helen Ross-Brown had immediately recognised the depth of the long-lasting love between the two men and had produced a heartrendering video with them that would ultimately become one of the most watched marriage equality videos made in Australia. Along with Peter and Bon, politicians from every party, advocates, and the stars of the recent television campaign marched down Oxford Street in the largest ever entry into the parade. The prime minister did not attend.

One international visitor who participated in the Equality Campaign's Mardi Gras entry was Californian senator Ricardo Lara, who had lived through Prop 8 in California in 2008. Prop 8 overturned the legal status of same-sex marriages until Prop 8 itself was overturned in 2013, and the rights of same-sex couples to marry were restored. Ricardo Lara lifted the spirits of staff and volunteers. He urged continued persistence and congratulated the team on a great campaign. It was wonderful to have Ricardo join in the Mardi Gras float.

While the campaign was getting back on its feet, the feedback from some in Canberra was that the issue was not a priority in the electorates of key MPs – and without that, the numbers could never be there for any parliamentary attempts to succeed. Working with Coalition insiders, the campaign developed a further list of electorates. Clint would continue his programme of visits in these seats to build support for whatever might happen. The tactics group also agreed to invest in a great deal of polling to show the government that the issue was alive and well on the ground in their heartland.

The polling would show the largest support ever recorded in the key Coalition seats of Bowman, Brisbane, Cook, Fisher, Goldstein, Moncrieff, New England, Pearce, Petrie, Robertson, Swan and North Sydney. A majority of voters in all twelve seats said 'yes' when asked if same-sex couples should be allowed to marry. A majority also said it was 'very important' to resolve the issue by parliamentary vote in 2017.

The campaign was making it increasingly hard for the government to ignore the issue. Alex thanked the team for working against all odds to bring the issue back to life in an email saying, 'We were in their electorates, their inboxes, their office in Canberra, their televisions, and stealing their headlines – thank you'.

Yet, the lack of action in parliament was particularly galling, given that we knew there were people urgently waiting to marry and that they were running out of time. Peter de Waal and Peter Bonsall-Boone were desperately hoping that parliament would act. Yet the dream they shared of having their relationship legally recognised through formal marriage was appearing less and less likely. On 14 April 2017, Good Friday, Peter and Bon wrote an urgent letter to the prime minister. It said, 'You can make our wish come true. But please do it quickly as Bon's time is fast running out!' Senator Janet Rice hand-delivered the letter to Malcolm Turnbull herself.

On 19 May 2017, the team were devastated to hear that Bon had passed away. Helen, Kirk, Shirleene, Sarah, Alex and Anna paid their respects on behalf of the team at a service filled with love and respect for a man who had given so much to the community for so long. Helen and Kirk also arranged for Bon's death to be covered so that others across the country would realise that a loving and good man who had spent fifty years with his partner had been denied the opportunity to marry. This was a very challenging task for them both emotionally, yet they did not hesitate to do it, grasping the significance and importance of showing the country what had been lost. Shirleene thought their commitment to doing this was one of the bravest things she had seen. Kirk describes this as a very hard time and perhaps one of the most difficult things he had to record in his career, due to his respect and connection to the men. But even after Bon passed away, Peter de Waal found the strength to keep campaigning so that others would not have to go through the same thing.

In addition to campaign actions, the group of Coalition MPs affectionately known as the 'Rainbow Rebels' would start agitating internally – but it wasn't easy. As Tim Wilson recalls, 'What we did was to expend an incredible amount of political capital, an incredible amount of emotional and physical energy to take the issue from where we were at the end of 2016, which was essentially one step back from dead and buried with no way back on the agenda, to back on the agenda'.

Work would begin across the Parliament with Labor and the Greens indicating they were working on incorporating the recommendations of the Senate Inquiry report into legislation. Importantly, so was Coalition Senator Dean Smith. The Rainbow Rebels, or the 'fab five', as Claire Dawson would call them, would begin turning up the temperature.

Corporate Australia also joined in and showed strong support. Qantas CEO Alan Joyce, the partner of the campaign's director of merchandise, Shane Lloyd, took on an especially significant leadership role. He would put the case that the government was falling behind the will of the people, and that it made good business and political sense to allow a parliamentary vote.[8]

This would lead to a remarkably inept attempt by the Coalition minister Peter Dutton to attack Alan Joyce, making headlines for telling him to 'stick to his knitting'. The reaction to this was swift, with the public backing Alan Joyce and telling Peter Dutton to instead start doing his job and get on with legislating for marriage equality. The hashtag #sticktoyourknitting started to trend across social media, and Greens Senator Janet Rice would famously bring her knitting to the Senate.

Significantly, Peter Dutton's comments dominated the media coverage of the government that week, pushing their announcement of the Snowy Hydro 2.0 energy project down to a second-tier story. Ironically, Dutton's actions had shown that the government could not get away from the issue of marriage equality, regardless of what they did or said.

Claire would counsel the team not to get too excited, stressing that the two most important things in politics, 'numbers and timing', needed to be the focus. The campaign needed to make sure the legislation was right. We needed more than just the Rainbow Rebels in the government to vote for it, and we needed to make sure that Labor or Greens didn't pre-empt any actions the Rainbow Rebels might take by bringing on an early vote, which would have led to certain defeat. All of this also depended on the opponents in the government not outplaying us, as they had successfully done to date.

In mid-March, while Tom, Anna, and Claire would do the rounds of Parliament House building support for resolving the matter through a parliamentary path, Clint and Alex would do the rounds of the press gallery. People could tell something was in the winds. Just as Alex and Clint were selling a message of hope, *Daily Telegraph* senior political editor Sharri Markson would alert them to a story she was about to break headed, 'Plan to hold national plebiscite on same-sex marriage via postal vote'.

To advocates, this was clearly an attempt to stymie the progress on marriage equality. To people like Peter Dutton and Scott Morrison, it was a way for the government to stick to their pre-election commitment despite the Senate voting it down – the government believed a postal vote wouldn't require a vote in parliament to enact it – nothing that would later become subject to a challenge in the High Court.

It was a direct, aggressive attack on the campaign. Alex would jump on Sky News just as the story broke and call the plan a 'sneaky and underhanded way of overriding the Senate'. Fortunately, a number of Coalition voices would also come out opposing the postal plebiscite, with Dean Smith calling the idea 'junk mail' and Deputy Prime Minister Barnaby Joyce telling Sky News that 'nobody would be happy with it'. Suddenly battle lines within the Coalition were drawn on the issue between those who wanted a postal vote and those who wanted a parliamentary vote.

The message that the government needed to deal with the issue had clearly gotten through, which was a victory for the campaign, but many in the LGBTIQ community felt once again that they were being treated as political footballs. Shirleene remembers, 'Yet again, something that should have been so easily dealt with was being pushed off the agenda'.

Given the campaign and the Rainbow Rebels had turned up the temperature, but we weren't yet ready for boiling point, a decision was made to lower the heat politically, but keep the electorate-based work going and keep working under the radar in Canberra. This strategy was proven right, when the opposite happened – marriage equality became front-page news for all the wrong reasons, and it galvanised the attention of our opponents. Christopher Pyne had been secretly recorded by someone unknown as he spoke at a private function, stating 'marriage equality would happen sooner than people think' and that the moderates within the Liberal party were 'in the winners' circle on marriage equality'.[9]

The right immediately reacted, accusing the moderates of working against an election commitment and creating a distraction. Although his comment had been recorded without his consent, Christopher Pyne issued an apology for his statement and was forced to retract it. This was another dip on the marriage equality rollercoaster for the LGBTIQ community – suddenly a senior government minister said it was going to happen, then backed down.

One person who didn't back down was Senator Dean Smith, who in July annnonced he was working on a legislative path to marriage equality.[10] Warren Entsch would share his journey to marriage equality and why he wanted it resolved in this term, and Trevor Evans put his case forward as well.[11] Tim Wilson and Trent Zimmerman would do a variety of TV and radio interviews where they expressed their hope to see marriage equality achieved.

Dean Smith's work on the legislation had finished and he had perfectly incorporated all the recommendations of the Senate Inquiry into law and had a Bill ready to go. It was critical to Dean that his Bill had the support of the campaign and his fellow Rainbow Rebels and when the Bill was announced, the campaign issued a media release with Alex and Anna welcoming it as a 'circuit breaker' and 'the most robust Bill the parliament had seen, with the greatest chance of passing'. What happened next, though, showed that the path to marriage equality was about to get more difficult than ever before as the team confronted their biggest challenge to date.

The High Court

No one could have predicted that a challenge before the High Court of Australia was just around the corner. As the temperature rose on the issue of marriage equality, the campaign kept up its efforts. To help drive home the message that the issue should be resolved through a parliamentary vote, we once again did polling, this time along with the Australia Institute, to show support for marriage equality in Cabinet ministers' seats, ahead of an upcoming Cabinet meeting where marriage equality was expected to be on the agenda. The polling showed that in these seats, voters – whether they were Labor or Liberal, young or old – wanted the issue resolved through a parliamentary vote by the end of the year.

On the ground, we encouraged supporters in key electorates to meet with their MPs and report back to the campaign. Adam formed a team who would send text message blasts saying, 'Your MP needs to hear from you' to people identified on our database as highly engaged. He and Lee Steph, who was based in the office as a digital campaigner, worked with Shirleene, Sarah Midgley, Carol Burger, Jay Allen, Chris Pycroft and Cam Hogan, Australian Marriage Equality's new treasurer from Lismore, to start sending out text messages. Shirleene remembers the response to the texts as very positive.

Respondents were asked a series of questions to gauge their interest and commitment to make sure we were putting the best possible people in front of MPs, once a meeting was secured. Claire briefed supporters on the best way to engage with specific MPs. Cam Hogan, who lived in an area we were concentrating on, met with her MP, Kevin Hogan (no relation). Dawn Hawkins from the electorate of Gilmore, who had proved to be an outstanding campaigner, met again with Liberal MP Ann Sudmalis. PFLAG in Perth met with Julie Bishop's office. This method proved successful and we were able to supply information to the Liberals' Rainbow Rebels to help them identify potential supporters in the party room.

The feedback coming back was mixed. Some MPs would support a parliamentary vote, others were still holding on to a public vote, some MPs felt the Coalition shouldn't and wouldn't deal with the issue this term and would develop a new policy ahead of the next election, others didn't want to talk about it. Meanwhile, Labor and the Greens were holding their fire – neither party wanted to bring on a vote that would fail.

The situation was coming to a head. Warren Entsch was getting sick of all the talk and wanted a vote. He went to the prime minister, telling him that 'we're going to bring it on'. Warren told us he 'made it very clear to the prime minister that if he didn't do it, we would give it to the Labor Party and they would do it and we would cross the floor'.

Tim Wilson describes the pressure he and others were under as 'horrific'. People attacked them in the press saying, 'We're going to get rid of you at the next election'. Pressure also came from the LGBTIQ community, urging the rainbow rebels to commit to crossing the floor. Tim remembers, 'There was a lot of pressure on us, people attacking us for different strategies and approaches, without ever thinking about what it was like to be in that situation'. Tim's husband Ryan remembers that: 'We had no choice but to have our name attached to everything, yet people flung mud. We never had the right to be anonymous yet they could say or do the most horrid things and wouldn't put their names to it'. Tim and Ryan remember being attacked in the media and accused of betraying a party they had been loyal to; a party they wanted to see deliver marriage equality.

The issue would again come down to numbers. Were the numbers there in the House of Representatives and in the Senate to have a marriage equality Bill pass with only a handful of Coalition MPs? Tim was concerned by what would happen if they risked their careers and the numbers weren't there. 'One of the big frustrations we had is we knew certain things which we could never say in public, like one of the key reasons it was such a high-stakes game is because we knew we didn't have the numbers or they were far from guaranteed.'

Insiders would keep a count of various scenarios and agreed getting the numbers was always going to be hard. We knew that because the government only had a majority of one, 'extreme discipline' was more important than if the majority was bigger. Any MP who crossed the floor risked catalysing accusations that the Coalition was a government in chaos and couldn't control its members. Claire Dawson, reflecting back on this period, does not believe there was ever going to be another path possible with this government. 'We were never going to have a free vote, we were always going to have a public vote. It was always going to happen.'

Tim says that although the Rainbow Rebels felt everyone should have a free vote, they knew it wasn't likely. For him, the worst-case scenario was: 'We could have forced a vote, and that would have been defeated in the Senate because two Greens senators disappeared overnight, meaning a vote would be defeated which would be a complete clusterfuck. So while we didn't agree with it, once it was clear that was the position, some people still wanted us to cross the floor. It would have ended, I'm absolutely confident, in a complete disaster, and that would have killed the issue for up to a decade'. The fear was that parliament would have voted down both a plebiscite on marriage equality and marriage equality itself at once.

The Cabinet decided the issue needed to be resolved and another party room meeting was pending. Tim's read of the room was that it didn't look good for a free vote, despite the campaign's valiant efforts. He said to the campaign, 'You need to decide whether you prefer a compulsory attendance vote that parliament defines through a vote, or a postal vote that cabinet decides on'. The rainbow rebels would go to the party room passionately arguing the case for a parliamentary vote. They lost, and the government agreed to try to pass the plebiscite legislation through the Senate. They also made it clear that, if that failed, they would impose a postal survey. Talking to us in 2018, Kelly Glanney reflected back on why the coalition party-room decided on a postal survey. She says, 'Clearly the main reason we had to go through this was more about the obvious culture war going on in the Coalition than what the vast majority of Australians wanted or would have chosen. We endured this painful Spanish Inquisition process not in the national interest, but because Malcolm Turnbull and Tony Abbott couldn't play nice'.

The campaign team was feeling the pressure of the uncertainty of the current political situation. To provide guidance and reassurance to the team, Alex enlisted the help of former Liberal

Party Senator Chris Puplick, who had long spoken out in support of marriage equality, had been through many tough, yet successful political battles and had helped the campaign with strategic advice at critical times for many years. Alex invited the team to his apartment for pizza and wine and a pep talk from Chris. In the talk, Chris stressed you could never predict what parliament might do but he continued to assure everyone their work would soon see Australia on the right side of history.

The government moved quickly, and on 9 August 2017, moved a procedural motion which would have then served to bring on the plebiscite Bill again. The government couldn't even get their initial procedural motion through. Later that day, they announced they would proceed with the postal survey.

Alex and Anna fronted the press and declared that the government's approach to marriage equality had gone 'well beyond a joke' and threatened to challenge the policy in the High Court. Some in the LGBTIQ community, including Justice Michael Kirby and his partner, Johan van Vloten, were so offended by the government's approach that they discussed a boycott. Alex remembers being lobbied by other key LGBTIQ leaders for a boycott. Others said, if a postal survey was coming, we needed to engage and we needed to win it. Both Claire Dawson and Tim Wilson thought that if the High Court ruled against the postal survey, the Coalition would not move to a free vote.

The threat of a boycott became useful in negotiations with the government. The prime minister had said the postal plebiscite would pass and wanted it to pass to resolve the issue in line with his election commitment, but for that to be the case it was critical to involve the LGBTIQ community. Alex knew they if they lost in the High Court they could not stop the postal survey from proceeding but felt that they could use the threat of a boycott to negotiate better terms for the postal vote.

Alex remembers being in a lift in parliament on the way to a press conference about the campaign's response to the postal survey. He was asked, 'Alex, you're not going to announce a boycott, are you?' Alex responded, 'We are not ruling anything in or out' and initially the campaign's official position was that we would see what was on offer but commit to challenge the policy in the High Court.

Claire would play the good cop and work with the government on a number of the details, including making sure people with disabilities and overseas Australians could vote in any postal survey. She found Finance Minister Mathias Cormann to be very pragmatic and a good operator in these negotiations in his role as Acting Special Minister of State.

The High Court challenge was critical in buying time. It was also important for advocates to know they had given everything to stop the postal survey from proceeding. The LGBTIQ community had been very clear in 2016 about the impact a public vote would have on them and no one wanted to go through one if we could avoid it.

Two cases were lodged in the aftermath of the Coalition's announcement. The first was brought by the Public Interest Advocacy Centre with Tasmanian Independent MP Andrew Wilkie, PFLAG and Rainbow Families' Felicity Marlowe. Their barristers were Ron Merkel QC, Kathleen Foley, Christopher Tran and Simona Gorey. Our case was brought by the Human Rights Law Centre and involved AME and Greens Senator Janet Rice. Our barristers were Katherine Richardson SC, James Emmett, Gerald Ng, and Surya Palaniappan.

There was some overlap between the two cases. The case brought by the Public Interest Advocacy Centre argued that Mathias Cormann as finance minister lacked the power to approve the funding because there was no real urgency. Secondly, they argued that the legislation giving the finance minister the power to make these sorts of allocations without parliamentary authorisation was itself invalid. Third, they argued that the exercise the ABS had been asked to carry out was not simply a statistical one, and therefore did not fall within the powers of the ABS. The case brought by the Human Rights Law Centre maintained that expending funds on the plebiscite was not constitutionally valid because it had not been authorised by legislation.

Anna remembers the two legal teams co-operating well to ensure that the evidence and arguments put forward to the court were complementary. It was very unusual to have a case of this scale and complexity brought before the High Court in such a short timeframe. She says, 'The teams of lawyers worked around the clock day and night to ensure that the complex cases were ready for the strict court deadlines. There weren't just the legal arguments to co-ordinate'. Anna credits Michelle Bennett from the Human Rights Law Centre for her hard work with LGBTIQ advocates and parliamentarians from different teams to co-ordinate a media strategy for the cases. Everyone had to be equally prepared for the possibility of winning or losing.

A core group of AME advocates, including Shirleene, Sarah Midgley, Liam Ryan, Carol Burger, Tim Peppard, Dawn Hawkins and Peter Black, went to the High Court's Sydney base to be present with Alex and Anna for the directions hearing. Anna knew the High Court challenge would be hard but remembers:

We decided it was something we had to do for the LGBTIQ
community because people were so scared and felt so
threatened by the idea of their rights being voted on and held
up – their relationships and the worth of their relationships
being held up for scrutiny for the entire Australian population
to judge – that we needed to do that for legal certainty.

Because, either way, even if we'd not run the challenge, there
would be question marks about its legal validity, and if we
didn't challenge it then if we won, who knows? The Christian
Lobby or the NO side, Coalition for Marriage, could have
challenged it and it was important to have that legal clarity up
front. And I think it was an important way of the community
working through its feelings, in a way, around the challenge.
And it gave us time to effectively pivot from our opposition
and our fear and anxiety to again finding that way of coming
together and fighting a positive campaign to win.

If the postal survey was not stopped in the High Court, the campaign decided that it would not boycott it. Losing the survey, even with people deliberately boycotting, would have been disastrous for the LGBTIQ community. Alex remembers getting a call from Bill Shorten saying, 'This policy is bullshit, but if we can't defeat it in the High Court, we will fight hard to win it'. Labor's support would prove to be critical in winning any public vote.

So the rollercoaster continued. This was an especially hard moment for staff and volunteers. Helen Ross-Browne had just come back from a break and remembers 'hearing or seeing Turnbull come out and tell us that he was a strong leader and that he was going to have a postal survey and I was devastated'.

She continues, 'He had been warned about the implications of a public vote for the LGBTIQ community and he went ahead anyway. That's not a show of strength'. The pressure was immense. The team knew that if the High Court challenge wasn't successful, the campaign would need to grow very quickly from twelve exhausted, hard-working people and a handful of volunteers who had been through a series of challenges over years, to a structure that could pull off a world-first – win marriage equality through a non-compulsory postal ballot.

The AME team, including Alex, Janine, Shirleene, Sarah, Peter Black and Tim Peppard, had all converged on the High Court's base in Melbourne to hear the case over two days in September. The court was packed with advocates from all over the country, desperate to find out if the postal survey would be going ahead. The world's media was watching and the pressure was mounting on the campaign team. Should we be successful, we would be heading right back to Canberra with a strong message that we would continue to make this an issue every day to the next election and beyond. If we lost, we had a plan to start campaigning immediately.

After the first day, advocates felt that the High Court was leaning away from striking down the postal survey. By the end of the second day, no one was feeling positive. Although it was not clear when the High Court was going to make its decision, a number of us decided to stay longer in Melbourne as we expected it to come soon. Less than twenty-four hours after the two-day hearing, the High Court announced its decision and it was unanimous. The postal survey would proceed. There was no time to dwell on the implications or let anxiety sink it. We had to start campaigning immediately.

Alex and Anna faced the media again, saying they were disappointed but now we all had to campaign to win the postal survey. Anna remembers the moment as a very bizarre situation: 'Of course we were disappointed to lose the court case but we had to win the campaign'. The other team who had lodged the other case expressed similar emotions. The rainy and overcast weather seemed to match the mood of many after the decision but there was not time to properly process this.

Anna and Lee Carnie, who had been dressed in clothes appropriate for court, 'put on our campaign t-shirts' and started handing out pamphlets and campaign material to people walking through the nearby Flagstaff Station. Everyone from the team who was there joined in. Shirleene remembers being impressed by Wil Stracke from Victorian Trades Hall, who was quick to jump into action. The campaign had started.

Alex spent the rest of the day doing a series of TV and radio appearances, trying to set a positive tone and urging people to do the job politicians had failed to do and to vote YES. Privately, he was upset by the court loss and felt overwhelmed. By the time he got on the plane home to Sydney, he was exhausted in every way possible. A Qantas flight attendant came up to him, gave him a handful of Lindt chocolates and three small bottles of red wine and said, 'You're going to need this'. Tears immediately cracked through the brave face he was trying to maintain. As soon as he landed though, he regrouped to do a live interview via Skype with the BBC to encourage expats to participate. It was essential that people knew the postal survey was on and that it would take everyone to win.

Campaign headquarters

While the High Court was deliberating, Australian Marriage Equality (AME) and Australians for Equality (A4E) had been preparing the groundwork to fight a postal survey in case the court ruled against us. The team knew that we needed to increase the resources available to fight this unique campaign and very quickly. If the survey went ahead, it was important to have the right internal structure and skills in the office in field, digital, advertising and creative and communications to help support and co-ordinate the massive efforts that would be required across the country.

The government had announced its intention to hold a postal survey on 10 August 2017. By early the next morning, Tim Gartrell was appointed unanimously by both the A4E and AME boards to lead the campaign through the impending postal survey and see out a successful vote in parliament. Tim, who had been the campaign director for the hugely successful Kevin07 campaign and then the Recognise campaign to have Aboriginal and Torres Strait Islander people recognised in the Australian constitution, had been strongly recommended by many people in Labor. Penny Wong had told Tom Snow that he would be great. She knew Tim had the ability to 'think meta as well as details. So, he sees the frame and the picture and the narrative and the emotional feel, but he's also good at the nuts and bolts. And very few people can do both'. He also won respect from the other side of the political spectrum. Claire Dawson saw his appointment to lead the postal survey campaign as a 'masterstroke'.

Alex, Janine and Tom met with Tim in Alex's office in the New South Wales (NSW) Parliament and outlined the enormity of the challenges ahead; he was prepared to tackle them. He brought with him a wealth of experience and skills, contacts and infrastructure as well as an incredible team from Recognise.

This was a critical and uncertain moment for the team, including staff and volunteers. We did not know if the survey would go ahead or not but if it did, we needed to be prepared to give it everything and to win it. The size of the task ahead was daunting to say the least, but Tim set to work to turbo-charge the campaign and provide direction and calm amid the chaos. While the High Court deliberated, he was building and developing the structure a national postal survey would require.

Tim and the co-chairs were quick to send an urgent call out for help and encouraged the team to reach out to their networks – volunteers who could give weeks of their time, campaign professionals willing to join the effort, and experienced union organisers who could be seconded to the campaign were all brought onboard. The team swelled from around ten full-time staff to up to fifty people in a matter of weeks and eighty at the height of the campaign.

While our pro bono legal team were still poring over case law and working incredibly hard at crafting their legal arguments, the team focused on creating a 'Get out the vote' campaign in case the postal survey could not be stopped. The digital team's mastery was on show, engaging young Australians who were not yet on the electoral roll en masse in a way that had never been seen before.

Tim Gartrell called Adam Knobel as an immediate priority the day after he had been hired. Adam remembers, 'We talked on the phone for a couple of hours – covering the lay of the land, what he needed to know about key players, the strategies and tools already in place, what I thought was missing that we needed to sort out. He let me know he had already found a bigger office – and I was blown away by how quickly and skilfully he operated'. Adam feels Tim grasped that Adam was 'carrying too much'. Adam remembers, 'He had suggestions for people he wanted me to meet over the next week. But he also wanted me to work up my list of proposed hires within the next few days. He was here to help in a collaborative and respectful way'.

Adam continues, 'Tim knew we needed to announce we'd be ready to win. He wanted to send an email out to supporters as soon as humanly possible. I'd been out that Saturday morning when he called, so sat down in a random gutter to quickly draft an email from Shirleene to supporters on my phone. Shirleene, Tim and I texted back and forth and we settled on the email. The subject line captured the announcement: 'In it to win it'.

Adam says:

The pace didn't really change from then until 15 November. By the end of the next week we had packed up one office and moved into another, hired new staff (the digital team would reach sixteen at its peak), and settled in for a full day strategy meeting the Saturday following this phone call, with a number of the new key staff already on board. Among it all, somehow, we were still keeping the enrol-to-vote campaign alive and moving.

Adam and his team collaborated with partner organisations, particularly youth organisations like Oaktree, AYCC and the National Union of Students. The Equality Campaign also worked with GetUp! to send text messages to 434 178 young people. Victorian Trades Hall and unions all across the country played a crucial role in this early stage in driving enrolments through their memberships and doing the groundwork that would be essential if we were to have any chance at winning the threatened survey. By the time the enrolment period closed, there were more people on the electoral roll than at any other time in Australian history.

This was backed up by media moments and campaign actions, which were played out across the country on university campuses, at public events and anywhere potential voters could be reached. Clint organised for former Olympic swimmer Ian Thorpe to attend the City2Surf Enrol and Update Kiosk. Sarah Midgley remembers meeting Tim Gartrell here for the first time, the day after he had started:

> As people approached the stall, Tim was listening and gauging
> reactions to the messaging. He was really keen on hearing
> people's thoughts as my friend Morgan and I approached
> passers-by asking them if they were enrolled to vote. At this
> point, there was a lot of confusion from the public about
> whether they had to enrol and how and when they could vote.
> When Tim came on board, he made the shift in focus to a 'get
> out the vote' campaign immediately clear. He was quick to
> point out his respect for the hard work that the team had done
> already – many for several years and even a few for a decade –
> to build public support for marriage equality.[1]

Until August 2017, Tim had been working on Recognise. As Shannan Dodson, who had worked as digital campaign director on Recognise, explains, the contribution Recognise campaigners made to the postal survey campaign is a very important context to understand. She points out that the Recognise campaign had been going for five years and had been 'about fixing the Australian Constitution to recognise Aboriginal and Torres Strait Islander people and deal with the race discrimination within it'. Tim's work with the campaign meant that he had access to a suitable headquarters for a nationwide vote, as well as a highly skilled team who were prepared to come onboard and join existing staff and volunteers to work towards victory.

Both Alex and Shirleene will never be able to stress enough the courage, strength and solidarity that the Recognise team showed; they were dealing with the denial of their own rights but still stood shoulder-to-shoulder with the YES team, doing all they could to help us win. We believe Shannan expresses it perfectly when she says, 'The YES team were handed a group of experienced campaigners that were busting to go into "full campaign mode" as they had been developing their skills over years but had never been able to properly practise them'. She says, 'seeing some of the most amazing campaigners from Recognise immediately fighting for the rights of another group was so impressive to me'. Shirleene believes that the Recognise team, including brilliant people such as Shannan who brought such skills, compassion and finely honed talent, were essential to the team. Shannan notes they were 'entrenched in the political space and had refined strategy and finesse over years'.

Shirleene remembers first meeting Tim at a dinner at Alex's mother's house with other AME volunteers. 'I really liked him right away. He wanted to get to know us all and he was very genuine about acknowledging the hard work that had been done over a long time by community campaigners. He knew that we were going through something very difficult and he showed us that he wanted to work together to achieve a victory. He took the time to find out who we were and what we could offer.' Sarah Midgley remembers ending that dinner thanking Tim, telling him that she hadn't slept properly for some time thinking about the task that lay ahead but she now felt she would be able to sleep a little easier, knowing he was at the helm in campaign headquarters.

While we would not actually know if the postal survey could be stopped before the High Court ruling on 5 September, this early period was critical in making sure that people were on the electoral roll before enrolment closed on 24 August. After that, people would not be able to add themselves or update their postal addresses and would not be able to vote.

Audrey Marsh, who came onboard at the YES campaign headquarters as deputy field director for NSW when it was clear the postal survey was going ahead, reflects on how difficult the enrolment period was for many people. While she realised she had to put aside her own feelings to be able to campaign, having people say no to your rights was hard. 'When I was handing out for the enrolment drive and people would say "no", I just thought, this is the worst feeling in the world. I'm standing here as a lesbian being like, "Hey, can I get married?" and people are going, "I don't care about this". I just thought that was so painful. That taught me that actually you've got to not think about yourself because you'd go crazy. But you should think about it as an important progressive milestone and the rights of people you love being so important.'

During this period, a relatively small team of staff and volunteers and seconded people at Barangaroo were readying themselves for a campaign the size of a federal election. Some had worked professionally on national campaigns before and the Recognise team brought with them essential skills that, without question, helped us win. Others had never worked on a campaign before. There were many LGBTIQ people in the office and this was a more personal campaign than ever before. The team was a strong one though, ready for the potential survey.

For the first time, we had a director of clearance and enquiries, with Ashley Hogan taking on the role. All material sent out by the campaign would have to be vetted and checked. By the end of the campaign, Ashley had been noted in Hansard as the 'Clearance Unicorn' for her ability to do the work of so many people so well. The creation of this role made it clear that our campaign was now on a very different footing. Alex, whose name was at the bottom of the campaign material being prepared, became a very visible name across the country, not only for those who supported marriage equality but also for those who did not.

While we waited for the High Court decision to come down, the campaign began a commitment phase that lasted from 24 August until the survey forms arrived, planned for the second week of September if the survey went ahead. This phase was about making sure people knew what was coming and were prepared to take action and return their forms. If not enough people responded the campaign would fail. In the midst of this, on 5 September, we found out that the High Court challenge had not succeeded. The campaigning continued with everyone fully aware of what was at stake.

Claire Dawson, the team's director of government affairs, immediately ramped up efforts in Canberra to work with the

Coalition and Labor on creating legislation that would provide some safeguards during the postal survey period, as it would fall outside of rules governing normal elections through the *Electoral Act* around advertising, authorisation and false claims. She remembers having a matter of days to consult with Mathias Cormann and Mark Dreyfus about the safeguards needed. Cormann's willingness to include an anti-vilification clause surprised many in the team as the Coalition had always opposed any restrictions on speech. Claire remembers:

> I think some of the people I worked with thought, maybe this
> was a bit of a trick. We've asked for this for so many years and
> they've never let us have it, but now we're at this position where
> we're about to have this survey and they're going to allow for
> this? And I said to Minister Cormann, 'There are people in
> the campaign who are really quite concerned about this'. And
> he laughed, 'You think your people are worried? How do you
> think my people are?'

As soon as we knew the survey could not be stopped, we focused all our energy and attention on winning the vote. Forms were expected to arrive from 12 September, and 7 November was the last date that forms could reach the Australian Bureau of Statistics (ABS) and be counted. We decided we were aiming for an overall target of a 60 per cent participation rate and a 60 per cent YES response.

The postal survey was an intensely traumatic period for many but one of the most inspiring elements to emerge was the number of people who came out from so many parts of society to ensure we won. This was reflected in the office and also in the broader community. As Adam remembers, 'We had people who worked for unions, for Greenpeace, for commercial advertising agencies, commercial consultancies, banks, for the Greens, the Labor Party and the Liberal Party. We had people who had never campaigned before. We had people from a variety of countries. We had people from different, incredibly diverse and different economic backgrounds'.

The unions were important in mobilising large numbers of people quickly and had been out on the streets handing out flyers as soon as the idea of the survey had first been mooted. The Greens and Labor Party were also particularly skilled at getting volunteers and staff out on the streets, handing out information about enrolling to vote, and this was important in the early stages of the campaign. Audrey Marsh emphasises that:

> Trade unions were the people with [experience of] non-compulsory postal votes, so they gave us the expertise there. But also, they are just remarkable organisers in a way that no other community has mastered. So, I think that their expertise and our greatest campaigners, in a field sense, came from the trade union movement.

As it was clear that the postal survey was going ahead, the Barangaroo office quickly expanded with staff and volunteers. Janine Middleton, based full-time in the office, had the immense responsibility of managing finances for a multi-million dollar campaign, sourcing and securing in-kind support and donations. Alex says, 'These behind-the-scenes responsibilities that Janine had taken on may not have been visible to the public but they were the backbone of the campaign'.

It was crucial to have a field team operating as soon as possible and Patrick Batchelor quickly came on board as national field director. He had been up in the Northern Territory with his partner Shannan Dodson, taking a break together after the five-year Recognise campaign was dismantled, when the possibility of a postal survey was announced. The two were just about to head off overseas on a six-week holiday. As mentioned, Shannan had excellent digital campaigning skills. Patrick had been working as national field director at Recognise and had previously been in contact with Adam Knobel and Tom Snow about general campaigning. Once the postal survey was announced, Patrick and Shannan decided they had to help, cancelled their travel plans and headed to Sydney.

Shannan Dodson points out that, 'For those of us who had been campaigning on constitutional change for years and years, it was all quite a blur to go through the shock and grief of that campaign ending with another campaign taking precedence'. She continues:

> It was quite a mixture of emotions because we felt we had lost a campaign we had been fighting for, for so long, and now we were fighting a campaign that the community it was about didn't even want. It felt like another injustice in which a vilified community was begging for their rights, just as we had been doing for years on end. It further reiterated that this current government were not interested in the rights of minorities, the oppressed or the vilified. That they would create every possible obstacle to prevent us having our rights realised.[2]

As Shannan explains about her commitment to the cause:

> Having marriage equality was a no-brainer for me, as not that
> long ago in our history, my white grandfather was imprisoned
> for being in a relationship with my Aboriginal grandmother –
> so the fact that even interracial marriage was not legal in this
> country is pretty recent. I wanted to use my skills for good,
> and although the postal survey was such a disgusting process,
> I wanted to fight that much harder to get a YES vote to prove
> that equality was something important to Australians. I was
> proved right – equality does matter, and Australians do want
> to see change.

Patrick had accrued a wealth of campaigning experience that
made him perfect for the role of national field director. He had
volunteered for the Obama primaries in Texas in 2007–2008.
He had also undertaken an internship with a United States con-
gressman and worked as a regional field director on the Obama
campaign in 2012. In between, in 2011, he worked on a marriage
equality campaign in Minnesota. The Minnesota Senate had
passed a Bill to place a proposed amendment to the State Constitution on the ballot that would ban same-sex marriage. Thirty
other states had passed similar ballots and Minnesota was the
first to turn the tide, with voters supporting marriage equality.
Patrick remembers:

> It was probably the best campaign that I've seen in terms
> of going from a position that really wasn't a winnable
> position to being a successful campaign. It was really
> just about empowering supporters and volunteers to go

out and have difficult conversations with people and personalizing everything.

As a strong ally of the LGBTIQ community, Patrick keenly appreciated how difficult this sort of campaigning could be and the importance of supporting people throughout the process.

The first task that confronted him was to assemble a field team that could cover the entire country and communicate with over one million voters, yet financial constraints meant he had a budget for just one full-time, paid organiser per state. He knew that 'if we were going to run a serious national campaign we needed at least fifty' nationally.

Georgia Kriz, who was seconded from the Australian Manufacturing Workers' Union, came on as NSW field director but Patrick emphasises that really, for 'the first couple of weeks she was the national deputy field director' and that she was 'just unbelievable at helping find and recruit' people to help from all across the country. In around ten days, she had helped assemble a national team of close to fifty full-time staff and 'we were only paying for six of them', which 'was only possible due to the generous support of the Australian trade union movement'.

Georgia remembers, 'My first five days on the job were just spent cold-calling political offices, unions and community organisations in every state and territory. The energy was wild. Everyone understood the urgency of the task and everyone was throwing staff at us. Unions in particular were wonderful. I'd call up and explain what I needed and and their response would inevitably be, "Whatever you need, comrade"'. Georgia is also keen to credit Patrick. She says 'I'll always remember his calm, compassionate leadership. He was an exceptional ally to all our LGBTIQ campaigners, particularly to the women on the team'.[3]

Audrey Marsh soon joined the Sydney headquarters as deputy field director for NSW, staying on a couple of weeks longer as field director when Georgia had to return to her regular job. Shirleene says, 'Georgia and Audrey brought with them this wonderful energy as a great team and they were absolutely tireless! It was really inspiring to see a younger generation doing everything they could to bring about a positive social change'. Audrey tells us that a major task of field campaigning in the early stages was setting up phone banking. Sarah Midgley used her annual leave to volunteer with the field team. Shirleene notes that it is the first and only time she has been based in the same office as her wife. It worked well! And it was reassuring to have each other close by as the NO campaign continued its hurtful words.

Joseph Scales from the Australian Services Union in South Australia, who had worked so hard within the Labor Party to move its platform towards marriage equality, gave up all his accrued leave and came to Sydney to help out however he could. His skill set and reputation had already meant that several people involved in the YES campaign had reached out to him. He thought, 'You know what? I care about this so much. I'd been part of it for so much of my adult life. I might feel frustrated if I don't feel like I've given it everything'.

As a union leader, Joseph was able to help get the Labor movement where the campaign needed them. Officially his title was 'Campaign Advisor', but he would prove to be an incredible asset in the office, working on the politics, in the field and out in the community campaigning. He also kept a watchful eye on the actions of our opponents, both official and unofficial. Ultimately, Joseph became something of a trusted bridge for the gaps that inevitably wax and wane between different teams in a campaign office.

Once the ABS started sending out the surveys, the digital campaign could reach likely YES voters and remind them to post their YES. Throughout the survey process, 1.45 million people visited a purpose-built VoteYES.org.au website to pledge their vote, find their nearest postbox, learn how to request a replacement ballot paper and discover how to get involved. Digital efforts were really important as it was an affordable way to reach people when the NO side had outspent YES by a substantial amount. Digital was able to reach likely YES voters up to seven times over a three-week period with reminders to post their YES, through highly effective targeted online advertising. And a successful crowdfunding campaign managed to raise $100 000 so that the popular 'Bachelor and Bachelorette' clip could be aired on television.

The strong creative team of Helen, Kirk and Leah continued to be responsible for creative production under the banner of advertising and branding. Their team drew more staff in during the postal survey but ultimately, these three were the key staff. Not only did they produce material crucial to letting people know about the postal survey and the importance of enrolling, the creative team worked incredibly hard to tell the stories of the people who were affected by the lack of marriage equality in this country. The creative team produced a total of 141 videos during the campaign period. This might be a record for any campaign's level of production and is a true credit to the skill of these three. Digital platforms such as Facebook provided an ideal outlet to share these important videos. All up, they were viewed a staggering 18.8 million times.

One of the stories captured by the creative team that moved many and also inspired people to post their forms was the 'Ring your Rellos' video, which featured a young woman called Lisa calling her grandmother and asking her how she planned to vote. Leah Newman, who was involved in the directing, production, post-production, editing and graphics stages of this touching video, explains that it was meant to encourage voters to have conversations and increase the YES vote through its personal approach.

In the office, Shirleene volunteered with the communications team, headed by communications director Clint McGilvray. Mike Fairbairn, who had previously worked for the Equality Campaign, came back to help out again. At that one table, there were people who supported each of the three major political parties but they all worked together single-mindedly, determined to do everything possible to see a YES returned. Shirleene spent the most time with Steve Offner and Georgia Tkachuk, experienced communication professionals who stayed with the campaign until the end and brought a steely determination and great skill set to the table. She says, 'Under the pressure of the campaign, we came to develop really strong friendships'.

The commitment phase of the campaign ended up being shorter than anticipated when the survey forms were posted out much more quickly than people expected. Adam remembers 'one of those first curve balls' was when the postal surveys started arriving in people's mailboxes. The team had been assembled, the survey was happening and it was critical that people returned their forms as soon as possible if we were going to win.

Australia campaigns

The story of the campaign to win the postal survey had two sides and it is impossible to tell one without the other. On the one hand, everyday Australians across the country gave it everything they had and campaigned inspiringly for YES. A nation put its heart and soul into winning. On the other hand, it was a difficult and anxious time for so many of those whose relationships and lives were being judged and who had to spend almost two months living with uncertainty about the results.

Australians were told that over sixteen million survey forms were being mailed out from 12 September and that they needed to reach the Australian Bureau of Statistics (ABS) by 7 November at the latest to be counted. For the YES campaign to win, we needed as many people as possible to send back their survey forms. Evidence from overseas and from other similar ballots showed that it was critical for people to post their ballots back within days of receiving them, otherwise there was a danger they would be neglected or forgotten. An anxious community was waiting to receive the forms.

As the survey began, a number of politicians provided crucial support for the YES campaign. Both sides of politics needed to show that marriage equality was a bipartisan issue if there was to be any chance of bringing home a YES. As soon as the postal survey was announced, Labor leader Bill Shorten delivered an extremely passionate speech in parliament, saying that the Labor Party would throw its support behind the LGBTIQ community and campaign strongly for YES.

Shirleene remembers feeling a huge sense of relief on hearing Bill Shorten's words, particularly that the Labor Party would continue to support marriage equality beyond the postal survey. 'It helped enormously on a personal level to realise that even if we couldn't get a YES across the line here, the Labor Party was still prepared to bring in marriage equality in their next term of government.'

A number of senior Coalition figures, including the Liberal Party president, Nick Greiner, and Prime Minister Turnbull, launched the 'Liberals and Nationals for YES' campaign and signed a joint statement pointing out how marriage equality aligned with conservative values. That same day, Labor's Terri Butler appeared on Sky News, pointing out that although the Labor Party had not wanted the postal survey and still believed it to be inherently discriminatory, now that the survey could not be stopped, a show of bipartisanship would be essential to win it. 'Now that we are in it, let's do it properly and try and have as much unity as possible and see what we can do to bring a united front.'

Politicians from all across the country joined in the YES effort. Clover Moore, lord mayor of Sydney, who had supported marriage equality since the very beginning, put the full weight of the City of Sydney behind the campaign. Banners supporting the YES campaign were hung up throughout the centre of the city for its duration. The lord mayors of Brisbane, Perth, Newcastle, Hobart and Wollongong also publicly supported a YES. The premiers of Victoria, Queensland, New South Wales, Tasmania,

South Australia and Western Australia, and the chief ministers of the Australian Capital Territory (ACT) and Northern Territory all declared their support for a YES vote.

Trevor Evans launched the Libs and Nats for YES campaign in Brisbane with Attorney-General George Brandis. Senator Louise Pratt from Labor and Senator Dean Smith from the Liberals both spoke in support of marriage equality at the same rally in Perth. At an Adelaide rally in September that attracted a crowd of 5000, Penny Wong, Christopher Pyne and Sarah Hanson-Young all spoke powerfully, providing a united front. Rally participant Laura Tanner from Kadina told the *Advertiser* newspaper that she had driven two hours from the country to make sure she was there. 'I wasn't going to miss out. It's too important and we've got to show our support.'[1] The next day, Penny Wong, Sarah Hanson-Young and Christopher Pyne launched an Adelaide door-knocking campaign together with Alex. So many people put their politics aside to campaign for a win.

Survey forms started arriving more quickly than the campaign had been told to expect. Fortunately, the infrastructure to campaign was set up and people were ready to campaign hard. While the national YES campaign headquarters was physically based in Sydney, other states and territories quickly established bases. Victorian Trades Hall sprang into action and became a major centre in that state. A crack team of field directors across Australia got to work. Apart from Patrick Batchelor as national field director and Georgia Kriz and Audrey Marsh as NSW director and deputy director, other state directors were Nita Green in Queensland, Jacob White in the ACT, Emmanuel Cusack in South Australia, Pat Honan in the Northern Territory, Alex

West in Tasmania, Emma Gibbens in Western Australia, and Wil Stracke from Victorian Trades Hall Council as field director in that state.

While the infrastructure was set up and there were excellent, dedicated staff and volunteers at the helm, campaigners knew that if a YES was going to be returned, it would be up to people all across Australia to get out the vote in their own states, territories and communities. The campaign could provide information and resources but a win would need everyday Australians to step up and do everything they could to make it happen. No one had wanted a public vote but now that it was here, losing would be unthinkable.

One of the first actions that the YES campaign set up was phone banking with the help of GetUp!. Phone banks ran in every state and territory and drew an extraordinary number of volunteers. Labor Senator Louise Pratt was just one of them. In Sydney, Audrey Marsh remembers:

> I knew the campaign was so powerful because we did not
> have enough room for the number of phone callers we had.
> I remember literally stepping over people who were making
> phone calls in the hallways, in the fire stairs, just everywhere
> … and every type of person doing it. They made those phone
> calls without a break for two and a half hours. I could feel the
> momentum of it at that time.

Wil Stracke in Melbourne had a very similar experience with the phone banks organised through Victoria Trades Hall. She remembers a diverse group of volunteers, many of whom had never campaigned before, coming in on weekends to make as many calls as they could. On one Sunday afternoon, ninety people showed up for a two-hour phone bank:

> We did not have enough lists, we did not have enough
> phones, we did not have enough food for people. We had
> people sitting on the front verandah at Trades Hall because
> we did not have enough chairs or rooms for them to make
> phone calls from, which was an amazing problem to have.
> It was fantastic.

The postal survey was a very difficult experience for many people but so many LGBTIQ Australians campaigned as hard as they could, as did allies, friends and family members who stood shoulder-to-shoulder with them. LGBTIQ people were in the very difficult position of having to campaign for their own rights, yet so many found the courage to do so or to support those in the community who were not coping with the process.

On 26 August 2017, 20 000 people gathered together in Melbourne for the largest marriage equality rally the country had ever seen. The following weekend in Sydney, that record was broken when 30 000 people gathered to support the reform. Shirleene, Sarah, Janine and Mark Adams set up a booth at Circular Quay with information on how to post a vote. As the crowds approached on their march from Town Hall and they realised that something truly historic was happening, Shirleene and Sarah raced up the street to see enormous throngs of people approaching, carrying signs, bringing an amazing sea of colour with them. Alex spoke on the stage and urged the crowd of supporters to take out their phones to text or phone a loved one, ask them to vote YES and return their surveys as soon as possible.

To his surprise, people did. Afterwards, the crowd, including a number of 78ers who had been at the first Mardi Gras, sang and danced joyfully. We celebrated as we handed out badges and stickers, urging everyone to post their YES. We were joined by Liam Ryan, Tim Gartrell, Shane Lloyd and Alan Joyce as we all soaked up the atmosphere.

Brisbane, Melbourne, Hobart, Adelaide and Perth were all determined to put on shows of support like never before. The rallies in these cities also exceeded previous ones in their scale, colour and sheer determination. Mums, dads, families and friends joined electrified crowds, making it clear that they expected action on this issue.

AME's Queensland director, Peter Black, urged the Brisbane crowd to post their YES and 'come together and get this done'. Peter was racking up some substantial miles across the state of Queensland during the campaign, speaking everywhere from Townsville to Toowoomba, from Cairns down to the Gold Coast. When he was in Brisbane, he volunteered at phone banks and helped spread the word wherever he could.

On 6 September, Janine Middleton and Tiernan Brady spoke at the National Press Club, emphasising the importance of supporting marriage equality. As a heterosexual woman of faith, living in Tony Abbott's electorate, Janine was in a position to powerfully challenge stereotypes. Carol Burger remembers watching this:

> She was amazing. You were able to relate to her, I think was the key point. But her story, I'm like, 'I can't even scratch that. I can't even say that, until I started at AME, I knew any gay people'. She's one amazing woman.

Once the ABS started sending out the ballots in bulk from 12 September, the message that was constantly reinforced was 'Post Your YES!' This message was heard loud and clear. In rural Victoria, AME's Carol Burger was one of the first of the team to receive her survey. While not generally a fan of running into town to pick up her mail, Carol remembers this was different:

> But this was the one thing that hit my mail box and I filled it out straightaway and posted it off. Sorry, all my other bills but this was, by far, one of the important things to do.

Although Carol is not someone who usually liked to be in front of cameras, we even managed to persuade her to take a photo of herself posting her YES so we could use it on social media to encourage others. She happily obliged.

Alex received his survey form before Shirleene and was one of the first people to receive his in the mail, as metropolitan Sydney had been sent a batch of ballots earlier than expected. He let Clint know, who would then organise for Janine and Alex to do a press event of them posting the very first ballots. When Alex got home, alone in his apartment, he stared at the envelope from the ABS and said to himself, 'There's ten years of advocacy in a fucking envelope'. The distressing reality that millions of Australians were receiving pieces of paper in the mail to judge LGBTIQ people suddenly hit him. Kirk remembers seeing Alex rattled for the first time: 'Alex was clearly unsettled, he was always bubbly and positive, and I had never seen him as distressed as he was that day'. Alex had to steel himself to be all smiles for the cameras and encourage everyone to post back their forms, saying, 'Within these envelopes are the hopes and dreams of millions of Australians'.

Shirleene remembers how strange it was to see the innocuous-looking letter holding the survey ballot in the mailbox and to know how much weight it held. 'Sarah and I both received them on the same day and we immediately ticked YES. We took a little while longer to post them back, I think firstly because we were so busy in this period but really because it was just such a strange feeling having to do it. But we knew how important it was that we all did it and we posted ours together.'

Penny Wong and her partner posted their surveys with their children as a family. She focused on what equality would mean for them and for Australia as a society. She says she gave the envelopes, 'to the kids and they put it into the box. And it became, for me, much more about them actually. I mean, you go into politics, you do what you do, don't you, because you ultimately want a better community, better world, better nation, better state. So, for me, this really was wanting them to grow up not ever having society say to them that your family is lesser'.

So many parts of Australia turned rainbow colours during the survey to encourage people to post their YES and to show support. People decked out their houses with rainbow colouring. In the south-eastern suburbs of Melbourne, Jack Barr and his housemates painted their fence on a main road in rainbow colours. In Enmore in the inner west of Sydney, one heterosexual man painted his entire house in rainbow stripes in a beautiful show of solidarity with the LGBTIQ community. In Francis Street, Yarraville, the occupants of another house painted its fence rainbow colours. Many houses set up rainbow letterboxes decorated with YES.

In every part of Australia, under remarkable pressure, people did extraordinary things to show their support for the LGBTIQ community and to bring home a YES. Parents handed out leaflets in the rain, supported by thousands of men and women dotted across Australian neighbourhoods. Workmates held morning teas to support marriage equality. There are so many stories of courage and action that we cannot possibly share them all. This was an effort driven by hundreds of thousands of people across the country. It involved millions of conversations and grassroots efforts everywhere.

Before the survey forms had even been sent out, Toni Johnson, from the group Albury Marriage Equality, had stepped into action and was visiting shops in Albury and Wodonga, asking them to put up signs in support of a YES, rainbow posters or decorations. She told a local newspaper, 'Balloons, streamers, it doesn't matter. I want it rainbow, lit up, until the postal vote goes through'. Toni even had her 84-year-old mother campaigning alongside her, helping her to convince an older generation to also vote YES.

In NSW, Dawn Hawkins from Marriage Equality Gilmore arranged a series of events including market stalls throughout the survey, and helped to set up and organise other groups to campaign in neighbouring areas. Having seen the flags the City of Sydney was flying to support marriage equality, Dawn fundraised and liaised with Shoalhaven Council to get flags with 'a simple rainbow' on them flown. 'It was simply about showing support to our community and creating that visibility so that people could walk along the street and think, wow, we really are being looked after here.'

Dawn went up to Kiama, where some fantastic fundraising events had been arranged. The community even co-ordinated people to spell out a human YES. She also decided that she was going to get out as far and as wide as she could to make sure she secured every YES she possibly could. Her extensive road trip has now become campaign legend.

Initially, Dawn started walking in the electorate of Gilmore, wearing her Equality t-shirt, carrying an A4 YES poster, so that interested people could approach her. She also went into shops to ask owners if they would like campaign material. She then hit the road, driving to Kiama, Berry, Nowra, Culburra Beach, Callala Bay, Mogo and Batemans Bay, before reaching Moruya, which was the end of the Gilmore electorate. At every single place, she stopped the car, opening up conversations, 'getting an understanding ... being honest and positive all the way through'.

While Moruya was her final stop in the Gilmore electorate, Dawn still had campaign material in her car and thought, 'Oh bugger it. So I just turned my car around and started driving to the border' through to the next electorate of Hume. She continued to drive through to Tuross Heads and Bodalla, Narooma and Tilba Tilba, continuing the conversations at each stop and meeting with local advocates and supporters. 'I knew that it was important for the community [to have] visibility. And here this is, this shows that your community cares and the people in this shop are willing to show that support for you.'

Once she reached Cobargo, the road trip took an interesting turn as the first thing she saw was 'this enormous rainbow flag flapping in the wind' and the entire town covered in rainbow flags. 'Shops, seats, just everything in this town.' After a little investigation, Dawn found out there was a story behind the rainbows. Two gay men, David and Kyle, who ran the Australia Post office in the town, had raised up a rainbow flag. An opponent of marriage equality contacted Australia Post, which, as a government business, was not allowed to put up another flag besides the Australian flag. When the men took down their rainbow flag, 'The community of Cobargo said, "If you can't, we will". So their whole town just had rainbows everywhere'. Cobargo is well known for a gnome village it has on the corner of the main street. David took Dawn on a walk, showing her 'This little gnomes-ville town. And they'd created rainbows all through the gnome town even!' At one point, David and Kyle even showed Dawn their lamb, resplendent with a rainbow heart painted on its wool.

After Cobargo, she continued her journey south, where the excitement of the response she was getting overwhelmed her and she decided to walk into a country pub. 'Just stinks of beer in the carpet and all the rest, I can hear the men talking inside, it's just that scene. And I went past and I thought, yeah nah, I'm going to do this.' Emboldened, Dawn walked in and stood in the doorway, holding her 'YES Equality' sign aloft, saying 'Who's with me?' She reflects:

> God knows what possessed me to do that. And the whole place went silent, it's like something you'd see in a movie. And then this one bloke just looked at me and he goes, 'Yeah love, I'm with ya'. And he picked up his beer glass and sort of cheered in my direction. And I sort of smiled, because in that one moment, I'm going oh fuck, what am doing! And once he did it, all the others went, 'Yeah, good on you!'

As she walked out, Dawn chastised herself, 'Never do that again'. After the pub stop, it was onwards to Bega, Merimbula and Pambula. She then found herself in Eden, 'which is the furthest south that I could go'. While it was becoming clear that the majority of the votes had been returned, Dawn kept checking in on people until the survey ended to see how they were coping. As her road trip ended and she headed back towards Nowra, she received a phone call, telling her that the rainbow street flags she had ordered had arrived and were proudly flying. 'I just welled up in tears to actually see this moment, to feel that support myself, to actually feel that my council really is with me. My community is with me.'

Tom Sebo, another seasoned and dedicated marriage equality campaigner, was based in Goulburn and worked as part of the Hume for Marriage Equality group. When the survey was announced, the group quickly began to prepare to win in that electorate. Tom had formerly been a journalist and brought with him a level of expertise in understanding how the media worked.

For Tom, the campaign in Hume was very strong thanks to an excellent local group who were experienced at working together. He says, 'The strength of our group was that that we'd been together for three years working on the campaign'. He worked closely with Warren Smith and Shelby Marks to build up a campaign that would speak to the area. From previous activity, they had a healthy group of contacts and they put a call out quickly to see who else wanted to be involved and to draw 'up a battle plan of what we needed'.

The team launched a Vote YES campaign at the Goulburn Club on Saturday 2 September, with a number of local speakers. As Tom was a member of the club, they could get affordable access to the space. From the start, Tom knew how important it was to maintain a positive tone and not to get dragged into any negativity.

In order to get the message out amongst the community, Tom secured the services of a young, local film-maker, Jack Bell, who made some excellent videos of 'just average people talking about why they support marriage equality'. Jack used the South Hill Gallery as a film set with the support of the gallery owners. The team also did lots of social media. 'Outside of that, it was just media and getting out there, getting in the streets. We did another business campaign and the second business campaign, we got fifty businesses' signed up and publicly supporting marriage equality.

Tom looks back on his part as 'an organising and liaising role' with the Sydney team. He had friends and contacts within the Equality Campaign. Secondly, he knew he needed to work within his own 'community to try and make this stuff happen. I guess the thing I'm really proud of about our campaign is it was a super low-budget campaign. I mean it was $1200. Which doesn't sound much but it's huge when it's coming out of our own pockets'.

On 16 September, the Hume team organised a rally at Belmore Park in Goulburn. They arranged public liability insurance through one of their number who was a union member, as 'unions were supporting the overall movement'.

That evening, a group of local musicians came together to play a show at the Goulburn Club. Hosts included music promoter Marky McColl and producer/rapper Brayden Judd. Performers included hip-hop artists, acoustic sets and a comedian.

Once the ballots arrived, Tom found he was met with support from workmates, friends and colleagues. His manager at work sent him a text message 'with his ballot paper with the big YES on it and his wife's one with the big YES on it and I was getting these messages from friends and from family sending me [pictures of] the ballot papers with the yes on them and stuff, which I thought was really nice'.

Local advocates in other parts of Australia were also doing everything they could across their own communities to see a strong YES returned. Friends and family members of the LGBTIQ community spoke about the importance of marriage equality for the people they loved. On the Sunshine Coast in Queensland, Colin Mildwaters and his wife Heather handed out 2500 letters asking people to vote YES in support of their son Grant, who is gay. It took them three days to complete the job.

Sharyn Faulkner from Geelong for Marriage Equality (GME) had campaigned hard against a public vote but once the High Court had ruled the postal survey was going ahead, she sprang into action. She formed the SAY YES GEELONG campaign, working with GME, Geelong Trades Hall and Surfcoast for Equality. After focusing on enrolments and making sure people's addresses were up to date, this campaign swung into the action of getting as many people as possible to vote YES.

SAY YES GEELONG used social media, were visible in public places such as shopping centres and markets, held phone banks and approached local businesses to put up posters. The group also encouraged people to have conversations, drop off letters explaining the importance of YES to neighbours, suggested that postal parties could boost the YES vote and suggested that people offer to help post back surveys if required. They emphasised the importance of personal safety and taking care of people during this stressful period. They also held public events, including an SMS YES night at the Piano Bar in Geelong on 5 October and an equality flashmob on 21 October.

Tim Peppard admired the grassroots campaigns run across Victoria, such as Sharyn's and Damien Stevens', a long-term grassroots campaigner from Shepparton.

In Toowoomba, long-term supporters such as William Rutkin and Thomas Coyne were also throwing their efforts behind campaigning. Thomas led a parade of seventy people through Toowoomba. Local grandfather Bob Spearritt, a former high school principal, even became a social media star when he was featured on AME's social media posting his YES. He was quoted as saying, 'I think everyone under the sun deserves a chance to marry the person he or she truly loves', which touched a lot of people.

Up in Alice Springs, Maya Newell and Dane Brookes took every opportunity to emphasise the importance of voting YES. The local Sunday markets proved a great spot to have conversations and campaigners even chalked up a rainbow on the Todd Mall in support. One of the highlights for Alex of the postal survey was flying to the Northern Territory to join campaigners like Andrew Addie and Daniel Alderman in Alice Springs and Darwin and thank them for their work. The Northern Territory campaign did not have the budget or infrastructure that existed in Sydney or Melbourne, however the passion and determination of the campaigners ensured it had the same impact. Meeting the campaigners up in the Northern Territory, and seeing them go door knocking in extreme heat to ensure 'VOTE YES' posters were in every cafe in town, reminded Alex of the early days of AME, a small team of dedicated people making a hugely positive impact.

In Kalgoorlie in Western Australia, George Foulkes-Taylor and her partner, Emily, saw the NO campaign printing and distributing upsetting material and decided to organise a grassroots YES campaign in response. The two designed flyers and paid to print them up. Twenty people from the community ended up contributing to their costs and once the flyers started going out, more and more locals asked for some to walk around their neighbourhoods. George and Emily estimated that around 3500 of their flyers ended up distributed around Kalgoorlie, with posters also put up in local business windows.

In Sydney, the Equality Shop on Oxford Street provided a vital hub for community support. Shane Lloyd had seen the importance of providing this sort of space when he envisioned its creation, and it served as somewhere people who were feeling vulnerable could come and know they were with friends or others could find out more information about the campaign.

Australians living overseas were also keen to show their support. Whether by voting over the phone or online, or getting a friend or loved one to fill in the survey on their behalf, we saw selfies from London to Los Angeles, Helsinki to Tokyo and beyond of Aussies overseas stepping up and helping out when it was needed most. Joe Murphy, who married his husband Nick Smith in New York in 2016, said, 'This survey allows us to vote YES to making the country we love a fairer and more equal place. We're going to make sure we vote and tell all our fellow expats to do the same'.[2]

On the evening of 21 September, Alex was at home thinking how well everything was going, but then received calls from Tim Wilson and Trent Zimmerman. They told him that Tony Abbott had allegedly been headbutted by a YES campaigner in Hobart, and they both urged the importance of acting quickly and defusing the situation. It had been a positive and respectful YES campaign and this random act of violence was the antithesis of everything people were working for. Alex got on the phone with Clint and Tim Gartrell, then immediately sent a tweet condemning violence. The NO campaigners and their allies in the right-wing media jumped on the incident and as Clint describes, 'They tried to create this false narrative that those campaigning for fairness and equality were somehow all thugs and therefore people should vote NO'. After discussing the strategy with Clint, Alex would text Australia's most listened-to conservative commentator, Alan Jones, saying, 'What a shocking incident in Hobart. This stupid clown who assaulted the former PM has nothing to do with our campaign, it's a terrible distraction from the tone of love and fairness we are trying to set'. Alan responded by booking Alex on his show first thing in the morning, reading out his text to his listeners and backing the campaign as one full of good Australians working hard. Alex was grateful for Alan's intervention: 'Some in the media were ready to just keep kicking us for the actions of someone who had nothing to do with us and were making all sorts of false allegations. Alan came to the rescue, backed the character of the campaign, and this sent a clear message that people were seeing through the bullshit of the NO side's tactics'.

After spending a day in back-to-back media appearances about the Abbott headbutt, Alex came in to headquarters for a briefing on the weekend's campaign plans. As he was leaving Patrick and Adam said, 'Remember, you are sending a text message to eight million people tomorrow'. Alex laughed and said, 'Can't wait'.

The weekend beginning on 23 September was action packed in many ways. The campaign sent out a text stating, 'The Marriage Equality Survey forms have arrived! Help make history and vote YES for a fairer Australia. VoteYes.org.au'. The campaign used randomly generated numbers and the texts were in line with previously used campaign tactics. The texts were also sent out at a time that the NO campaign was using dubious robo-calls to suggest same-sex marriage could lead to changes to sex education and threats to religious freedom.

Alex had spent the day door-knocking in Paddington and Woollahra with volunteers. The feedback was so positive, Alex wasn't looking at his phone or Twitter, so when he did he was shocked. Some NO campaigners had started a targeted offensive to troll Alex with messages like 'Stop raping my phone', even urging people to hunt him down and headbutt him. The media jumped on board and everyone from the ABC to Andrew Bolt chastised the campaign for sending a four-line text message, while the NO side were taking out full-page ads packed with offensive misinformation.[3]

Alex was booked by *ABC News 24* with only forty minutes' notice to 'defend the text message'. The hosts grilled Alex on why he would dare send a text message to people, and on air he replied, 'Hang on, we had this process imposed on us, we have to do everything we can to win it, and that includes using all technology available to us'. At the end of the interview, the hosts said, 'Next week we will have someone from the NO side'. Alex asked to speak to the executive producer, saying, 'You give me forty minutes to get here and the NO side gets a whole week's notice; I hope you will at least share that interview on social media'. The ABC refused. What followed was a two-week targeted offensive by NO campaigners to call and harass Alex's office; his staff could not answer the phone, because every time they did, someone would shout abuse at them. The police had to check Alex's office regularly due to safety concerns, and two people were investigated.

Adam Knobel and Ashley Hogan from headquarters had to deal with the great bulk of this with some assistance and Alex and Shirleene commend them both for the strength they showed under such difficult circumstances. Shirleene remembers logging in to AME's Facebook inbox and being shocked at some of the vitriol the campaign received. Ultimately though, the decision to text was a good one. 170 000 people who received the texts clicked through to receive more information and 20 000 people expressed an interest in volunteering for the campaign as a result. Also on the weekend of 23 September, campaigners activated Australia's largest door-knock. Over 2000 volunteers assembled across Australia intending to knock on over 100 000 doors. We ended up reaching 102 000.

Shirleene and Sarah volunteered with Joseph Scales at the North Sydney door-knock. Shirleene had not realised that Joseph had been working within the Labor and union movement for years to advance marriage equality. But as soon as she saw him so effectively organising his door-knocking team and motivating them with kindness, she turned to Sarah, impressed, and said, 'He has definitely done this before!' We were all delighted with the numbers of people turning out, giving up their weekends to do anything and everything they could to help bring home a YES. At this event, many volunteers who completed knocking on the doors they'd been assigned came back and asked for another round to keep helping. This weekend saw engaged couples, like Mark Evans and Andrew Sklar, literally knock on their neighbours' doors asking them if they would vote YES so they could get married. Young people were out in force and behind the campaign. It was incredibly inspiring. So many people told us that they would do whatever was needed to win.

Despite the drama and stress of the Abbott headbutt and the text message, this weekend was a momentous time for the marriage equality movement. Alex would address the morning staff meeting to thank and acknowledge the amazing team who had organised for more people to campaign for marriage equality than had ever happened before. Alex remembers thinking, 'We had certainly come a long way since 2010 with a handful of volunteers with a few flyers'.

In early October, the Cairns LGBT Alliance, who had spent the previous weeks making phone calls, door-knocking, letterboxing and waving placards at drivers, produced their own video, calling for a YES vote. The volunteers in the video spelt out the word YES and unfurled the country's largest rainbow flag. In Rockhampton, the Capricornia Equality Alliance secured a ute and a driver for the annual Pineapple Fest. They decked it out with rainbow flags and Vote YES posters and proudly drove it in the street parade.

From Tuesday 3 October, the ABS began releasing weekly totals approximating the number of ballots that had been posted back. The first release estimated that 57.5 per cent of ballots had been returned. While this was encouraging, we knew we had to keep emphasising that complacency could cost us this campaign and that each and every supporter needed to return their YES.

On 8 October, Alex organised a 'Post Your YES' street party near Oxford Street in Sydney. The atmosphere was incredibly joyful, with signs, rainbows and crowds blowing bubbles. Sarah Midgley remembers this as a momentary respite from the hectic campaigning. John-Paul Young, Ricki-Lee Coulter, DJ duo Peking Duk and Alfie Arcuri, who had won *The Voice*, all performed. Alex urged the crowd to return their surveys as the campaign was reaching its mid-point.

On 21 and 22 October, as the survey deadline drew even closer, another series of marriage equality rallies were held. Clouds and rain did not deter a Brisbane crowd from coming to Queen's Park. Shirleene was amongst the speakers, along with Bridget Clinch and Shelley Argent. As she spoke, she looked out into the crowd and she saw a familiar face. Graham Perrett, the federal member for Moreton, who had been such a key part of Shirleene's journey into marriage equality, was standing there, supporting the cause as he had done for so long. It was a special moment.

In Tasmania, there were many people working hard to bring home a YES. Alex West took leave from her role in Tanya Plibersek's office in Sydney to return to her home state for the duration of the postal survey. Advocates including Rodney Croome, working with the group Tasmanians United for Marriage Equality, put together a series of videos featuring a diverse cross-section of Tasmanians speaking about the importance of marriage equality and organised other actions. A weekend of action on 20–22 October saw yarnbombing 'knit-ins', rainbow chalkings and a giant postbox. Hotel SOHO also hosted a gig by Tas Musos for Marriage Equality.

On 29 October, Shirleene spoke at the Western Sydney Says YES rally and attended the Parramatta Pride Picnic afterwards. This occasion had been organised by a group of 78ers, including Gay Egg, Steve Warren, Mark Gillespie and Peter de Waal. It was a privilege to speak alongside them and others, including Geoff Thomas, who had shared his personal story about addressing homophobia and loving his son unconditionally on *Q&A* years earlier. In her speech, Shirleene tried to emphasise the importance of posting back your YES and also supporting one another. William Brougham, a very active volunteer throughout the postal survey period, remembers this occasion well. He says:

> It was smaller than the rallies we were used to at Town Hall or Taylor Square in Sydney but there was no less passion, pride or conviction in the campaign for a YES vote. It was an afternoon of support and solidarity with a strong message of equality.[4]

William was very moved by Geoff Thomas sharing his journey. He says, 'It was a powerful and poignant speech in which he drew comparisons with his own fear and courage in Vietnam to that of his son's coming out'. Shirleene had gotten to know Geoff through numerous events and actions over the years, appreciated his long-term advocacy and always valued catching up. On the march down to the Parramatta River Foreshore, he described how he had previously decked out his ute with the Equality Campaign symbol and a message asking supporters to get in touch with politicians. He had then driven it across two states. When the postal survey was called, Geoff drove the ute to as many public places as he could to open up conversations and emphasise the importance of a YES vote. He also volunteered as an observer to monitor the vote-counting process. Penny Sharpe also helped organise observers for the vote counting. Statistics provided by the ABS indicated that 77.7 per cent of Australians had returned their survey forms by the end of October. This was a tremendous return rate and a testament to all.

While there was an extremely uplifting side to the way Australians supported LGBTIQ people, we need to address the negative aspects. The survey was a very stressful experience for many Australians. Children in rainbow families had to live through a period where their families were judged. Many LGBTIQ people suffered increased anxiety and depression. There were many accounts of abuse.

The YES side did not often mention the levels of abuse that extremists directed their way but it certainly happened. From bricks through windows to increased levels of stress LGBTIQ people experienced because abuse had increased their pain to an intolerable level, the postal survey was an intensely difficult experience for many.[5] Some people were abused in the street, while others were the target of hateful graffiti and discrimination in the workplace. Some were even threatened with extreme violence. From the start, the NO campaign tried to portray LGBTIQ people as 'bullies' for wanting to change the law, yet so many LGBTIQ people were traumatised through the postal survey and in its aftermath.

Penny Wong keenly felt how difficult a process the postal survey was for so many. As an extremely visible public figure, she had to care for her family but she also felt an obligation to appear resilient for many in the community who had come to depend on her as a figure of strength. She remembers feeling, 'There's this thing of "I have to protect my family", but also that sense where you have to keep projecting hope and strength and resilience because that's what the community needs. And that was even when I didn't feel it or when I felt really upset, and that's draining and it's tiring. I think it was hard for a lot of people'.

In Western Australia, Louise Pratt experienced the NO campaign tactics in a personal and hurtful way. She says, 'My son was down the supermarket with one of his gay dads, and one of the anti-marriage equality campaigners passed my son a pamphlet against gay parenting'. She had always perceived that a public vote would bring out these extremist elements and it was upsetting that she was proved correct.

In early September, Kevin Rudd's godson, Sean Foster, was punched in Bulimba in Brisbane after trying to prevent a man from pulling down YES signs.[6] In Western Australia, around the same time, Glen Forrest mother Julia Burch hung the YES flag on the front gate to her property to show support for her gay son, but it was defaced by a passer-by in what she described as a 'hateful and hurtful' act.[7]

Tom Sebo, who loves his community and found their overall response to the campaign very positive, was able to describe an incident where 'one of our campaigners was wearing a YES shirt and had some bloke call him a faggot and another one of our campaigners had a YES sign in his window and someone threw a rock at his window'. Some corflutes in the area were defaced and ripped off fences but Tom 'just called them up and went, "Hey, do you want another one?" Then we went and just put another one right back up. I just thought, I can play this game forever!'

Even Dawn, who had been resilient enough to drive through her entire electorate and then head into another on a road trip, while also continuing to campaign on the ground in the Gilmore electorate and surrounding areas, found the campaign very tough at times. What really hurt her was seeing her community upset and traumatised by the process. Shirleene remembers experiencing both sides. 'In some cases, I saw people I never would have imagined helping out and providing incredible support. At other times, doing things like wearing a YES EQUALITY t-shirt at the train-station while reminding people to return their ballots could result in someone screaming at you. That sort of direct and aggressive level of confrontation while campaigning had never happened to me before, even in 2012.' The trans and gender diverse communities bore the brunt of much of the NO sides' attack campaign. Highly-regarded trans advocate Kelly Glanney says, 'It was incredibly traumatic to see our community become the ideological punching bag of the far right'.[8]

Joseph Scales noted that even experienced campaigners started to feel a toll that they weren't used to. He notes the role of allies on the team in lifting up the LGBTIQ campaigners at these times; and how people leant on their fellow LGBTIQ friends who 'got it'. 'My best mate Tom Mooney, a longterm Rainbow Labor activist, was equally in the midst of the campaign as an advisor to Penny Wong. Our daily chats almost always ended with, "You doing ok?" That checking in really helped.'

Right across the country, many people who had never previously lobbied for social change engaged with this issue. Yet LGBTIQ people were finding the experience very difficult; there are some who may not recover and we know of others who did not make it through. Sarah Midgley still remembers seeing the sadness on a young lesbian woman's face in the Sydney suburb of Leichhardt as NO was splashed directly above us by skywriters. She stopped to talk to us as we were in our YES shirts with advocates, including actress and producer Lisa Campbell, doing a media event. The young woman mentioned her family was voting NO and how incredibly hard it all was.

On 7 November, the final day surveys could reach the ABS and be counted, Alex and Shirleene spent the last few hours outside its Sydney headquarters to encourage any last-minute voters to post their YES. We were joined by the wonderful journalist Lane Sainty. We were keen to make sure that voters knew they had to hand-deliver their surveys inside the building and couldn't just post them in the mailboxes placed outside. We had a few close calls when we intruded on people posting bills and other unrelated letters but think we probably did also stop a few ballots from going into the mailing system. A lovely woman, Claire Maloney, arrived at 4.22 p.m., with eight minutes to spare and sprinted through the building, lodging her vote as the last YES voter in New South Wales.

Alex says, 'It was extremely special to share the last hours of voting with Shirleene; we had been through so many tough times in the campaign together. During the postal survey we worked together doing everything from stuffing envelopes to addressing town halls to writing a weekly blog for the *Huffington Post*. This was such a fitting way to end the postal survey campaign, knowing that the movement had done everything we could and now all we could do was wait'. Australia had stepped up in a way we could never have imagined. With every person who went out of their way to post back their YES, who wore a badge, who put on a sticker, who talked to their friends and families about the importance of a YES vote, this had been Australia's campaign. We knew that around 77.8 per cent of surveys had been returned, an extraordinary response.

Shirleene remembers, when the last possible ballot had gone in, 'it was time to take a moment to reflect with Alex. He had worked so hard for so long. We ducked across the road from the ABS and grabbed a quick glass of wine. We had been on a long journey together and the waiting ahead was not going to be easy!'

Reinforcements

While Australians all across the country from all parts of society were working hard to win marriage equality, we also knew we had reinforcements and they had been building for years. In many ways, highly visible and respected Australian celebrities were well ahead of politicians in supporting marriage equality and were much more in tune with the Australian public. This turned out to be very useful during the postal survey. Not only were the Labor Party, the trade union movement, the Greens, members of Libs and Nats for YES and politicians from across the country stepping up, other well-known figures were prepared to use their positions to help show that marriage equality – and winning the postal survey – was something that would unite us all.

Around the 2011 Labor Party conference, many celebrities started to speak out in support of marriage equality. This was thanks to the work of Stephan Elliott, the writer and director of *Priscilla: Queen of the Desert*. Confused about why more celebrities weren't publicly supporting marriage equality (at that time the biggest names were actor Rob Mills and comedian Wil Anderson), Stephan reached out to Alex and drove to his office to meet and strategise. Alex remembers that 'Stephan knew everyone. While we could struggle getting through to someone's agent, Stephan would call the celebrity directly and push them to support us'. Following this, actors such as Guy Pearce, Hugo Weaving and Olivia Newton-John sent quotes for Alex to use in media articles and signed a petition, along with film critics Margaret Pomeranz and David Stratton. Over time many celebrities would come on board including Kylie Minogue, Dannii Minogue, and Jimmy Barnes. It was big news every time someone did, as it highlighted how out of touch politicians were to oppose something that was not only the right thing to do, but hugely popular to support.

Right up to and all the way through the postal survey, reinforcements in the form of celebrities, sports figures and well-known identities played an important role. People like Cate Blanchett would record videos urging people to vote. Lisa Campbell and David Campbell, David and Emma Pocock and Mia Freedman were all very generous allies, providing much needed support. Well-known LGBTIQ Australians, with whom the community had gone on a journey, resonated extremely powerfully. These included Kerryn Phelps and Jackie Stricker-Phelps, long-time marriage equality advocates who worked hard to campaign during the postal survey. As Kerryn was a highly respected medical doctor and former president of the Australian Medical Association, she was able to refute the harmful misinformation the NO campaign was spreading about sexuality and gender identity. She appeared in the very first advertisement filmed as the postal survey kicked off, asking Australians to ignore the hurtful misinformation and untruths being spread about the LGBTIQ community.

Christine Forster, a Liberal councillor for the City of Sydney, also campaigned tirelessly for the YES side. Christine and her partner Virginia were unstinting with their time, making themselves available to campaign or speak publicly whenever required. Although her relationship with her brother, prominent NO campaigner Tony Abbott, was often raised, Christine handled questions gracefully, pointing out that it was possible for family members to have different viewpoints. Christine's niece Frances Abbott also gave her support to the YES campaign, speaking in a video about how much she hoped she could see her aunt marry in Australia soon.

Elders from the LGBTIQ community, including a great many 78ers who had been at the first Mardi Gras, campaigned hard, determined to show their solidarity. Many of those who had led Australia's response to the HIV and AIDS epidemic, including William Rutkin in Queensland and Jamie Gardiner in Victoria, were also strong and supportive advocates during the survey.

Trade unions and members of the Labor Party were also vital in providing desperately needed on the ground support. Penny Wong says, 'It was profoundly moving that here's all these Labor activists and people out of the unions and Young Labor people and other people out of the branches who basically provide most of the muscle and organising capacity for the YES campaign and that was a great thing. Because our party should be about reform and progressive reform, and at our best we have been'.

Alex pays credit to those in the Coalition who played an active role in supporting the campaign. He says, 'Thanks to the leadership and determination of Luke Barnes and Andrew Bragg from the Libs and Nats for YES, the ground game in blue-ribbon Coalition seats helped us win almost every Liberal and National electorate. Despite the constant attacks from people across the board the hard left to the far right, they just kept knocking every door they could determined to get to YES'.

Many businesses across the country also joined in to show their support for the campaign. Janine had engaged with an impressive list of some 4000 organisations in support of marriage equality. Elaine would lead the 'corporate challenge' project to encourage major Australian corporations to do whatever they could to encourage people to vote YES. Elaine remembers, 'Whether it was call centre staff staying back after work to phone bank for YES, CEOs emailing all staff advocating for YES, or morning teas raising money from YES cupcakes, people across corporate Australia and their LGBTIQ networks did all they could to help us win'.

Sports stars and teams were also keen to be involved in the YES campaign. AFL teams, including the Western Bulldogs, North Melbourne, Collingwood, Sydney Swans, St Kilda, Geelong, Gold Coast Suns and Greater Western Sydney and the Brisbane Lions all supported the YES vote, as did Cricket Australia. The NRL, Football Federation Australia, the National Basketball League and Netball Australia were also amongst the many supporters.

Some of Australia's most loved celebrities also worked hard on the campaign. Ian Thorpe, one of Australia's best-known sporting superstars, who had come out as gay only a few years earlier and moved the nation when he did so, filmed two advertisements for the YES campaign. One with his partner Ryan showed just how quick it was to enrol or check details in the Australian Electoral Commission's system. The second showed him posting his YES. He also came to public events to personally convey this message. He spoke with passion and reason at a Twitter event and in media throughout the campaign on the issue. At the 6am City to Surf enrol-to-vote drive, when people asked for selfies with Ian, he would say, 'Only if your electoral details are up to date'.

American singer Macklemore provided a high profile boost to the campaign. Janine remembers his support during the campaign well, as she had led efforts to get him to sing his hit song, 'Same Love', at the NRL Grand Final. After reaching out to the NRL, 'within forty-eight hours it was all agreed'. Unfortunately, Tony Abbott stepped in, arguing in the media that Macklemore should be banned from singing a song that touched on marriage equality during the campaign.

Although this became a huge media story, Janine emphasises that 'the NRL held firm with no influence from us, they held firm'. Macklemore refused to withdraw the song from his planned set list and 'Same Love' went to number one in the charts. His performance received rave reviews and was a wonderful moment of cathartic release for so many people across Australia who were campaigning so hard for marriage equality.

Macklemore generously gave all the proceeds of 'Same Love' sold in Australia that month to the YES campaign, 'which was fantastic', says Janine. She spoke to his manager afterwards, who told her that Macklemore saw the performance as one of the highlights of his career. For Janine, the importance of Macklemore singing at the event was that his song and his message would reach the entire country. 'I always hoped with things like that and with things like the corporate involvement that the LGBTIQ youth or even adults, if they felt more included and less isolated because they could see that Australia was coming together to support them, then that might help them through the hate of the campaign.'

One of the most iconic and well-known supporters of marriage equality throughout the duration of the postal survey was unquestionably Magda Szubanski, who played a unique role. By

2017, Magda was loved across the country and had been for nearly three-and-a-half decades. Her warm personality, quick wit and ability to make Australians laugh had won them over. Sharon Strezlecki, a character she had created for the popular television show *Kath and Kim*, had become a national icon and that was just one of many of her well-loved creations. Her powerful book, *Reckoning*, had also displayed her fierce intellect. When the postal survey was called, Magda, who had a very strong sense of social justice, did not hesitate to come forward and offer to do anything she could to help. She had been friends with Alex since she came out publicly in 2012 and she had long used her profile to advocate for LGBTIQ people. She had appeared at many fundraisers for AME over the past several years, donating her time and energy to move the issue forward.

When the postal survey began, Magda appeared at the launch of the Melbourne Get Out the Vote campaign. She appeared on television shows such as *The Today Show*, *The Project* and *A Current Affair* to urge Australians to post their YES. The campaign heard back from people across the country about how fantastic it was to see someone with Magda's profile and standing in mainstream Australia advocating proudly for YES. Magda remembers, 'I knew that I had that responsibility and the privilege of being able to give a voice to the hurt and the pain and the anguish, but also the beauty and the joy and the decency of our community'.

As the gruelling and protracted postal campaign dragged on, Magda bravely used her role as an iconic figure to win over undecided voters and support the LGBTIQ community in one of the most memorable media moments of the campaign. The moment came at a time when many people were feeling increasingly overwhelmed by the NO campaign's tactics, which had relied on a constant bombardment of misinformation and untruths. Lasting damage has been caused by what was put in Australian mailboxes and beamed into Australian homes.

It was in this context that *Q&A* scheduled an episode devoted to the topic of marriage equality for 23 October, which was in week six of the campaign. The stakes surrounding the episode were significant. The audience figures would be extremely high, and it was going to be the last major chance to address and dismiss the NO side's arguments as the red herrings and deceptive comments that they were and to keep the issue on track.

Two factors were most important about the *Q&A* episode. The time to return ballots was fast running out so the *Q&A* appearance would represent the last chance to shoot down any doubts in voters' minds and get them to post those envelopes back. Secondly, the LGBTIQ community was hurting and they needed someone who understood their pain and was able to stand up and defend them. So much was riding on the episode.

In this high-stakes atmosphere, Magda was asked to appear alongside the 'big guns' of the NO campaign. These included Glenn Davies, the Anglican Archbishop of Sydney, who had arranged a $1 million donation to the NO campaign, and Karina Okotel, NO campaign spokesperson, federal vice president of the Liberal Party and a lawyer. These were formidable opponents. Representing the YES side would be Jesuit priest and law professor, Father Frank Brennan and Magda, who agreed to appear, despite knowing she would be the only LGBTIQ person on the stage in a studio where 50 per cent of the audience were NO voters.

As she had watched the campaign unfold, Magda, who knew there was widespread support for marriage equality across the community, had realised 'just how hard and mean the fight against equality was going to be from the NO side and I got quite a fright'. Tragically, Magda's mother passed away in between the initial interviews she had done for the campaign and the scheduled *Q&A* episode. In an incredible show of strength, she never wavered in her commitment to appear on the episode.

Magda knew just what was at stake. She remembers, 'Of all the appearances and interviews I had done I knew that *Q&A* was the Big One. It was the last opportunity for a major push back against the avalanche of untruths and disinformation. But it would also help set the tone for negotiating the terms of the peace once the vote was over'.

Magda's preparation was intense. Her razor-sharp intellect had anticipated the duplicitous paths the NO side would try to take on the episode. She says, 'I had already spotted gaping holes in the NO arguments and had a very strong sense of the direction I wanted to take the debate but I needed information. The opposition had steered the fight down a very legalistic path and I was not across all the semantic ins and outs. I told Alex I would need some help to get up to speed and he put me in touch with Shirleene Robinson'.

Shirleene remembers working with Magda as an absolute campaign highlight. 'I was just so impressed by Magda's ability to outthink the other side with strategy and get across an enormous volume of information fast! The NO campaign had absolutely no idea who they were going up against! And although she was under such enormous pressure, she was always so kind and generous.'

Magda knew the NO campaign was trying to appear sensible and hide their prejudice in a veneer of logic. She says, 'Even to me, some of the NO arguments seemed initially "reasonable". But on closer inspection they just fell apart. Australians are a smart, sensible people. I believed they deserved to have the truth and facts and then be left to make up their own minds'. Magda was determined to deliver that truth. 'People had warned me not to get dragged down "rabbit holes". But that's not in my nature. I needed to go right to the end of every burrow and examine every crack and crevice and find out for myself what I truly felt about the issue. That way, when I made the case I could do so with utter conviction.'

Shirleene helped find the research that Magda needed to have at her fingertips and to be intimately familiar with. Magda says, 'Shirleene is a gun researcher. She speaks fast and researches even faster. Every question and line of inquiry I put to her she would be on it like a cruise missile and back to me with a long list of articles and information within hours'.

Magda continues, 'Shirleene and I became a tight team during those months. It can be very lonely when you are the only one out there under the glare of the studio lights, staring down the barrel of the camera. Knowing she and Alex and the rest of the team had my back and that I was armed with thoroughly researched facts made me feel so much stronger'.

On the night of 23 October, though, we knew that Magda was walking out on the *Q&A* stage totally alone and that all the weight and pressure was resting on her shoulders. As Australia watched on, she was composed, made excellent points and refuted everything the NO side had said brilliantly. She even had the audience laughing at times!

As soon as it had ended, her performance on *Q&A* was praised across media and the internet as absolutely outstanding. Twitter and social media lit up with praise and with LGBTIQ people thanking her for standing up for them. On Twitter,

@Matt_in_London reflected the sentiment of so many when he wrote, 'Imagine sitting on a panel while people debate your basic worth as a human being on national TV? Every LGBT person in Australia is indebted to Magda Szubanski after that'. Newspapers the next day covered it extensively. News.com.au said that Magda had 'nailed it' and 'hit back with a seemingly limitless supply of well-researched statistics and arguments'. The *Sydney Morning Herald* noted that she was 'tested from the get-go', having to deal 'with slings and arrows', but that 'she marshalled facts with feeling, letting nothing slide and laying everything out, including the personal experience that drives her but which she never allows to emerge as fury.'[1]

The untruths and the cruelty had been publicly unmasked by one of Australia's most loved icons. That television appearance is regarded as the most famous media moment that came out of the postal survey campaign. Magda remembers, 'It became one of those moments, which of course, you never know are those moments until you're in them'.

Alex says, 'Magda's *Q&A* appearance was a critical moment in the YES campaign. Not only did she prosecute the case for YES better than anyone could, she stood up for the LGBTIQ community on national television at a time when the NO side's attacks were coming thick and fast. Magda became the superhero of the YES campaign. After seeing her on *Q&A*, so many in the LGBTIQ community told us that they slept better that night. Shirleene and I said, Wonder Woman is on our side with her lasso of truth!'

We saw that when Magda spoke about the importance of a YES, people listened. Julia Banks, Liberal MP for Chisholm and a member of Libs and Nats for YES, wrote an opinion piece in the *Sydney Morning Herald*, explaining how a story Magda had told in her appearance on *Q&A* had touched her deeply:

> I'm sure I'm not the only person in Australia who has enjoyed
> that wonderful feeling of a belly laugh brought on by watching
> Magda Szubanski herself or in character mode. Magda has
> made me laugh so many times over the years. And recently
> she made me cry. This happened when she told the story of her
> friend with a cancer diagnosis who was denied being with her
> partner during a treatment. I cried not only for her friend but
> for all those Australians who would have similar experiences.[2]

There is no doubt that Magda lifted the spirits of YES campaigners wherever they were. Magda continued her involvement with
the campaign team right through until the final vote was passed
in the House of Representatives.

People such as Magda and Ian Thorpe resonated so well with
people across the country because Australians fell in love with
them before they knew they were gay. These celebrities were loved
and respected for the achievements and their personalities. Their
sexuality did not define their success. Australians would ultimately question why it should deny them their rights.

Results day

The fifteenth of November 2017 was a day like no other, and few who saw the postal results come in will ever forget it. When it began, no one knew what to expect. Even now, we both have complex emotions as we reflect back. Right before 15 November, polling, along with the excellent rate of returns, indicated a YES was likely. All the way through, Tim Gartrell in the office, who knew how to read campaigns better than anyone, had been calm, reassuring and in control. Yet so much depended on a victory and a loss would have broken the country's heart.

The night before the announcement, on 14 November, Alex sat alone in his office in New South Wales (NSW) Parliament, poured a glass of red wine and, with a spoon, ate an entire rainbow cake that a supporter had sent him. Shirleene did not go to campaign headquarters but instead spent the day at her university workplace. There was nothing else she could do to prepare. Alex and Shirleene both felt it was impossible to know exactly what was in the envelopes that had been mailed back across the country. Waiting was going to be very hard for everyone. To add to the apprehension, Alex and his husband Victor, and Shirleene with her wife Sarah were both going to be followed by documentary crews, keen to capture their reactions and see history unfold through a personal lens.

Shirleene decided to go to Brisbane with Sarah to hear the results announced. It was the city where she had grown up and gone to university, where many of her friends and family lived, and where she and Sarah had met and their first marriage equality action had taken place. She also knew many of the local advocates who had worked for so many years across the state. Peter Black, who had campaigned tirelessly across Queensland, also wanted to be in his home city of Brisbane to see the results come in. Together, the three of us, who had formed a close friendship, would stand together, waiting to see how Australia had responded. We were joined by many from the Queensland field team and a great number of long-time community advocates.

The team knew the chief statistician from the ABS was going to announce the results at 10 a.m. Sydney time. But there was one person from the YES campaign who knew the results an hour earlier than the rest of the country, although she was in lockdown and could not communicate them with anyone else. The ABS decided that they would let a small group from each side of the campaign – three from YES and three from NO – see the results in their Canberra office before they were released publicly across the country. Although they would have access to the information, they would be in a locked room, with all devices switched off, no WiFi and absolutely no way of sharing this material.

The YES campaign sent Claire Dawson, the campaign's director of government affairs. She was accompanied by two volunteers to assist. One was from the Labor side of politics and the other from the Liberal side, though that day they were on the same side and were offering their assistance in a private capacity. The three were escorted to a small room with a very serious atmosphere. She remembers:

They had a suitcase in the room with big locks on it. They
opened up the suitcase, they pulled out an envelope, within
that envelope was another envelope, and then finally out of
that came sheets and sheets of paper, which they handed to my
colleague Ross. And I said, 'Okay is that ...' they knew there
would be three of us. I said, 'Do we have three sets?', they said
'No, no that's just one set of everything'. I said, 'Great, we only
really want one number, can you tell us where that is?'

After some rummaging through masses of papers, the small team
found the figure they were looking for. Australia had voted YES
with a national vote of 61.6 per cent! Claire remembers 'there were
cheers and there were smiles' and then they got down to examining all the data, states and electorates. After they had spent some
time doing this, the chief statistician began making his public
announcement and the team was allowed access to their devices
and WiFi and were able to start sending information out. Claire
reflects, 'It was a remarkable thing to be part of and to witness'.

There were many ways that individuals and communities
decided to hear the results come in that day and they all mattered. The campaign set up some official events in capital cities,
the largest being in Sydney, so that people could be together if
that would help them. There were also a range of community-run
events, where campaigners who had worked together opted to
remain together in their regions. But we also knew that many
people would have to work, would want to be at home with loved
ones or take some time for quiet reflection and self-care.

As the campaign's headquarters were in Sydney, this was
where many who had been deeply involved would watch the results
come in together. A lot of planning had gone into the results day

at Prince Alfred Park to make sure it was a success. This was led by Elaine Czulkowski and Brian Murphy, who played a vital executive support role during the campaign. Both were respected as people who could get things done and in an inclusive way. They were helped with bumping in on the day of the event by Helen, Janine and a team who were all there at 5 a.m. Georgia Kriz and Audrey Marsh were helping with a team of volunteers they had marshalled. Georgia remembers, 'It was almost a relief to spend the next few hours prepping – anything to distract us from our nerves'. Looking around, it felt like every single media outlet in Australia had come along to film.

Alex had not slept much the night before the results. He would be the first person to speak after the results announcement and on the morning, was still was not sure of what he would say. The documentary crew arrived at Alex and Vic's place and Alex would then head to Prince Alfred Park. Between multiple media interviews Alex wanted to hug everyone he saw from the campaign. When it came to Elaine, with whom he had handed out his first marriage equality flyer, he burst into tears.

In Sydney, Auntie Millie Ingram would provide the Welcome to Country, followed by a welcome from Lord Mayor Clover Moore, who had been on the marriage equality journey from the very start. Janine then spoke about the significance of the day and the sacrifices everyone had made to get there. It was a day of mixed emotions for Peter de Waal, whose hand Janine would hold on stage; as mentioned in the chapter 'Uncertain future', the day had come too late for him to be able to marry his late partner Bon. Tiernan Brady would also speak before the announcement, acknowledging the mixed emotions of nervousness and excitement that people were feeling.

Magda Szubanski, who had been a towering figure of strength throughout the survey, delivered desperately needed words about the community's resilience and ability to get through whatever lay ahead together. Malcolm McPherson, who had helped to organise the 2005 march for marriage equality, which brought out around 800 people, could hardly believe how far the movement had come or the size of the crowd (or that he was standing next to Magda, whom he admires greatly). Back in 2005, he had spoken from the back of a truck.

In the lead-up to the announcement, crowds in cities across Australia all watched the same video, which had been beautifully prepared by Helen, Kirk and Leah in the office. It ended with the message, 'Love always wins anyway'. After that, screens switched to the live announcement from the ABS, where chief statistician David Kalisch read out his detailed speech. Anyone who watched this would remember that it was not a fast process. Magda Szubanski says, 'What a nerve-wracking win! And he was really dragging out that announcement'. Shirleene remembers her apprehension increasing as the speech continued. 'Because he justified everything so carefully I wondered if there was going to be a surprise result.' But finally, he announced the overall number of voters; 12.6 million. He then went on to announce that there had been over 7.8 million YES votes returned.

In that split second, which seemed to take an eternity, people were asking themselves, does this mean we won? In Sydney, Shane Lloyd processed the numbers faster than anyone and told his partner Alan Joyce, 'We've won'. John Paul Young performed 'Love is in the air' live. Magda Szubanski tells us that, once she heard the numbers, 'My overwhelming feeling was just relief because it would have been so terrible if it had been a NO or in the low fives. It would have been terrible'. Jay Allen describes the announcement as 'surreal. I was just shell-shocked, I think'.

Carol Burger, who had found the postal survey an outrageous and horrible process, remembers the moment in Sydney when she realised that YES had won:

> Obviously, I'm terrible at maths because I'm like, 'Is that it? Is that a win for us?' But I think other people automatically calculated a lot quicker than me and they're like, 'I think that's it'. Then the 'NO' and I just burst into tears. I was so happy, and exhausted, but happy in that what I've been doing in the last however-many years has come to that moment, basically that the population of Australia has said, 'Yes, we agree'. It was a very powerful and moving moment.

Janine Middleton emphasises this point also. She says, 'to be part of changing history, to see history made, is really truly emotional. It was a great day for all Australians. I think all Australians are very proud of themselves'. On the Sydney stage, Alex delivered the message that 'love has had a landslide victory'. Anna congratulated Australia and acknowledged the people for whom the campaign had been especially tough, including the transgender and gender diverse community.

Shannan Dodson, who had been such an important part of the campaign, was very happy that YES had won and that Australia had delivered a result that meant so much to LGBTIQ Australians. She tells us, 'I try to see that majority of Australians who voted YES as being a true representation of where this country wants to go'. Shannan's insight is extremely powerful, accentuating something Shirleene and Alex would like to stress. For too long, this country has neglected the rights and recognition we owe our Indigenous people. Yet, despite this, Indigenous campaigners with skills we desperately needed reached out to us and stood with us when we urgently needed their help. This debt and solidarity must never be forgotten. Shannan says, 'I hope now the marriage equality folk can return the favour and campaign for the rights of our communities – because we can use all of the help we can get!'

In the immediate aftermath of the vote in Sydney, a core campaign group gathered together behind the stage and began their critical work. They nicknamed themselves 'Team Nerd Force' and they were poised to kick into action the very second that the ABS publicly released the survey figures. Tim Gartrell, Joseph Scales, Patrick Batchelor, Ashley Hogan and pollster Jim Reed were set up with laptops on a camping table; Adam Knobel, Shannan Dodson and the digital team were beside them, ready to communicate their data analysis to our campaigners at events across Australia and through the campaign's social media channels.

Team Nerd Force, consisting of the best campaigners Australia has, had already made preparations to instantly start populating data into spreadsheets that showed the strength of the YES vote, tweeting and sharing results from each electorate around the country. A photo of this group in action remains one of Shirleene's personal favourite images from the entire campaign. The other member of Team Nerd Force was Claire Dawson, who made contact from Canberra as soon as she regained access to her phone. The digital team had prepared one email to send out in case of a NO and another in case of a YES. Drafting the NO email had been a terribly weighty responsibility but now it could be discarded. Australia had spoken.

Team Nerd Force did not get to spend time with the crowd celebrating as they headed back to the office immediately after the work at the park was done. They needed to send out statistics and information to the spokespeople across the country and anyone who was going to be talking about the results publicly. Joseph says, 'So we did some really interesting analysis very quickly'. Digital and Team Nerd Force had so much work to do but Australia had delivered them the results they needed to get things happening.

Similarly, the work continued for the creative team. They had put together crews across the country to try and capture as many reactions in as many cities as possible. Helen remembers this as a huge logistical job and they took on a production manager to help. The crucial thing was to get the footage returned from all the cities back to Sydney headquarters 'so that it could then be edited. Then Leah and I would go through that footage and pull out what we needed and then Kirk and an editor put it into a film'. The pressure was tight because the campaign wanted to have footage and reactions from around the country ready to show by 6 p.m. that evening.

Balancing the incredible emotions of the result with then having to go and film was a challenge. Helen remembers:

> I had a bit of a cry but then I had to go and do some filming and ask people, 'How do you feel? What do you think about this?' And the first people I stopped to interview I just burst into tears and somebody else had to take over; I actually was incapable of doing anything until I got back to the office and got into edit mode because I just spent my time crying.

It took the team in the office five hours to turn the footage around. Once that was done, Helen remembers the kindness of Lee Steph, who put a shot of whisky on her desk. Helen says, 'When I'd gone through the last set of footage, I just sat on my own and that's the best whisky I've ever drunk in my life because I just sat and just was quiet and I enjoyed this amazing whisky that she'd given me, so I did have a moment'.

Tom Sebo travelled in to Sydney from Goulburn to see history unfold. As he had been very anxious the night before, he had been unable to sleep. After finally dozing off, he slept through his alarm and then had a mad dash to make it to Sydney. Once he reached Central Station, his phone battery was running out and he couldn't find Prince Alfred Park until he was 'rescued by journalists from *Pedestrian*' who steered him in the right direction.

Tom watched the results announcement and caught up with the team but because his phone wasn't working, could not see how the electorate of Hume had done. 'So I went into this random bar and plugged into a random power point and then it turned back on and then I saw a bunch of nice messages from my friends and my family … one of the first messages I opened up said, Hume, 59 per cent.' Tom remembers, thinking 'you fucking beauty! You know, we did it!'

Meanwhile, at the same time that Sydney was waiting for the announcement, Shirleene, Sarah and Peter Black were together in Queens Park in Brisbane, which was filling up. Shirleene recalls this as one of the most 'excruciating' waiting periods of her life. A big screen with a clock counting down had been set up, which unfortunately only added to the nerves. One saving grace was that friends and advocates were able to be together to see the results come in. Shirleene remembers seeing people with ashen faces, clearly deeply anxious. It was a mood both Shirleene and Sarah shared, though they tried to project positivity. Peter also put on a brave face, though he clearly felt the tension too.

One special person made it to the Brisbane announcement just in time. Geraldine Donoghue, AME's first national co-convenor, did not want to miss the results. She tells us:

> It was peak hour and we were stuck in traffic and I was
> thinking, we've got ten minutes to go, we're not going to make
> it and I said to Beck, 'I'm almost at the point of getting out of
> the car and asking cars to just move aside unless they [are]
> directly impacted, move the hell aside, we're coming through'.
> I was like, 'I'm not missing this moment'. Anyway, so we
> eventually got in. So, I'm coming screaming through into there
> and we get there and we kind of join everyone at the back and
> they were just about to do the announcement and we had,
> there was about a minute to go. And all of a sudden, I said to
> Beck, 'Oh my god, I feel like vomiting, I feel physically ill' and
> I looked around and I've never seen that many grey faces.

Just before the results were announced and Brisbane cut to the same video that was about to play in other cities, Peter stood up on the stage to speak to the crowd. Shirleene and Sarah both remember his incredible courage and strength as he did this. No one knew what was about to happen. One young woman had already come up to Sarah and told her that a friend had lost her life to suicide during the postal survey. There was huge pressure on everyone. Peter looked out at the crowd, spoke calmly and reassuringly and told everyone that regardless of whether the result was a YES or a NO, the LGBTIQ community was loved and supported and that we would get through it together. He also explained that there was a tent set up with staff ready to offer counselling to anyone who might need it.

Shirleene was scheduled to speak right after the result was announced. She had not prepared a NO speech, feeling that she would have to speak from the heart if that was the case. Sarah, who had never really relished public speaking, had agreed to come up on the stage with her after the announcement, so that the two could be together at that moment, whatever happened. Sarah also took on more media interviews throughout the day so that Shirleene could focus on what was about to happen and fortify herself for what she might need to say. Shirleene was contending with the possibility she might have to address a crowd who had just been dealt a terribly savage blow in the shape of a NO result.

But once the Brisbane audience heard the chief statistician announce the numbers, the cheers rang out. Shirleene remembers calculating, 'Seven million YES votes is more than half of 12 million!' She looked over at Sarah and Peter to confirm that they had also registered this (which they had) and then she – and then Sarah – began spontaneously jumping, a completely unexpected reaction. In what Tim Gartrell would call their 'jump for joy' moment both leapt and embraced mid-air. Shirleene remembers, 'We then grabbed Peter, a man for whom we feel such enormous respect, for a hug. We were able to soak in the win and let the anxiety slip away'. Geraldine Donoghue realised 'from the minute they said how ever many million that was over 50 per cent so I started screaming … and all you hear is silence from the crowd and just me going WAWAWAWAWA and then eventually everyone goes off'.

As in Sydney, John-Paul Young's 'Love is in the air' song played before Shirleene and Sarah headed for the stage. Looking out, we saw just what the victory meant to the community – but we also registered exactly what it had cost people. As part of her speech, Shirleene told the crowd, 'What we have achieved here together as one people will send such a powerful message to future generations that we are all equal under the law'. As more and more statistics came through, Peter read them out to the Brisbane crowd. Realising that Queensland had returned a higher YES vote than NSW was a shock to Shirleene, who had grown up in Joh Bjelke-Petersen's Queensland.

Shirleene, Sarah and Peter were truly honoured to be able to share the Brisbane moment with William Rutkin, a friend and a wonderful advocate for the LGBTIQ community for almost fifty years. He had been the youngest member of CAMP, one of the first gay rights groups in Australia, in Brisbane in the 1970s and then went on to become the longest serving president of the Queensland AIDS Council during an era when a great deal of stigma surrounded HIV and AIDS, particularly in Queensland. He had devoted his life to making things better for LGBTIQ people and had been one of AME's strongest supporters through good times and bad.

He told the crowd that 'I almost burst into tears thinking about how far our community has come and the trials that we've been through in that time to today, where finally we've found our place in the sun'. Before leaving the park, the team was able to tell the crowd that every single Australian state and territory had returned a YES vote. What a wonderful affirmation from across the country and what a extraordinary mix of emotions we were all feeling.

In Melbourne, more than 1000 people gathered near the steps of the State Library of Victoria. Speakers included Tim Peppard, AME's Victorian director; Ro Allen, the Victorian commissioner for gender and sexuality; Wil Stracke; Jacqui Tomlins; Jason Tuazon-McCheyne; Ali Hogg, convenor of Equal Love; and Anthony Wallace, campaign manager of Equal Love. Opposition Leader Bill Shorten took to the stage, saying that 'unconditional love has had the last word'.

Wil Stracke remembers that lots of emotions were stirred up:

> I think it was a massive relief. It was a massive relief. So there was relief, elation, some people kind of … the crying that comes with the end of a period of tension. It was a crying in happiness. Everyone's emotional responses were different.

Victorian Trades Hall put on an after-party at a pub across the road with a stage. Wil says:

> So for us, I'm glad that we did that. I'm glad that we did that party because it felt like the full stop. Because that announcement time was really weird. So it felt like people who wanted to celebrate could come here and people who wanted to go to their own community bars and venues could do that, or people who wanted to reflect could do that.

Anna Brown, who had been in Sydney for the results in the morning, travelled back for the evening celebrations in Melbourne as she wanted to celebrate with friends and the community there.

In Canberra, as hundreds gathered in Haig Park, AME received approval from the ACT government to close part of

Lonsdale Street in Braddon, near Hopscotch Bar, so the celebrations could continue. Politicians who were in the Senate that day were also glued to the television as the announcement was made. Louise Pratt, who was being filmed at the time, remembers being 'exhausted but very nervous. It was hard to be away from my partner Bek that day because she was on the streets of Perth with all our friends and family'. Penny Wong, in the same committee room with Louise and other parliamentary YES supporters, who had been so stoic for so long, allowed herself to cry once it was clear that more than 60 per cent of Australians had returned their YES.

In Perth, hundreds gathered at Northbridge Piazza for the results. Stephen Dawson, a Labor minister in the Western Australian Parliament, was with his partner Dennis Liddlelow in the crowd. Stephen declared, 'It's a fantastic result. I'm very proud of Western Australians and also Australians in general. This is a momentous day for the LGBTIQ community'.[1]

In Adelaide, rain did not prevent hundreds of supporters gathering together to celebrate at Hindmarsh Square. Labor Premier Jay Weatherill declared the results were 'a victory for love'. Caitlyn Georgeson, from the SA Equality Campaign, described the reaction from the crowd as 'more relief than anything ... I don't know if it was the rain or what it was. There was a lot of celebration but mostly it was relief'.[2] Ian Hunter, an openly gay state Labor MP, danced on stage with joy. In Darwin, the official results event, hosted by AME and The Territory Says Yes, was held at Oaks Elan Darwin. In Hobart, an announcement event was held at the Cascade Hotel.

We both want to acknowledge the complexity of emotions felt across the country on this day. Yes, many people felt overwhelming relief and happiness. There was also enormous anxiety and stress on that day and over the course of the campaign. The postal survey was difficult and it was unnecessary. Opponents targeted people on the very basis of who they were. We must acknowledge that transgender and gender diverse people were heavily attacked by the NO campaign and that enormous damage was done and that the cost continues.

We must also recognise the pain felt by those who found out that their electorates had voted NO, and those managing their cultural identity alongside faith, sexuality and gender identity. As Francis Voon, faith and multicultural outreach co-ordinator for the Equality Campaign, notes, 'No sooner had the YES result been announced than the media highlighted certain areas that voted overwhelmingly NO. They claimed ethnicity and religion as the reason that these areas returned NO votes'. This ignored the favourable results returned in multicultural seats, including Graham Perrett's electorate of Moreton and many electorates in Victoria. Negative reporting and the process of the survey itself has had ongoing ramifications, which Francis outlines:

> Not only do LGBTIQ people in these communities continue
> to feel unsafe even today, but as an LGBTIQ person of an
> ethno-religious background reflected rather brokenheartedly
> to me, 'We had always had this uneasy feeling we may not have
> been really accepted in our own neighbourhoods, but now we
> know exactly what per cent of our neighbours are against us
> and our relationships'.

There is ongoing healing to be done in the aftermath of the survey. This will take time and require energy and commitment. Already, though, as we move past the scare campaign we had to live through in 2017, polls have shown support for marriage equality increasing. A poll by research group Essential from 13 March 2018 showed 65 per cent of respondents supported marriage equality, a significant increase of four percentage points since the one it conducted less than four months earlier.[3] We should take great confidence in this. As Australians see the joy and happiness that marriage equality brings, we know that the support will continue to grow and flourish just as it has internationally.

Dawn Hawkins, who had worked so hard across the south coast of NSW, was not initially sure that she wanted to be with many people when the announcement came in. But she did want to be with her community. She agreed to go to a breakfast with two women she felt very safe with in Huskisson. This small event snowballed as more and more people indicated they wanted to attend. Dawn also arranged another event in Nowra for supporters there. At her event, she remembers, 'a wonderful sense of community and such a cross-section of community'. Just as the announcement started to come through in Huskisson, the wi-fi shut down. As soon as it was resolved, Dawn logged on to her computer: 'For me, I just had to see Gilmore. Once I'd seen that, then I was right, then I could celebrate'.

Dawn was not the only one concerned about the Gilmore result. Both Alex and Janine independently had a moment where they thought 'What about Dawn and Gilmore?' Dawn had worked so hard for the campaign, the team would be devastated if there was not a majority result in her electorate. Dawn was buoyed to receive calls from both Alex and Janine.

After the official announcements in Brisbane and Melbourne, Shirleene, Sarah and Peter and Tim Peppard all flew in to Sydney, so that they could be with the rest of the team for the afternoon and evening. Of that flight out of Brisbane, Shirleene says, 'The funniest thing was that we were all desperate to see what was happening and what the results across the country were but we were completely cut off from the world and communication for just over an hour at the most pivotal time in the whole movement thus far. It was surreal'.

Once travelling team members made it to Sydney, they went to a rally in Taylor Square, where Magda Szubanski spoke to roars of approval from the crowd, alongside Clover Moore, who had been at the first rally in support of marriage equality and was at the first one held after Australia had said YES. Tanya Plibersek and Alex, as well as representatives from the 78ers and Rachel Evans, who had organised the very first marriage equality rally, also spoke. Oxford Street was a mix of exhilaration, colour and exhaustion all night long.

Kirk Marcolina told Shirleene she would feel the emotions of the results day much more powerfully than the ones that would occur later with a parliamentary vote. While she disputed this at the time, she now concedes Kirk was right. The Sydney evening celebrations, being with friends and fellow advocates, coupled with the sheer relief of knowing the YES result, were more emotionally powerful than the drawn-out final vote in the House of Representatives. Brian would drive the YES plinth back to his home on the back of a ute and was honked and cheered with praise the whole drive. Elaine says she will never forget walking home from the campaign's after-party at the Beresford Hotel in Sydney with fellow campaigner Chris Pycroft, and seeing the joy and relief on people's faces.

The Australian people should take enormous pride in the

YES campaign they drove from the grassroots up and the win they delivered against the odds. The postal survey was never designed to favour supporters of marriage equality. Yet people from all across the country stood up, showed their support and most importantly, posted back their YES vote in overwhelming numbers. And together, the people won. As Qantas CEO Alan Joyce pointed out, 'If this was a general election, it would be the biggest landslide in Australian electoral history'.[4]

There were also international celebrations, reported in newspapers from Israel through to India. Australia House in London even put up a rainbow flag in the aftermath of the survey results. Warren Entsch, who had driven the movement for marriage equality within his party for so long, was in New York at Manhattan's Australian Hotel when the announcement was made. He describes being with a 'fantastic crowd' at a venue 'packed to capacity' and that 'it was a very emotional time over there when it came through'. He told the crowd that for a long time, in Parliament, 'No one wanted to hear from me. I was very much a single vote.'[5]

Not any more though. Over seven million Australians had stood with Warren and said YES. And, proving that he was very much in tune with his electorate, Leichhardt had also returned a 63 per cent YES vote. In incredible scenes, paying tribute to the Australian result, New York's Empire State Building lit up in rainbow colours for that evening.

Back in Australia, both Alex and Anna boarded flights to Canberra to make sure they were ready for an early start in Parliament House the next day. Anna would join Corey Irlam to have dinner with Dean Smith, who would proceed with his Bill the next day. Alex popped in to the Canberra celebrations where

Sarah Hanson-Young and Tim Wilson were waiting for him to join them.

The team had always known that the work to achieve marriage equality was not going to stop with the YES result. Parliament now had to do its job. Claire Dawson, who had been thrilled to see the YES come in early that morning, knew the legislation still had to get through both the Senate and the House of Representatives. She remembers:

> While I was incredibly excited and relieved, to me it was so not over. I know from my years working in parliament and politics and watching Bills get through parliament that we essentially had one challenge over and we really had two more. That was getting it through the Senate and then getting it through the House of Representatives, knowing that that's not always an easy process.

At the forefront of her mind was the possibility of amendments, which would derail the passage of the legislation. Knowing there was going to be an enormous amount of work in the weeks ahead, Claire 'went home that evening and I had a really big glass of red wine and a big deep breath and thought, "Right. Tick. We've done that". But I also just really wanted to get myself prepared for what we had ahead of us'.

The Senate makes history

As soon as the postal survey results were in, it was time for action. For far too long, too many politicians had managed to avoid reflecting the will of the Australian people. Now though, change was in the air; the Australian people had made a decisive statement and LGBTIQ senators and their allies were going to lead the charge. Before the results of the survey had even been announced, though, political game-playing around the legislation was starting.

The campaign had learnt that the Victorian senator James Patterson would intervene, in what Alex describes as 'the ultimate act of political bastardry'. Before the results of the postal survey were even announced, on 13 November, Senator Patterson announced that he would be proceeding with his own same-sex marriage Bill, but it would be one with much 'stronger religious protections' than Senator Dean Smith's Bill. Patterson's Bill was an attempt to introduce new forms of discrimination against LGBTIQ Australians. It would essentially allow businesses who had a conscientious or religious objection to deny service to people whose weddings they did not approve of. Essentially, after putting Australia through the postal survey and leaving them with the expense of the process, some in the Liberal Party found it appropriate to proceed with a Bill that would increase discrimination against LGBTIQ people and others. Fortunately, the Dean Smith Bill had emerged from a substantial and in-depth cross-party process. Labor Senator Louise Pratt, who had been the deputy chair on the select committee on the exposure draft of the Marriage Amendment (Same-Sex Marriage) Bill, emphasises just how important that earlier cross-party work had been in drafting the Dean Smith legislation. She says:

> The intellectual integrity of the [Smith] Bill was right and I think that was a pretty major achievement because we wouldn't have been able to get through that Senate debate, really without that groundwork that had been done in that Bill starting nearly twelve months before.

Tim Gartrell, Alex, Clint McGilvray and Anna Brown developed a strong communications plan, which accused Senator Patterson of 'wanting to take Australians back to a time where a shop could have sign saying who they would serve and wouldn't serve'. Key Labor voices including Penny Wong and Tanya Plibersek also strongly criticised Senator Patterson's Bill. Tanya Plibersek told ABC Radio National that the Patterson Bill was 'one more delaying tactic from the people that brought you the $122 million waste of money postal survey'.[1]

The Patterson Bill also sent a strong message that supporters of the fairer and more robust Dean Smith Bill that had emerged from the earlier cross-party committee draft would need to act fast. Alex and Anna met with Senator Penny Wong, who told them with regard to the Coalition, 'Just avoid their party room' as every time it went there, the situation for marriage equality got worse. She stressed the importance of starting the process with Dean's Bill the day the results were out. The Bill was co-sponsored by eight other senators from Labor, the Greens, Nick Xenophon Team and Derryn Hinch's Justice Party.

On 14 November, Dean gave notice in the Senate that he would introduce the Bill on 15 November, with debate commencing on 16 November. Seeing the Bill in Dean's hand, and knowing it was going into the Senate, had a very emotional impact on Anna Brown, who suddenly burst into tears and was consoled by Lee, Corey Irlam and Claire – the three people with whom she had worked so closely. Corey had long provided political and policy advice as a member of the team, bringing with him a strong history of working on LGBTIQ reform.

Joseph Scales and Patrick Batchelor had been hard at work in the meantime, putting up 'Australia said YES' signs wherever they could within the parliament, and asking senators to put a poster up that said their state 'said YES'. They wanted to reinforce that message that the vote had come back, it had been overwhelmingly strong, and that the country was watching and expecting action – and soon. Indeed, Patrick was busy through the week mapping out the last potential public and field activities to assist in maintaining that pressure.

For many, the most moving part of the day was seeing LGBTIQ Senate members lead the debate. Dean Smith spoke first, followed by Penny Wong, Louise Pratt and then Janet Rice. Dean Smith became emotional as he told the chamber that, 'I never believed the day would come when my relationship would be judged by my country to be as meaningful and valued as any other. The Australian people have proven me wrong'.[2]

Penny Wong referred to the difficult journey she had been on since 2004, when the *Marriage Act* was amended to prevent same-sex couples from marrying, and her decision to stay in the Labor Party and work for change from within. Louise Pratt referred to her own loving relationship and family when she said, 'I know we share the feelings of other same-sex couples who look forward to the focus turning from a massive public debate about our lives and our identities and turning towards each other, for the love we share for each other and for our children'. Janet Rice spoke of the discrimination she and her partner Penny had experienced after Penny had transitioned to live as her authentic self. 'You don't know the pain of having to let go of your partner's hand because you're not sure of the reaction it might get from people around you.'[3]

Claire Dawson and Joseph Scales, from different sides of politics, worked closely together as the Senate debated; both talk about the enormous trust they developed. Claire had of course already spent over a year leading this complicated work. Joseph recalls Claire laughing down the phone to him soon after he joined the team at the Sydney HQ. 'It's so nice to have someone I can just speak in political shorthand with!' Their new friendship across the political spectrum sometimes bemused others in the team. Claire and Joseph ran complex vote or 'whipping' spreadsheets, predicting every possible outcome.

Claire and Joseph also tracked the various conversations the team was having with senators, ministers and shadow ministers and staffers. Political advisors or 'staffers' are rarely acknowledged. Indeed, a good staffer never wants to be the story or recorded in the history books. But it would be remiss if we did not acknowledge the network of LGBTIQ staffers from across the political spectrum who supported the campaign from the inside, providing helpful understandings of their MP or senator.

Many of them in their private capacity were warriors and rebels for marriage equality inside their own parties, too. All this intel, along with Claire and Joseph's diverse political experience, and Claire's expertise on the political mood towards our issues, would be a useful guide for where to deploy the team to visit senators and ensure we had got them across the line.

Claire and Joseph were given access to the Greens Party room to work from, where Claire remembers:

> We had various lists of numbers, we had the speakers lists for the debate, we kept an eye on timing and we didn't actually get into the voting stage of the Bill, which is, so you essentially have the second reading, where people put their position of a Bill. Then you get into the committee stage where you debate the Bill clause by clause, and that's the point where you can amend it. There were various amendments that were proposed by opponents of the Bill.

Claire remembers being there until midnight every night, having to listen to hurtful and appalling statements about the LGBTIQ community, but it ensured that they were clear and confident on the individual positions of every single senator. The attitude of the whole team in Canberra was, 'This is not a done deal yet'.

Penny Wong made it very clear that she and the Labor Party were not going to support the Bill if any amendments were added on that would introduce new forms of discrimination. She remembers emphasising the point that "'I'm not going to vote for wholesale amendments to the sexuality/discrimination laws in this country, I'm just not. Not even for marriage equality" and I think probably most of the people on that side of the debate would have agreed, we're not prepared to pay this price'. This move ensured the passage of marriage equality through the Senate without hostile amendments. Despite the taunts from some government members, the Labor Party held firm throughout.

Anna and Lee Carnie were under extra pressure as the Bill was being debated because, as it was a private members' Bill, Dean Smith did not have a government department or a ministerial staff team to assist him. That meant Lee and Anna acted as advisors, with explainers and tables of key issues. They had to be ready to provide information about any aspects of the legislation that might need to be addressed. Anna remembers, 'I was able to provide some information back about, "Well, this case has decided this, but the Bill doesn't actually do that" and really explain what the actual effect of the legislation was'. Most critically, 'We just needed to get it through unamended'. Anna credits the solid trust on the Bill that existed between Penny Wong, Dean Smith, Louise Pratt and Janet Rice as being 'a really important ingredient of the success'.

The speech Alex was looking forward to the most was Sarah Hanson-Young's. Sarah played a truly historic role in the marriage equality movement, moving more Bills in support of marriage equality than any other politician, often with little or no support from across the political spectrum. But unlike those many other attempts, this time, she knew 'this was the Bill that was going to pass'. As others spoke, she listened very closely. 'I really wanted to soak that up. I wanted to take all those moments in and really listen to people's words because people who spoke were people who, ten years earlier, did not support it and to hear a totally different response was quite an amazing thing to sit there and listen to.'

Sarah would deliver her speech on Alex's birthday, exactly eight years to the day since they had first met. He advised Sarah as she wrote her speech and she included some lines Alex had always wanted to use, but had not been able to as he had to be diplomatic with all political sides. With reference to Senator Patterson and other conservative senators, who had now turned the Patterson Bill into a series of amendments to be tacked on to Dean's Bill, Sarah Hanson-Young told the Senate, 'Unfortunately, we have a handful of ultraconservative, right-wing MPs and senators who are trying to spoil the celebration and ignore the will of the people'. With deeply felt emotion, she paid tribute to Bob Brown, who had given her responsibility for the LGBTIQ portfolio when she was first elected to the Senate. She said:

> When Bob retired, in 2012, I said to him, 'Bob, I'm really
> sorry that we weren't able to reverse that awful law before your
> time was up'. Today I stand here with my Greens colleagues,
> finishing the job that Bob Brown started. Boy, this parliament
> has come such a long way.[4]

Sarah Hanson-Young would then host a very special birthday party for Alex in her office in Parliament House, joined by many of the AME team and Alex's mother, followed by a dinner on the terrace at Parliament's dining room. Quite a few of the team had not been inside parliament itself before. Their work had been out in the community or electorates, so to be in Canberra for this was a special experience indeed. Sarah would invite the press gallery, MPs and senators from across the parliament to celebrate. Alex thinks one of the most special moments for him was when Liberal senator Simon Birmingham acknowledged how hard the campaign had been for people and thanked them all for staying strong in the face of adversity. Alex thought back to that first time he came to Federal Parliament with sweaty hands, nervous and intimidated. Now he was celebrating with friends who had become family. The celebration was a brief reprieve and time to be with friends whilst all the chaos of the debate continued. Indeed, during dinner, Sarah would have to run back down to the Senate to help vote down amendments.

The final Senate vote would come the next day, 29 November. The campaign team was in three different places. One group was back in Sydney, working hard on digital and other aspects of the campaign. The second group, including Tim Gartrell, Shirleene, Sarah Midgley, Peter Black, Tim Peppard, Carolyn Greenwich, Brooke Horne, Shane Lloyd, Jay Allen, Tiernan Brady and Elaine Czulkowsi, were at the National Press Club, supporting Magda, who was giving a speech. The third group were in the Senate itself.

Shirleene and Sarah Midgley had read Magda's speech the night before and were keen to see her deliver it. We knew how much of her heart and soul she had put into it. While Magda was speaking, everyone in the Press Club knew the vote was coming in. As usual, Magda delivered an incredible speech and it brought many to tears. As part of her address, she said:

> There is an old Polish saying: 'We are fighting for our freedom and yours'. Increasing the rights of LGBTIQ people does not come at the expense of others. On the contrary: any effort that enhances empathy, that promotes human dignity and cherishes respect, that sees beyond superficial difference to the deep, shared sameness within, is a treasure to all of us.

She continued, adding 'we all know that love is hard to find. That when you do find it, you must cherish and nuture it. And sometimes yes, it must be enshrined in the law'.

Magda received thunderous applause and a standing ovation, believed to be one of the first given by the Press Club. Shirleene says, 'Seeing this was a real privilege. It was just a beautiful moment'.

Once Magda had finished speaking, Tim Peppard pulled up the action that was happening in the Senate on his phone, and being close to Magda, showed her as well. The cameras started to gather around them, and then Tiernan jumped up to join Magda onstage. Shirleene and Sarah were standing enjoying the historic moment, chatting with Tim Gartrell, who urged them to have another 'jump for joy' moment when the Bill passed, just like they had done in Brisbane. He also encouraged them to share the moment with Magda, and they, and Elaine, embraced all on the stage with her, overjoyed.

As guests of Sarah Hanson-Young, Alex, Janine Middleton and Tom Snow sat together on the floor of the Senate watching the legislation pass unamended and burst into hugs and cheers. Rodney Croome, Peter Furness and Ivan Hinton-Teoh were also watching from the floor of the Senate. Alex would grab Sarah Hanson-Young for another massive hug. Claire Dawson, a seasoned political expert, who had seen many votes on many issues pass over the years, knew this particular vote passing was something truly special and she was not going to miss witnessing it. Mobile phones aren't allowed in the public gallery, so she 'just dropped my phone' at her work space 'and I ran upstairs and I went into the public gallery. So I was sitting in the gallery, looking down onto the Senate chamber floor as the vote happened'.

Penny Wong, who had worked so hard for so long to achieve marriage equality, describes the moment the Bill passed through the Senate as being 'incredibly moving. More the Senate debate than the House for me, because I guess I was sort of running it with people. I just felt relief and jubilation'. She pays tribute to the Australian population, who had been on such a difficult journey. 'We collectively had done this, and that the country had done it, you know? And that's a good thing to be part of, isn't it? And we've all been part of that'.

The team who had been inside the Senate, along with the politicians themselves, would then hold a joint press conference. Here, Penny Wong said, 'It is always a privilege to stand in the chamber but there are days when you feel like you are part of changing the nation'. Alex would deliver a teary and heartfelt thanks to Dean Smith, saying, 'From one gay man to another, thank you. This wouldn't have happened without someone with your determination, from your side of politics who showed such amazing courage'.

After the Senate vote and Magda's press club speech, everyone reconvened at parliament in a Greens meeting room. Shirleene remembers the feeling of excitement, returning to parliament, realising that we were closer than ever before to marriage equality becoming a reality. She says, 'I walked into the building talking with Brooke Horne about how surreal it all felt and the amount of adrenalin and endorphins we'd burnt through over the past week. It was really nothing like I had ever experienced before. It felt almost like we were walking on Mars, on uncharted territory. There had been so many attempts over so long and each time, we had been defeated. Now, finally, we were getting there'. The Greens party room was filled with advocates and supporters, some of whom had been active since 2004. Alex provided a toast to the amazing work Anna, Lee and Corey had undertaken for so long on marriage equality legislation. A sense of history was in the air and we knew there was just one more vote to go.

The House finally represents

After the legislation had made it through the Senate without any hostile amendments, supporters were beyond overjoyed. As the country had now reached a point where marriage equality appeared closer than ever before, people from across Australia converged on Canberra. So many of those who had worked so hard for so long were determined to be there to see the injustice of 2004 rectified. Others who had friends or families who were affected or who wanted to see a better, fairer Australia also made the journey. Many others watched online or on television. A sense of historical change was in the air; we were on the verge of something truly remarkable. Yet substantial challenges still lay ahead.

The ALP had made it clear that it had compromised sufficiently on the Dean Smith Bill and that they would encounter very real difficulties voting for amended legislation that introduced new forms of discrimination. In effect, this meant the House of Representatives needed to pass the Dean Smith Bill unchanged, and vote down the next set of hostile amendments.

The political team from the campaign had been hard at work and focused on the situation in Canberra since the postal survey had ended. They still had a great deal of work to do, but an increasingly excited Alex would keep distracting them with his stories, gossip, or historical references to things that had happened in the campaign. Alex remembers how skilled Claire was in quarantining him and keeping him busy. 'Every time I came up to the room they were working in, to prevent me from distracting them all, Claire would have a pre-prepared task for me, ones that would often take me to the other side of the building. She would say, "Alex, it's really important you bring Adam Bandt this 'Melbourne Says Yes' poster. He needs it for his office urgently"'.

Managing such significant legislation was far more complex than many realised. Whereas the Senate would deal with private members' Bills and motions more regularly as no one party controls the numbers, the situation was much less common in the House of Representatives. The challenge would need to be managed by Warren Entsch, Tim Wilson, Trent Zimmerman, Dean Smith and Trevor Evans. The ALP would also need to hold tight and make sure that none of its members backed any amendments.

Trevor remembers the challenge of putting forward a private member's Bill:

> As a backbencher, as someone who's relatively new, you
> walk into the House knowing that a minister is in charge
> of this process with the full weight of their advisors
> and departments and lawyers behind them. There was
> no such thing here so a lot of work went into preparing
> and coordination.

Fortunately, the Senate had shown that Labor were working well together and no one from that side had shown any inkling that they would support any amendments. Claire Dawson and Joseph

Scales kept their eyes closely on the numbers. Anna Brown and Lee Carnie were ready with any legal advice required.

With the country watching, speeches in the House of Representatives began on Monday 4 December. Fittingly, a little after 10 a.m., Warren Entsch, wearing a rainbow tie, rose to introduce the legislation into the House of Representatives. As he explained, his lengthy advocacy for LGBTIQ people had been a lonely path for a long time. Back in 2004, he had been one of the very few who had questioned why legislation discriminating against LGBTIQ people needed to be introduced. He had worked hard for many years to address other inequalities LGBTIQ people faced in the law.

In 2007, Warren had left politics. In 2010 though, he came back from retirement because he felt 'I had unfinished business'. On 4 December 2017, he told the House, 'I hope some of that business can be dealt with this week because a clear majority of Australians back this because they believe in a fair go. They are sick of politicians playing games with real people and real lives'. Just one of the people whose life had been changed by Warren's compassion was Kate Doak, who was acknowledged in his speech. She tells us:

> Hearing my favourite 'Croc Hunter' tell our story to others is something that I always cherish, regardless of what the setting is. Telling our story saves lives, so whether it's during a debate on marriage equality or other LGBTIQ rights within the parliament or a conversation with a constituent on the streets of Cairns, I always feel proud and grateful whenever my mate Warren and his wonderful staff tell it. Life is there to be lived.[1]

After Warren's powerful speech, Brisbane Liberal MP Trevor Evans seconded the motion.

There were many significant moments and speeches throughout that week. On Monday, Bill Shorten, the Leader of the Opposition, rose to support the Bill. He said, 'I think this is an uplifting moment in our nation but we need to be mindful to match our joy with humility. Humility to acknowledge that for so long on marriage equality, Australia has trailed the world'. He spoke directly to the LGBTIQ community: 'We seek your forgiveness, we salute your courage and we thank you for including us in your historic moment'.[2]

Earlier that day, Tim Wilson told Alex to make sure that he had a good seat during his speech, although he did not reveal the full reason why. Alex made sure he sat next to Tim's partner Ryan, who he knew had made many sacrifices to support Tim. Tim spoke very generously about Alex's role in the campaign, but then Tim made history by being the first parliamentarian to propose to his same-sex partner on the floor of parliament. A beaming Ryan said 'Yes!' as the gallery and the parliament burst in to applause. The proposal was broadcast internationally. Alex says, 'You can't underestimate the positive impact this visibility had and will have for LGBTIQ people around the world, especially those for whom marriage equality might still be a long way from being achieved in their country'.

There were some incredible moments of deep courage and compassion that will stay with many of us forever. On Tuesday 5 December, Labor's Linda Burney, whose gay son had died during the postal survey, returned to parliament for the first time since his death to deliver a speech that resonated across the country. It was stirring and powerful, and spoke to the hearts of everyone who had ever experienced injustice and discrimination. Linda had been a long-term supporter of marriage equality. She had given up her time to attend a marriage equality workshop in her electorate in 2016, delighting the members of her community who attended. Shirleene and Sarah remember the faces of those who came to that event lighting up when they saw that their federal MP was on their side.

In her speech in the House of Representatives that day, Linda Burney declared, 'I have long been a supporter of marriage equality. I have never had a second thought. It seemed to be so obvious to me'. She made the point that she did not support the postal survey process. 'It was expensive, divisive and hurtful. But what I found most disgusting about it was that it forced LGBTIQ loved ones to beg for their own civil rights, a truly humiliating and shameful exercise.' Those watching on in the gallery knew they were listening to someone who understood so deeply what it meant to be an treated as outsider in their own country:

> I support marriage equality as someone who has, and has
> had, loved ones who identify as LGBTIQ. To them, marriage
> equality would mean so much. I honour these people, and
> in particular, my late son Binni. And I support marriage
> equality as someone who is a member of a community that
> has experienced great discrimination and injustice and
> understands what it means to be rejected, understands what
> intergenerational trauma feels like and what hurt and distress
> does to you.

Following her speech, the *Sydney Morning Herald* reported on her bravery, stating, 'the parliament had rarely seen such a moment'.[3]

Rural Indi Independent Cathy McGowan, wearing a beautiful pair of rainbow earrings, also delivered a speech that received widespread acclaim.[4] She was determined to thank the young people who had worked so hard to see a strong YES result for marriage equality returned in her electorate.[5] She also took the opportunity to point out that there was still a way to go on issues of gender diversity and inclusion, a journey that she herself had been educated on. Later, when someone implied that rural Australia was not as supportive of marriage equality as the cities, she took exception, correctly pointing out that the results across the great majority of regional Australia had been positive.

Less impressive for most was the prime minister's speech, where he said that same-sex couples were better off married than 'living alone comforted only by their respective cats'. He would then go on to say, 'I am the first prime minister of Australia to be unequivocally and consistently in support of legislating same-sex marriage', even though he had voted against it in in 2012. Many felt that Turnbull was trying to take credit for a reform that others had put their blood, sweat and tears into. Magda Szubanski would tell journalists, 'Having had so much feedback from people in terrible pain, to see the prime minister gloating and taking credit was a little bit hard to swallow'.[6] Alan Jones would tell us that he was 'sickened' by Turnbull's attempt to claim credit, and in contrast to the leadership shown by everyday Australians, Jones felt Turnbull's contribution was 'juvenile, and pedestrian at best', and that 'people like Penny Wong and Tim Wilson can take credit, but not the prime minister'.

As the week progressed, the team were still working hard and doing all they could to keep an eye on amendments. Joseph, Claire, Lee and Anna kept up the hard work. Claire, who was more experienced than anyone in the team at parliamentary process, would say, 'We won't know till the final vote, we can't take anything for granted'. There was another indication that the numbers to block amendments were there on Tuesday 5 December, when Christopher Pyne publicly announced he would not be supporting any. Anna remembers feeling a great deal of relief. 'That was a real game changer.' She knew that Pyne's move, as a senior member of the government, would embolden others and give unsure backbenchers the confidence they needed to also vote down the hostile amendments.

By mid-week, the public galleries were filling up, with people from across Australia coming to parliament to see the vote. A strong contingent from the campaign were also arriving. Shirleene arrived on Tuesday and so did Adam Knobel. Shirleene had to spend an anxious day away from Sarah Midgley in Canberra before she arrived on Wednesday. They had shared so many marriage equality moments as a couple it felt strange to be apart at this time, when we were on the cusp of reform.

Slowly, the team came together in Canberra. Helen Ross-Browne, Ashley Hogan and Leah Newman drove down together. Leah had brought her 13-year-old son, Ryan, with her to watch the vote. She remembers, 'I really wanted him to understand how big that moment was and to be able to hold that for the rest of his life too'. Dae Levine and Liam Ryan, who by this time were both working in Los Angeles and had the most vast distance to travel, were determined to be there and secured flights. Liam remembers:

> I think it was incredible for us to regroup and I think I
> definitely felt overwhelmingly a sense of togetherness and
> people who had moved on and formed other organisations

for the most part were there and I don't think anyone wasn't included or recognised.

Wil Stracke, who had led such a powerful campaign for the postal survey through Victorian Trades Hall in Melbourne, made it there with her partner Lisa. Dawn Hawkins, whose efforts in the electorate of Gilmore and whose spectacular road trip had won such admiration, had thought she might have to miss the Canberra vote for financial reasons. When she realised that the money just was not there, 'The boys up at the Art Bar in Kiama threw a fundraiser and raised $1300 in that one night ... for four nights in Canberra, which was quite amazing'. Tom Sebo and Shelby Marks from the Hume campaign 'made a decision we wanted to go over' too and joined up with the team.

We could also see other campaigners – many of whom we had worked with over the years or whose actions we deeply appreciated – in the gallery. Shelley Argent watched all the speakers until very late each evening. Rodney Croome, Sharon Dane and others who had played such a crucial role in AME were also there. Jacqui Tomlins and Sarah Nichols-Tomlins and Jason and Adrian Tuazon-McCheyne, whose question on the legality of their Canadian marriages had seen the Howard Government introduce the 2004 *Marriage Act Amendment*, were there with their families. Felicity Marlowe made it to Canberra to represent all the rainbow families who had been affected but could not be present.

Penny Sharpe, who had been so important in advocating for change within the Labor Party, was there. Louise Pratt, who could have sat on the floor as a senator, chose instead to sit in the public gallery with her partner Bek. Sean Leader, who had spent years driving grassroots change from within Rainbow Labor, was also present.

Prominent LGBTIQ Australians would also begin arriving in Canberra the day before the final vote, including Ian Thorpe and his partner Ryan, Kerryn and Jackie Stricker-Phelps, Christine Forster and Virginia Edwards, Bill Bowtell who had played a critical role in developing Australia's world-leading response to the HIV and AIDS epidemic, and Magda Szubanski. Alex and Tom Snow would play the role of chaperones, taking people from office to office, and Clint would co-ordinate a number of interviews for the press gallery.

Shirleene was delighted to see that Graham Perrett was an Opposition Whip, which meant he would be immersed in the action on the floor and counting the numbers on all the unsuccessful attempts to amend the Bill. It was wonderful to see someone she had shared a political journey with – and formed a friendship with – play a leading role in the process of legislating for marriage equality.

The week marriage equality passed was a gruelling one for spectators in the gallery. More than 110 MPs spoke for over twenty-eight hours on the proposed Bill. Former prime minister Tony Abbott was one of many who attempted to insert amendments. At times the debate was painful and bordered on abusive for many in the LGBTIQ community who were listening. On the very last day of the debate, Bob Katter made accusations that gay people were 'murderers' and 'responsible for giving AIDS' to society through donating blood. It felt as though opponents of marriage equality wanted to seize every possible opportunity to inflict further hurt on a community that had already been through so much. Leah Newman, one of the most resilient and calm people you could ever meet, exclaims, 'Oh, it was excruciating!'

By Thursday, it was clear that if the vote was going to pass, it had to pass that day. Shirleene, Sarah and Alex all walked up to parliament together. The campaign was holding a media event to urge politicians to finally get it done and celebrate the work that had got us there. There was a lot of dancing and media interviews. Alex and Anna would lead the press conference, saying, 'Later today, marriage equality will be the law of the land'. Shirleene and Sarah walked over to chat to Tim Gartrell, who was watching it all unfold, and thanked him for his work.

Overcome with emotion, Alex was holding back tears during the event, but afterwards this turned into uncontrollable sobbing. He was grieving that everyone in the family that had formed around the movement would soon be going their own way. Alex explains, 'Like any family, we had ups and downs, good times and bad times, good members and challenging members. I did not expect the happiness of achieving marriage equality to be matched by the sadness of losing that'.

Shirleene and Peter Black headed inside to a breakfast parliament was holding to mark World AIDS Day with some other members of the team. Terri Butler, as Shadow Minister for Equality, who had been working so hard all week, came over to say hello and wished us all the best for the day ahead. She, Mark Dreyfus and Anthony Albanese had prepared for the tranches of amendments. As she points out, if just one of them had got up, 'It would have spelt, at the best trouble, and at the worst, potential disaster for marriage equality'. Terri remembers thinking, justifiably, 'If one of the amendments gets up, then we have a whole new ball game, because there's additional licence to discriminate in a

Bill'. She continues, 'You might be the world's biggest supporter of marriage equality but not be prepared to open up further discrimination against LGBTIQ people'.

The gallery seats were almost full after lunch on Friday. This meant that those who sat through Question Time – including Shirleene, Sarah and Peter Black – knew that if they got up and left, they might not get back in to see the historic vote pass. Shirleene and Sarah had deliberately opted to sit with Peter. The three had been together in Brisbane when the postal survey results were announced, had been at the National Press Club when the Senate vote passed and now it looked like they would share the moment of the House of Representatives passing the legislation. Sarah and Shirleene were worried that Tim Gartrell might not have secured a seat but were very happy when they looked down and saw him standing on the floor in the advisor's box.

At times, hearing some of the comments about the LGBTIQ community provoked loud responses from people in the public gallery. The Speaker sent a message that we had to be quiet or risk being asked to leave. At various points, Bill Shorten, Penny Wong and Anthony Albanese came up to let people know that they understood the speeches were painful but we all really did have to be quiet or we could be asked to leave and would miss the legislation's passage.

Finally, it became clear that the last set of amendments had failed. One of the questions on everyone's lips with a vote imminent was, would the Bill just pass on the voices or would opponents call for a vote? Tim Wilson certainly wanted a vote and would help organise for one to occur. He remembers:

One of the things we strategised on the day was trying to make sure there was a vote, because what we didn't want to do is have it passed on the voices, which means there wouldn't have been a final vote, so it would have been anti-climatic; we wanted the history to record the strength of the vote. So we thought, 'How do we do this?' A vote could only be called by someone voting against the Bill and we actually approached David Littleproud, because we knew he was a NO, and said 'Can you organise a division for us?' He told us he was planning to. After the third reading, the clerk read out the title of the Bill and the public gallery knew that marriage equality had passed.

Carol Burger remembers thinking, 'History is being made right now and I'm in the gallery where it's happening!' Dae Levine, who had travelled across the world to see this happen, captures the emotion so deeply felt. 'It's a once-in-a-generation thing to see in a parliament. It's a once-in-a-lifetime thing to see as a campaigner. And I feel tremendously privileged to have been there for that moment and I will never forget it.' Australia working together had achieved something truly remarkable. As Penny Wong reflects, 'I think there are moments in the life of the country which are profoundly important in terms of how they shape identity and character. Some of us for better, some of us for worse, and you can identify them. There are things that do go to the heart of who we are, I think, and this was one.'

This sentiment was strongly felt in the public gallery, who broke out into loud and sustained applause and then song. The first verse of the Seekers' song, 'I am Australian', began, tentatively at first but then loudly and more emphatically. Politicians like Bill Shorten and Tanya Plibersek, Cathy McGowan and

Andrew Wilkie looked up and watched something that might never happen again in the House of Representatives. Louise Pratt, as a senator sitting in the public gallery, had been able to bring a rainbow flag in with her, and unfurled it, adding beautiful colour to the moment. She says, 'I wanted that rainbow flag to be there in that moment'. On the floor itself, supportive MPs also produced rainbow flags. In a truly moving moment, Warren Entsch swept Linda Burney up into an enormous bear hug. This glorious, spontaneous image of bipartisan solidarity would be beamed around the world. Linda tells us that, 'I went over to Warren to congratulate him for all his work, in what had been an unfriendly journey for him over many years. In an act of pure joy, he picked me up for a cuddle and a swing'. She continues, 'That moment was one of the few times in a parliament's history where we all came together to do something good and have a meaningful and positive impact on people's lives'.

As this was happening, Alex was sitting next to Ian Thorpe, whom he hugged and thanked, and then he embraced Elaine, Janine and his mother Carolyn. All were in tears apart from Alex, who was still stunned. He proceeded outside to the hall where people would congregate to celebrate. He saw Tim Wilson and ran up and hugged him, then kissed Warren Entsch and Bill Shorten, and ran up to Penny Wong to hug and thank her. He saw Sarah Hanson-Young and hugged her, and then Anna. But there was still a final press conference to do, which Anna and Alex would lead, and they would be joined by politicians and advocates from across the entire political spectrum.

Alex remembers that being a very long press conference, and during it, emotion once again got the better of him, and while others were still speaking he snuck out. Sarah Hanson-Young noticed him leaving and went over to see how he was going. Crying again, Alex would tell her, 'I need to be with Vic'. Not wanting to endure another day of Canberra's games, Vic was back at home in Sydney. Sarah Hanson-Young snapped into action and rushed Alex down to the front entrance, where she put him in a car to make sure he got to the airport on time. Alex made his flight, with fellow Australians for Equality board member Andrew Parker waiting at the gate with his boarding pass. Sitting next to Alex on the plane was one of his role models, former High Court Justice Michael Kirby, who would calmly ask Alex, 'So, how did today go?' Later that night Alex and Vic would celebrate over a quiet dinner.

Shirleene, Sarah and Peter sat in the public gallery of the House of Representatives until most people had filed out. Amongst the handful of people still left were Malcolm McPherson, Sharon Dane, Shelley Argent and Rodney Croome, who had been there in 2004 when the Howard amendments were passed and who had formed AME before that. As Shirleene walked over to thank him, he jumped over a row of chairs and pulled her into a hug. It was a very emotional and moving end to a long day and a long journey.

In the aftermath of the vote, everyone in the public gallery had to walk past a crowded hall and join an enormous line-up to reclaim their baggage, phones and other items that had been kept in storage all day. It was clear that people were feeling mixed emotions. Finally, marriage equality had been achieved. Wil Stracke remembers, 'We pelted outside and ran into Jason Tuazon-McCheyne. And did the dance of "Oh my God, we changed the world"'. Adam, who had been sitting next to Wil during the vote, 'started feeling a bit weepy' and then, as he walked out of the public gallery, ran into Dae, who had been one of the earliest staff members hired to join him back when the campaign was based above the bookshop. The pair were overcome with emotion.

For a building that is meant to be a place of the people, parliament can be an exclusionary place. It can be very difficult – understandably, for security reasons – for people to get in and out of certain areas without passes and escorts. In the aftermath of the vote, supporters, politicians and campaigners were gathering in the Mural Room, yet just getting in there proved very challenging for many who did not work in the building.

Once up there, Leah Newman remembers:

Everything felt a bit strange. People who had been there so long began breaking down in different ways. Not everybody was experiencing that moment how you would think, in celebration. We'd all been sitting in the gallery with no water the entire day, so that was excruciating and now everything seemed so surreal. I think everybody just broke open at the seams. The campaign maybe broke open at the seams in that final moment. We were holding it all together for so long, and there were so many personalities in the campaign all rubbing up against each other. We'd managed, only just, to pull each other through it, and in that last moment, everything fell apart.

Shirleene also remembers that aftermath as a very strange experience. For years, she had joked with Elaine Czulkowski about the enormous celebrations that would happen once marriage equality was finally achieved. Yet many did not have the energy or spirit to celebrate that night. Liam Ryan recalls 'the feeling was just exhaustion – emotionally exhausted'. The campaign had been equal parts gruelling, exhilarating and entirely unpredictable. It was wonderful to see long-time advocates celebrating and being recognised. Parliament, after a people-led campaign that swept the country, had finally reacted and introduced legislation which would forever change the country. A great many politicians had dedicated years to seeing this legislation pass and it had truly been a cross-partisan effort.

For Adam, there was one last job to be completed in the Mural Room. It was 'to quickly throw open my laptop and read and amend and finally send that last email to the list saying, "That's it. It's done. We got the Senate vote. Now we've had the House of Representatives vote. You did this. We did this together".' He emphasises, 'Sending that email was hugely important to me. This was an email to the people who won marriage equality – the thousands of volunteers all around the country who stepped up and fought for change. This was their moment'.

At this point, amongst the celebrations, Shirleene and Sarah sat together, slumped against a window, completely spent. There was a moment of levity. We enjoyed seeing Peter Black and Mark Dreyfus comparing their equally spectacular rainbow socks. Jay Allen, Dawn Hawkins and Peter all came over to offer their company. Being part of the marriage equality movement meant meeting some of the best people there are.

Janine Middleton, who deserves immense credit for the care she showed for her team, took one look at the group at the end and decided that some needed food and a little time out from parliament. While some went out for food and drinks, Shirleene and Sarah were dropped off at their hotel by Shane Lloyd. Peter, whose partner Joe is based in Canberra, messaged Joe and told him he was coming to join him for dinner. Peter says Joe 'sort of took one look at me that night and knew that it was going to be an early night. I think I looked just pretty exhausted and over-whelmed by it'.

Dawn also felt overcome and drained. She remembers, 'I just took a seat out the front of Parliament House, looked around, took a few deep breaths, was really just taking in the moment. I was just done, I was spent. I had absolutely nothing left. There was seriously nothing left but an absolute history of stories and expe-riences and emotions and people. And in that moment, I really felt everyone with me, you know?'

Those who continued to celebrate into the night partied hard. Some politicians surprised everyone with excellent renditions of ABBA. Tom Sebo, who had to be back at work in Goulburn at six the next morning, still decided he was not going to miss the celebrations. He remembers, 'Dean Smith stood on the chair ... he was right there. I was standing here and he's standing on the chair and him and Penny Wong are having some banter and it was just great'. History had been made and the people had won.

To have and to hold

Alot happened in the days after the House of Representatives vote. On a practical level, the very next morning, Attorney-General George Brandis, accompanied by the prime minister, went to Government House so the Governor-General could sign the *Marriage Amendment (Definitions and Religious Freedoms) Act* into law. All those advocates, supporters, friends, families, along with politicians who had been gathered together, began leaving the nation's capital. It would take thirty days before all Australians in same-sex relationships could marry but the change, so long fought for, had been won.

Unfortunately, the morning after the vote passed, Dawn Hawkins, who had given so much to the campaign, literally driving across two electorates, went down to her car and found it wouldn't start, 'and I couldn't get myself home'. It sank in that she was 'going to need to be towed'. She tells us:

> That was the end of Canberra. And I drove out in a tow-truck
> with a tow driver with my car on the back of a truck. And I
> took a photo of it and said, 'If you believe in psychological
> symbolism, this is me leaving Canberra! I'm broken, I'm done,
> I can't even get myself back home under my own steam!'

Fortunately, later that day, things looked up for Dawn as the momentous change she had helped drive – literally – became apparent. She had pre-arranged a celebration for that evening in Huskisson, although the last thing she felt like doing was going out. But she made it and walked in to a full house with a community celebrating. At one point, a man in his late sixties she had not met before came over to her and asked her if she would have a quiet word with him and his partner. She remembers:

> They said to me, 'Thank you'. Because tonight they made a promise to each other. That tonight, for the first time, they got out of their car when they arrived at the party, they held hands as they walked through the pub. And their promise was that they would not let go. And they didn't.

For Dawn, this gave her 'a very real picture of what I'd been fighting for ... it was probably the most perfect thing that could have happened to me that night'.

Although this was often cruelly obscured over many years of political debate and obstruction, the marriage equality movement was always about people and always about love. On 15 December 2017, two Queensland women, Jill Kindt and Jo Grant, became the first same-sex couple in Australia to marry under this country's laws. They had been together for eight years but Jo was terminally ill with cancer. Jill stood by Jo's side, caring for and loving her, just as she always had, in her end stages. Their time was fast running out and they needed help if they were going to be able to marry. That help came.

When the marriage equality legislation received assent in 2017, there was still a thirty-day waiting period before same-sex couples could marry, meaning that weddings across the country could take place from 9 January 2018. But because of Jo's health, the couple were approved, registered and married, all in the one day. Under such emotional circumstances, people were prepared to do all they could to help. Queensland Attorney-General Yvette D'Ath told parliament how one staff member from Births, Deaths and Marriages had driven from Brisbane to a roadside service station on the Sunshine Coast to give a celebrant the paperwork the couple needed to wed.[1]

Jo Grant passed away on 30 January 2018. But for forty-eight days, she had been able to call Jill Kindt her wife.[2] Yvette D'Ath told parliament that Jo 'passed away knowing she got to fulfil her wish to get married to the person she loved' and that this 'was ultimately a love story of the deep bond between the two women and the will of the Australian people to legally recognise that bond'.[3]

We know of a number of other couples across Australia who also desperately raced against time to express what had always been in their hearts. In Victoria, on 17 December 2018, Cas Willow and Heather Richards, who had been together for almost twenty years, married at the Peter MacCallum Cancer Centre, where Cas was receiving treatment for breast cancer that had spread to her brain. The hospital's service providers and contractors donated catering, goods and services.[4] On 29 December, Cas passed away. In an obituary notice, Heather was able to call the woman she was mourning her wife.[5]

Others were able to marry before 9 January 2018 because of special circumstances, including pre-arranged family visits from overseas for civil ceremonies that had already been arranged. Sydney couple Lauren Price and Amy Laker and Melbourne couple Amy and Elise McDonald married on the same Saturday, 16 December 2017, for these reasons.

Same-sex couples who had married overseas or in foreign consulates or embassies gained legal recognition slightly differently. *The Marriage Amendment (Definitions and Religious Freedoms) Act 2017* signed into law at Government House by the Governor-General included a clause that meant when the law came into effect, the thousands of couples who had married overseas or at foreign embassies and consulates would be recognised as married under Australian law at the stroke of midnight on 9 December 2017. This included Alex and Vic, and Shirleene and Sarah. Alex would later tell Attorney-General George Brandis this made him the celebrant of the largest mass wedding in Australia's history. Shirleene reflects that, slightly embarrassingly, she and Sarah technically slept through their 'Australian wedding' at midnight. It had been a long and tiring few months!

From 9 January 2018, which was a Tuesday, all same-sex couples in this country were able to marry and so many wonderful ceremonies were held that day from one corner of the country to the other. The first was between Craig Burns and Luke Sullivan, who had been together for three years. They married shortly after midnight on the Northern Rivers Hinterland in New South Wales. Both were athletes, Luke a Commonwealth Games sprinter, so it seemed fitting that they had made it to be first across the line that day.

In Melbourne, Ron van Houwelingen and Antony McManus, who had met thirty years before and had been a driving force behind Equal Love in Melbourne, exchanged vows at the theatre where they initially met. They had participated in sixteen legally unrecognised weddings over the past years, to highlight the exclusion of LGBTIQ couples from the institution of marriage. Finally, they were able to make it official and legal.

Wil Stracke, who had worked so hard on this campaign with Victorian Trades Hall, married her partner, Lisa, in February 2018. The two had already had a very meaningful but legally unrecognised ceremony back in 2016, which Wil remembers as 'being a mixture of joy overlaid with a tinge of angry political defiance'. The 2018 wedding was not as meticulously planned. 'We filled in the forms, booked a park and messaged everyone with a "hope you can make it, no stress if you can't" vibe'. On the day itself though:

> It hit us that we were finally getting married. That morning we lay in bed together, holding hands. Then we got up, got dressed, wandered down to the park and surrounded by our family and friends, got really, legally married. We were wearing the same clothes and used the same vows as we had in 2016 but it felt completely different. No politics, this time, just love. All the relief, all the joy. All the happiness. Best day of my life.

One more significant change to the law must also be mentioned. It was critical that the *Marriage Amendment (Definitions and Religious Freedoms) Act 2017* addressed a particular difficulty experienced by married transgender and gender diverse people. In a number of states and territories, transgender and gender diverse people must be unmarried before they can change their gender marker on their birth certificate. Many married transgender and gender diverse people have had to make an unimaginable choice between divorcing their partners or living with identification that does not reflect their gender identity accurately. As part of the

Marriage Amendment (Definitions and Religious Freedoms) Act 2017, Australian states and territories were given twelve months to remove these cruel 'forced divorce laws'.

At the time of writing this book, four states and one territory had corrected this grave injustice. All must amend it by December 2018. When Queensland amended its legislation in June 2018, Roz Dickson spoke of its profound personal significance. She had transitioned at the age of forty-seven, had been with her wife Kathy for twenty-eight years and had two children. Roz said: 'I want to stay married, particularly for our children. When I transitioned to live as a woman I became happier in myself, a more fulfilled and content person to live with and a better parent to our young children. This law means I will finally be able to change my birth certificate to reflect who I am'.[6]

The movement for marriage equality has shown that love really does conquer all. It can open the hearts of a country and it can bond two people together, in sickness and health, for better or for worse, for life. It brings families and communities together. Three years ago, Kerry Flanders suffered a stroke that left her with aphasia, which means she is unable to speak. Her partner for the past twelve years, Jaye Cartwright, talks of the deep and abiding love the women share. While words are challenging, the two women can look into each other's eyes and communicate deeply. They have long wanted to marry and, after the legislation passed, they were finally able to do so in March 2018. It was important that they exchanged their vows on Koori land, an important part of Kerry's identity, near her favourite place, a fishing pond. In attendance was Dawn Hawkins, who was asked to be ring bearer. Dawn tells us she was incredibly honoured to perform this role and that it was a deeply moving ceremony to be part of. 'It felt so symbolic after being the marriage equality advocate for the area to be presenting them with their rings. It was a beautiful gift they gave to me on their wedding day!' Jaye beautifully conveys the true meaning of love and commitment, telling us 'we had already been together for twelve years and felt we were married all along. It's a social justice issue. We just wanted to be treated as equal, so the magic day came and we got married. We loved each other then and we love each other now and until the end of time'.[7]

The formal movement for marriage equality in this country began in 2004, when a very small and committed group stood up against an enormously powerful, well-funded opposition. With great courage, they pointed out the terrible injustice that had been done to LGBTIQ people, time and time again. As time passed, more and more Australians from all backgrounds came to understand the cause and why it mattered and joined them. While opponents tried to delay, to obstruct and to prevent marriage equality, they failed. They failed because marriage equality was always a positive movement, it was always about love, and was truly the people's movement. Now this is the people's victory.

There are very few times in life when you see something that means so much to so many people achieved. It might happen once or maybe twice in a lifetime if you are lucky. This journey has been extraordinary and it has been a privilege for both of us to have seen it unfold. As we both sit here, six months on from the announcement of the public vote, and write our final words in this book, we feel grateful that, like so many thousands of Australians across the country, we could play a role in something that has changed this country for the better, forever. Australia, this is your achievement. Congratulations and thank you!

Sources

This book, much like the marriage equality movement, relies on the personal stories and memories generously shared by a number of advocates, campaigners and politicians. Most, but certainly not all, of the stories we've drawn on were captured through interviews. Some have asked for anonymity and we have respected that. In the first few months of 2018, in the aftermath of the campaign, we travelled widely and sat down with many people who were welcoming and open. Emotions for many (including both of us) were still raw and fatigue had yet to lift. Yet we found the process of reflection through discussion deeply rewarding and extremely moving. We hope the interviews we have gathered and the material we share in this book provide an early glimpse into the thoughts and feelings of some advocates and campaigners during and after a major campaign for social change. Some interviewees provided further reflections on their experiences after their interviews, which we appreciated. Others requested light amendments to their quotes, which have been incorporated. As we've worked on this book, it has been a great joy to see Australian couples marrying and receiving the recognition they have been denied for far too long.

This is by no means an exhaustive book, and nor is this set of oral history interviews. It is a memoir from two people who were lucky enough to volunteer alongside and meet truly extraordinary Australians during their involvement in the marriage equality campaign. We anticipate many other perspectives and different voices will also emerge. After all, the marriage equality campaign involved an entire country. There are so many other people we would have loved to interview but were not able to at this time due to various constraints. We hope to capture more stories and also hope that many others will record and write about Australia's journey to marriage equality. We also hope, in time, to revisit some of the interviewees below to consider how their perspectives might change in years to come, once they have a chance to reflect on what might have been a once-in-a-generation campaign.

Interviews

National Library of Australia

Jay Allen interviewed by Shirleene Robinson, 20 March 2018, National Library of Australia, ORAL TRC 6935/13

Patrick Batchelor interviewed by Shirleene Robinson, 6 April 2018, National Library of Australia, ORAL TRC 6935/22

Peter Black interviewed by Shirleene Robinson, 9 January 2018, National Library of Australia, ORAL TRC 6935/1

Anna Brown interviewed by Shirleene Robinson, 2 April 2018, National Library of Australia, ORAL TRC 6935/20

Carolyn Burger interviewed by Shirleene Robinson, 28 March 2018, National Library of Australia, ORAL TRC 6935/18

Claire Dawson interviewed by Shirleene Robinson, 22 March 2018, National Library of Australia, ORAL TRC 6935/14

Shannan Dodson interviewed by Shirleene Robinson, 6 June 2018, National Library of Australia, ORAL TRC 6935/25

Geraldine Donoghue interviewed by Shirleene Robinson, 24 March 2018, National Library of Australia, ORAL TRC 6935/15

Luke Gahan interviewed by Shirleene Robinson, 10 March 2018, National Library of Australia, ORAL TRC 6935/12

Tim Gartrell interviewed by Shirleene Robinson, 22 February 2018, National Library of Australia, ORAL TRC 6935/8

Dawn Hawkins interviewed by Shirleene Robinson, 26 and 27 March 2018, National Library of Australia, ORAL TRC 6935/17

Ashley Hogan interviewed by Shirleene Robinson, 19 February 2018, National Library of Australia, ORAL TRC 6935/7

Adam Knobel interviewed by Shirleene Robinson, 13 February 2018, National Library of Australia, ORAL TRC 6935/6

Sean Leader interviewed by Shirleene Robinson, 25 March and 14 April 2018, National Library of Australia, ORAL TRC 6935/16

Malcolm McPherson interviewed by Shirleene Robinson, 25 January 2018, National Library of Australia, ORAL TRC 6935/2

Audrey Marsh interviewed by Shirleene Robinson, 22 February 2018, National Library of Australia, ORAL TRC 6935/9

Janine Middleton interviewed by Shirleene Robinson, 7 February 2018, National Library of Australia, ORAL TRC 6935/5

Leah Newman interviewed by Shirleene Robinson, 4 February 2018, National Library of Australia, ORAL TRC 6935/3

Helen Ross-Browne interviewed by Shirleene Robinson, 1 April 2018, National Library of Australia, ORAL TRC 6935/19

Liam Ryan interviewed by Shirleene Robinson, 1 March 2018, National Library of Australia, ORAL TRC 6935/10

Joseph Scales interviewed by Shirleene Robinson, 2 March 2018, National Library of Australia, ORAL TRC 6935/11

Tom Sebo interviewed by Shirleene Robinson, 5 February 2018, National Library of Australia, ORAL TRC 6935/4

Penny Sharpe interviewed by Shirleene Robinson, 4 April 2018, National Library of Australia, ORAL TRC 6935/21

Wilhelmina Stracke interviewed by Shirleene Robinson, 12 April 2018, National Library of Australia, ORAL TRC 6935/23

Francis Voon interviewed by Shirleene Robinson, 6 June 2018, National Library of Australia, ORAL TRC 6935/24

Other interviews

Sue Boyce interviewed by Shirleene Robinson, 25 March 2018, authors' collection

Bob Brown interviewed by Alex Greenwich, 28 February 2018, authors' collection

Terri Butler interviewed by Shirleene Robinson, 15 February 2018, authors' collection

Elaine Czulkowski interviewed by Alex Greenwich, 20 March 2018, authors' collection

Warren Entsch interviewed by Shirleene Robinson, 15 February 2018, authors' collection

Trevor Evans interviewed by Shirleene Robinson, 11 April 2018, authors' collection

Geoff Field interviewed by Alex Greenwich, 16 March 2018, authors' collection

Larry Galbraith interviewed by Alex Greenwich, 17 February 2018, authors' collection

Kelly Glanney interviewed by Alex Greenwich and Shirleene Robinson, 30 July 2018, authors' collection

Sarah Hanson-Young interviewed by Alex Greenwich, 24 April 2018, authors' collection

Alan Jones interviewed by Alex Greenwich, 24 April 2018, authors' collection

Dae Levine interviewed by Shirleene Robinson, 23 February 2018, authors' collection

Clint McGilvray interviewed by Alex Greenwich, 12 February 2018, authors' collection

Kirk Marcolina interviewed by Alex Greenwich, 9 April 2018, authors' collection

Tim Peppard interviewed by Alex Greenwich, 5 April 2018, authors' collection

Graham Perrett interviewed by Shirleene Robinson, 15 February 2018, authors' collection

Kerryn Phelps and Jackie Stricker-Phelps interviewed by Alex Greenwich, 16 June 2018, authors' collection

Louise Pratt interviewed by Shirleene Robinson, 5 April 2018, authors' collection

Magda Szubanski interviewed by Shirleene Robinson, 13 April 2018, authors' collection

YES YES YES

Tim Wilson and Ryan Bolger interviewed by Alex Greenwich, 5 April 2018, authors' collection

Penny Wong interviewed by Alex Greenwich and Shirleene Robinson, 18 May 2018, authors' collection

Acknowledgments

First and foremost, Alex and Shirleene would like to thank all of those people who so generously shared their stories with us. Without their honesty and courage, this book would not have been possible. We also thank the thousands of Australians who have contributed to achieving marriage equality in so many ways at different times. Your bravery, resolve and dedication inspire us both. You may never have sought recognition and your efforts may not have received the acknowledgment they deserved but they made all the difference. Combined, they moved an entire country.

Alex and Shirleene would both like to thank all those they have worked alongside at Australian Marriage Equality – people across the country who were part of this grassroots organisation, the board, members and those who came before. We thank everyone who joined us from Australians for Equality to become the Equality Campaign, and then the YES campaign. You are an incredible group of people and it has been a privilege getting to know you all. We have built friendships we know will endure. We are very grateful to the thousands of volunteers, campaigners and donors who supported us over many difficult years. We also thank the incredible Recognise and GetUP! team who helped us when we needed it most. We thank the unions, corporates, state, territory and local governments, grass roots campaigns and NGOs who partnered with us for so long. We thank Magda Szubanzki who campaigned alongside us when the stakes were so high without any hesitation. And of course, thank you Australia!

We are also very grateful to the staff of the National Library of Australia, who provided practical and in-kind support, which means a great majority of the interviews we conducted will be available for future generations. We look forward to seeing this collection grow further. We especially acknowledge the support of Shelly Grant, curator of oral history and folklore, for efforts in developing this collection and her commitment to oral history in this country. Rhys Cardew gave up his personal time to help us turn around audio and Alisha Baker was always organised, patient and helpful. Kevin Bradley has always supported efforts to increase the scope of the NLA's collection. We also thank Margy Burn, assistant-director general, Australian Collections and Reader Services.

The team at NewSouth Publishing have been supportive and enthusiastic from the outset and incredibly kind. Our extraordinary executive publisher Phillipa McGuinness provided the initial interest and the ongoing encouragement that was crucial to this book's completion. We also thank our dedicated editor Jocelyn Hungerford, publicist Harriet McInerney and project manager Emma Hutchinson.

We thank Anisa Puri, a wonderful research assistant (and friend) who worked under tight time constraints to ensure oral history interviews conducted for this book were processed incredibly efficiently. Sean Leader, an extraordinary Labor historian, was both generous and patient in explaining finer details of ALP policy and process needed for this book. Two friends we came to know and value on the campaign deserve extra special thanks. Joseph Scales was a wonderful source of knowledge and showed enormous grace and kindness in providing valuable explanations of the finer details we required, almost always at incredibly short notice! Thank you so much for everything! Adam Knobel also deserves a special thank you for so graciously giving up his time to provide valuable information, feedback and encouragement. We are very grateful!

Alex wishes to acknowledge his fellow co-chairs and board members of the YES campaign and the amazing team he worked alongside for so long. He greatly thanks AME co-chair Janine Middleton, who stuck by his side through everything. Without her, he would not have seen the finish line. He thanks Elaine Czulkowski for her ongoing friendship and commitment and for never, ever giving up. Alex thanks the corporate leaders and their partners who encouraged him and stood up for marriage equality when political leaders wouldn't, including Alan Joyce, Michael Ebeid, George Frazis, Paul Zahra, James Collins, Geoff Selig, Mark Nielsen, Brad Cooper, Paul O'Sullivan and so many more. He gratefully acknowledges those who mentored, advised and guided him over the years; Bill Bowtell, Chris Puplick, Larry Galbraith, Peter Stahel, Bob Brown, Ben Oquist and Evan Wolfson have helped him learn so much. Alex is immensely grateful to Clover Moore for her support, guidance, and always being an inspiring role model. He thanks Tim Wilson and Ryan Bolger for their honesty, friendship and determination. He thanks Sarah Hanson-Young for her friendship, the laughs, the hugs, for providing a shoulder to cry on and for letting the movement work out of her office for a decade! He thanks his NSW Parliamentary and City of Sydney colleagues for their work and support. Alex acknowledges his wonderful electoral staff, Tammie Nardone, Roy Bishop and Leanne Abbott – you are the best! He thanks Shirleene Robinson – there could have been no one better to write this book with! It has been wonderful sharing this journey with you and with Sarah Midgley. Alex also wants to express his appreciation to his friends for their support and his family – his mother, father, brothers Victor and Nick, and sister Paris for all their encouragement. He especially pays tribute to his mother Carolyn who has been by his side campaigning throughout. Finally, with all his heart, he thanks his husband Victor for his love.

Shirleene would also like to thank all the marriage equality campaigners she has been privileged to work with, from the teams mentioned above through to grassroots community advocates. She hopes she has acknowledged your wonderful efforts in person, as listing everyone who has helped over the years would require a separate book! She thanks Alex for his leadership role, for believing in this book and his ongoing friendship over many years. The list of interviews included in the sources section of this book lists many people we have formed meaningful friendships with, so Shirleene has tried to avoid restating those names. She thanks William Rutkin, an understated but remarkable man who has made her home state of Queensland a much better place. She thanks the tireless Rodney Croome and Sharyn Faulkner. She also thanks history friends Lisa Featherstone, Lisa Ford (for practical and personal support), Rebecca Jennings (who listened when it mattered most), Andy Kaladelfos, Ann McGrath, Scott McKinnon, Clare Monagle, Robert Reynolds, Kay Saunders and Yorick Smaal.

Graham Perrett: since that first coffee more than a decade ago, a lovely and lasting friendship has formed. Thank you for your encouragement and sharing the journey! Thank you also to another Queenslander, Terri Butler, to fellow history buff Louise Pratt, to Penny Sharpe and to Andrew Bartlett, who have all been tireless advocates. Tim Gartrell, forever grateful for all you did at such a critical time (and for helping us to 'jump for joy').

Shirleene also thanks dear friends Philippa Griffiths (we owe you always!), Emily Wilson, Jim Wilson, Helen Wilson and Rod Wilson, Jacopo Sabbatini, Julie Ustinoff, Nick Henderson, Adam Duffy and Rebecca Stones, Kay Harrison and Sophie Partridge, Morgan Spearritt, Sarah Taylor, Ky Menzies and Paris Lehn, Jen Peden, Samantha Glennon-Bond, Maria Nordenberg and Nikea Ranger. Shirleene is grateful to Sydney's Pride History Group, including Mardi Gras 78ers, who remind us all of how far we have come. She also thanks her three families who have influenced the course of her life, perhaps in ways they don't realise (the Robinsons, the Vaughans and in-laws, the Midgleys). Finally, Sarah Midgley, words cannot express how important you have been to the campaign and to me. You gave so much for so long, quietly. You were strong when I was not. You continue to believe we have a responsibility to create a better world. You are the best person I know.

Notes

1 The journey begins

1 Graham Willett, 3 October 2016, *ABC News*, 'Australia's Secret History of Sexual Fluidity', <www.abc.net.au/news/2016-04-09/secret-history-sexual-fluidity/7253856>.

2 Robert French, *Camping by a Billabong: Gay and Lesbian Stories from Australian History*, Blackwattle Press, Sydney, 1993, pp. 99–109.

3 *The Australian*, 8 August 2017, <www.theaustralian.com.au/national-affairs/john-howard-defends-malcolm-turnbull-on-samesex-plebiscite/news-story/c8af28fc2bf4bca6babe3331caf7963d>.

4 *Sydney Star Observer*, 8 January 2004, p. 9.

5 Surname unknown.

6 *Sydney Morning Herald*, 5 June 2004, <www.smh.com.au/articles/2004/06/04/1086203634298.html>.

7 Australian Marriage Equality, 'New Group Calls for Reform: Supporters to Write to Senate Inquiry', 28 June 2004. Possession of authors.

8 Luke Gahan speech notes, July 2004. Possession of authors.

9 Iain Clacher, 'G W Bush Conservatives for Gay Marriage', *On Line Opinion*, 30 June 2004 <http://www.onlineopinion.com.au/view.asp?article=2329&page=0>

10 John Howard, 'Address to the National Marriage Forum, Great Hall, Parliament House', 4 August 2004, <pmtranscripts.pmc.gov.au/release/transcript-21439>.

11 Australian Christian Lobby, 'Tremendous wins for faith and family', 8 August 2004.

12 *Sydney Morning Herald*, 10 August 2004, <www.smh.com.au/articles/2004/08/10/1092102440370.html>.

13 Australian Christian Lobby, 'Marriage defined', 13 August 2004.

14 'Same-Sex Marriage Ban a Milestone for Values', *ABC News*, 14 August 2004 <http://www.abc.net.au/news/2004-08-14/same-sex-marriage-ban-a-milestone-for-values/2025340>.

15 *Sydney Morning Herald*, 15 August 2004, <www.smh.com.au/articles/2004/08/14/1092340534557.html>.

2 Building support

1 Luke Gahan, 'The ins and outs of marriage (and divorce)' in Victor Marsh (ed.), *Speak Now: Australian Perspectives on Same-Sex Marriage*, Clouds of Magellan, Melbourne, 2011, p. 63.

2 Australian Labor Party, 'National Platform and Constitution', 2007, p. 208, <parlinfo.aph.gov.au/parlInfo/download/library/partypol/1024541/

upload_binary/1024541.pdf;fileType=application%2Fpdf#search=%22library/
partypol/1024541%22>.

3 Matt Young, 'Penny Wong makes moving speech in Senate over same-sex marriage
legislation', *The Australian*, 16 November 2017, <www.news.com.au/lifestyle/gay-
marriage/penny-wong-makes-moving-speech-in-senate-over-samesex-marriage-
legislation/news-story/7f62465885163c50783a4ffd597edcc7>.

4 Sarah Price, 'Sydney lesbian pair register their union', *Sydney Morning Herald*, 5
February 2006, <www.smh.com.au/news/national/sydney-lesbian-pair-register-
their-union/2006/02/04/1138958945398.html>.

5 Lisa Millar, 'Lesbian couple to wed in Brisbane', *The World Today*, ABC Local
Radio, 5 May 2006, <www.abc.net.au/worldtoday/content/2006/s1631508.htm>.

3 Breaking through

1 Sarah Price, 'Big business joins push for same-sex marriage', *Sydney Morning
Herald*, 27 April 2008, <www.smh.com.au/news/national/big-business-joins-push-
for-samesex-marriage/2008/04/27/1208743316176.html>.

2 Sarah Hanson-Young, 'Greens send telegram of support to Feast's wedding of the
year', 18 November 2007, <sarah-hanson-young.greensmps.org.au/articles/greens-
send-telegram-support-feast%E2%80%99s-wedding-year>.

3 Louise Pratt, First Speech, 27 August 2008, Australian Senate, <parlinfo.aph.gov.
au/parlInfo/search/display/display.w3p;query=Id%3A%22chamber%2Fhansards%
2F2008-08-27%2F0159%22>.

4 Australian Marriage Equality Submission to the Senate Legal and Constitutional
Affairs Committee Inquiry into the Marriage Equality Amendment Bill 2009,
<www.australianmarriageequality.org/2009/10/13/ames-senate-inquiry-
submission/>.

5 Australian Marriage Equality Submission to the Senate Legal and Constitutional
Affairs Committee Inquiry into the Marriage Equality Amendment Bill 2009.

6 The Senate, Legal and Constitutional Affairs Legislation Committee, Marriage
Equality Amendment Bill, 2009, <www.aph.gov.au/Parliamentary_Business/
Committees/Senate/Legal_and_Constitutional_Affairs/Completed_
inquiries/2008-10/marriage_equality/report/index>.

7 'Big crowds turn out in support of gay marriage', *Sydney Morning Herald*, 2 August
2009, <www.smh.com.au/national/big-crowds-turn-out-in-support-of-gay-
marriage-20090801-e52g.html>.

8 'Rudd firm on gay marriage stance', 29 July 2009, *ABC News*, <www.abc.net.au/
news/2009-07-29/rudd-firm-on-gay-marriage-stance/1370872>.

9 Interview in authors' possession.

4 The power of marriage

1 Flyer in authors' possession.

2 In authors' possession.

3 In authors' possession.

4 In authors' possession.

5 Claire Connelly, 'Gay rights group plans anti-Labor campaign',
Daily Telegraph, 1 July 2010, <www.dailytelegraph.com.au/
gay-rights-group-plans-anti-labor-campaign/news-story/
e29e31cd89cff7c7e4d82a6efd51646d?sv=1b8ac9f5d0140c86b5f75c8170ccc773>.

6 Jonathan Watts, 'Australian election: Greens key to success of new government',
Guardian, 7 September 2010.

7 'Tony Abbott joins Q&A', *ABC News*, 16 August 2010.

8   Alex Greenwich, 'Cameron support for marriage equality welcomed: overwhelming response to conscience vote call', 25 October 2010, <www. australianmarriageequality.org/2010/10/25/cameron-support-for-marriage-equality-welcomed-overwhelming-response-to-conscience-vote-call/>.

9   'Prime minister restates opposition to gay marriage', *The Australian*, 6 November 2010, <www.theaustralian.com.au/national-affairs/prime-minister-restates-opposition-to-gay-marriage/news-story/efe6f733e8922dfb3ba533d6c13df-d4a?sv=65359bb1b1707b08c515f9a6d9ba3e50>.

10 Andrew M Potts, 'Marriage equality inevitable', *Sydney Star Observer*, 10 November 2010, <www.starobserver.com.au/news/national-news/new-south-wales-news/marriage-equality-%E2%80%98inevitable%E2%80%99/33120>.

11 Andrew M Potts, 'Marriage equality inevitable', *Sydney Star Observer*, 10 November 2010, <www.starobserver.com.au/news/national-news/victoria-news/coalition-mp-in-favour-of-marriage-2/34101>.

12 Patricia Karvelis, 'Catholics told to lobby against gay marriage', *The Australian*, 20 October 2010, <www.theaustralian.com.au/national-affairs/catholics-told-to-lobby-against-gay-marriage/news-story/9fa3b34439c3cad2a959f4de76afafcc>.

13 In authors' possession.

14 Alex Greenwich, 'GetUp! and Australian Marriage Equality launch national television campaign for same-sex marriage', Australian Marriage Equality media release, 14 February 2011, <www.australianmarriageequality.org/2011/02/14/getup-and-australian-marriage-equality-launch-national-television-campaign-for-same-sex-marriage/>.

15 Alex Greenwich, Australian Marriage Equality media release, 14 February 2011.

16 Matt Johnston and AAP, 'Gay couples to share $31K dinner with PM', *Advertiser* [Adelaide], 16 June 2011, <www.adelaidenow.com.au/news/gay-couples-to-share-31k-dinner-with-pm/news-story/9eb1c440bfad578ecc68ec5d7fceee17?sv=f932e9326 8819e337614a54c6f1542e>..

17 DJ Dan Murphy, 'I DO: Australian Marriage Equality', YouTube video, <www. youtube.com/watch?v=6WmnRxsPWuw>.

18 Andrew M Potts, 'Marriage equality inevitable', *Sydney Star Observer*, 10 November 2010, <www.starobserver.com.au/news/national-news/new-south-wales-news/marriage-equality-%E2%80%98inevitable%E2%80%99/33120>.

19 Peter van Onselen, 'Gillard pushes conscience vote on gay marriage as a deliberate sop to the Left', *Daily Telegraph*, 20 November 2011, <www.dailytelegraph.com. au/news/opinion/julia-gillard-pushes-conscience-vote-on-gay-marriage-as-a-deliberate-sop-to-labors-left/news-story/1e144d9ec148fd7ce0f7a5d244e9f62b>.

20 In authors' possession.

5   Rainbow warriors

1   Penny Wong, 'Speech to the South Australian ALP State Convention', 27 November 2010, author's possession.

2   Lenore Taylor, 'Win for Rainbow Labor, but one it will have to wait for', *Daily Advertiser*, December 2011, <www.dailyadvertiser.com.au/story/941082/win-for-rainbow-labor-but-one-it-will-have-to-wait-for/>.

3   Terri Butler, 'BILLS – Marriage Amendment (Definition and Religious Freedoms) Bill 2017 – Second Reading', House of Representatives, 4 December 2017, </Hansard/Hansard_Display?bid=chamber/hansardr/72ab0aa3-c3f2-48e1-b365-7e7ac525ceb6/&sid=0103>.

6 Weddings on Australian soil

1   *Senate Journal*, No. 74, 8 February 2012, <parlinfo.aph.gov.au/parlInfo/search/display/display.w3p;query=Id%3A%22chamber%2Fjournals%2F20120208_SJ074%2F0016%22>.

2   Andie Noonan, 'Senate Inquiry shores up "landslide support"', *Star Observer*, 2 April 2012, <www.starobserver.com.au/news/national-news/new-south-wales-news/senate-inquiry-shores-up-landslide-support/75167>.

3   Lisa Martin, 'Two Libs break ranks on gay marriage', *Sydney Morning Herald*, 25 June 2012, <www.smh.com.au/national/two-libs-break-ranks-on-gay-marriage-20120625-20y8n.html>.

4   'Committee reports on gay marriage bills', *Sydney Morning Herald*, 18 June 2012, <www.smh.com.au/national/committee-reports-on-gay-marriage-bills-20120618-20it4.html>.

5   Martin, 'Two Libs break ranks on gay marriage'.

6   'Last Piece of the Puzzle', *Sydney Morning Herald*, 1 September 2012, <www.smh.com.au/politics/federal/last-piece-of-the-puzzle-20120831-255ub.html>.

7   Dan Harrison, 'Push for Gillard to review gay marriage', *Sydney Morning Herald*, 14 May 2012, <www.smh.com.au/politics/federal/push-for-gillard-to-review-gay-marriage-20120513-1yl0j.html>.

8   Jonathan Swan, 'Senator Wong condemns Christian Lobby's Stolen Generation Comments', *Sydney Morning Herald*, 21 May 2013, <www.smh.com.au/politics/federal/senator-wong-condemns-christian-lobbys-stolen-generations-comment-20130521-2jyn3.html>.

9   Lisa Martin, 'Two Libs break ranks on gay marriage', *Sydney Morning Herald*, 25 June 2012, <www.smh.com.au/national/two-libs-break-ranks-on-gay-marriage-20120625-20y8n.html>.

10 Malcolm Farr, 'Julia Gillard and Tony Abbott help defeat same sex marriage bill 98–42', News.com.au, 19 September 2012, <www.news.com.au/national/julia-gillard-and-tony-abbott-help-defeat-same-sex-marriage-bill-98-42/news-story/d55ea5e7bf55be504066ed46b0e6eeed>.

11 Senator Louise Pratt, 'Marriage Amendment Bill (2) 2012, Second Reading', 17 September 2012, <parlinfo.aph.gov.au/parlInfo/search/display/display.w3p;query=Id%3A%22chamber%2Fhansards%2Fcb9ee569-ca11-453b-bbc3-38d3893c8e82%2F0006%22>.

12 'Gay marriage bill defeated', *Sydney Morning Herald*, 19 September 2012, <www.smh.com.au/national/gay-marriage-bill-defeated-20120919-266a8.html>.

13 Sarah Midgley, communication to Alex Greenwich, authors' possession.

14 Jonathan Swan, 'Marriage equality bill fails but Lib crosses floor', *Sydney Morning Herald*, 20 June 2013, <www.watoday.com.au/federal-politics/political-news/marriage-equality-bill-fails-but-lib-crosses-floor-20130619-2ok20>.

15 Jonathan Swan, 'Senator Wong Condemns Christian Lobby's Stolen Generation Comments'.

16 Sue Boyce, communication to authors, authors' possession.

17 'Full text: David Cameron's Conservative conference speech', *BBC News*, 5 October 2011, <www.bbc.com/news/uk-politics-15189614>.

18 Australian Marriage Equality, 'Media release: election sees increased marriage equality support in new parliament', 9 September 2013, <www.australianmarriageequality.org/2013/09/09/media-release-election-sees-increased-support-for-marriage-equality-in-new-parliament/>.

19 Siobhan Heanue, 'Australia's first gay marriages conducted', *ABC Radio*, 7 December 2013, <www.abc.net.au/am/content/2013/s3907122.htm>.

20 Sean Nicholls, 'Same-sex marriage bill defeated in NSW Upper House', *Sydney Morning Herald*, 14 November 2013, <www.smh.com.au/national/nsw/same-sex-marriage-bill-defeated-in-nsw-upper-house-20131114-2xicv.html>.

7   Communities and corporates

1   Louise Pratt, Valedictory Speech, Australian Senate, 24 June 2014, <www.openaustralia.org.au/senate/?id=2014-06-24.117.1>.

2   Jill Stark, 'Geelong councillor Jan Farrell marriage equality's secret weapon', *Sydney Morning Herald*, 1 November 2015, <www.smh.com.au/national/geelong-councillor-jan-farrell-marriage-equalitys-secret-weapon-20151030-gkmt8m.html>.

3   Sarah Midgley, communication to Alex Greenwich, authors' possession.

4   Jim Reed, 'The tide has turned on same-sex marriage', *ABC News*, 31 July 2014, <www.abc.net.au/news/2014-07-31/reed-the-tides-have-turned-on-same-sex-marriage/5637770>.

5   Jacqueline Maley, 'Same-sex marriage a vote turner in 2015', Sydney Morning Herald, 3–4 January 2015, <www.smh.com.au/politics/federal/advocates-plan-samesex-marriage-push-in-federal-electorates-for-2015-20150102-12gzhu.html>.

6   Liam Ryan, 'Why it's important to remember the children in Australia's marriage equality debate', Lifestyle, Foxtel, undated, 2016 <www.lifestyle.com.au/health/why-its-important-to-remember-the-children-in-australias-marriage-equality-debate.aspx>.

7   Brittany Murphy, 'Marriage equality group gains traction', *Goulburn Post*, 5 June 2015, <www.goulburnpost.com.au/story/3125549/marriage-equality-group-gains-traction/>.

8   Adam Holmes, 'Bendigo small businesses back marriage equality', *Bendigo Advertiser*, 5 June 2015, <www.bendigoadvertiser.com.au/story/3128823/bendigo-small-businesses-back-same-sex-marriage/>.

9   'Marriage equality is serious business', *Goulburn Post*, 22 July 2015, <www.goulburnpost.com.au/story/3226289/marriage-equality-is-serious-business/>.

10 *Goulburn Post*, 22 July 2015.

11 Transcript: 'Obama's remarks on Supreme Court ruling on same-sex marriage', *Washington Post*, 26 June 2015, <www.washingtonpost.com/news/post-nation/wp/2015/06/26/transcript-obamas-remarks-on-supreme-court-ruling-on-same-sex-marriage/?utm_term=.848e72977749>.

12 Australian Marriage Equality, 'Media Release: Shepparton Businesses Back Marriage Equality, 29 July 2015 <www.australianmarriageequality.org/2015/07/29/media-release-shepparton-businesses-back-marriage-equality/>.

8   Lights on, hopes fade

1   Cameron Atfield, 'Queensland MPs lead marriage equality charge', *Sydney Morning Herald*, 7 September 2015, <www.smh.com.au/politics/federal/queensland-mps-lead-marriage-equality-charge-20150907-gjh2w7.html>.

2   Cameron Atfield, 'Queensland MPs lead marriage equality charge', *Sydney Morning Herald*, 7 September 2015, <www.smh.com.au/politics/federal/queensland-mps-lead-marriage-equality-charge-20150907-gjh2w7.html>.

3   Teresa Gambaro, 'Marriage should be a choice for all', *SBS News*, 17 August 2015, <www.sbs.com.au/news/teresa-gambaro-marriage-should-be-a-choice-for-all>.

9   Early days of preparing for a plebiscite

1   Kelly Glanney, communication to Alex Greenwich, authors' possession.

2   Judith Ireland, 'Facebook boost for same-sex marriage YES campaign', *Sydney Morning Herald*, 1 March 2016 <https://www.smh.com.au/politics/federal/facebook-boost-for-samesex-marriage-yes-campaign-20160229-gn6awf.html>.

3   Hayley Warden, 'Marriage equality about people not politics', *South Coast Register*, 18 June 2016, <www.huffingtonpost.com.au/2016/03/01/marriage-equality-facebook_n_9360854.html>.

4   Rick Morton, 'Federal election 2016: "Ugly" Irish gay marriage defence rejected', *Australian*, 30 June 2016, <www.theaustralian.com.au/national-affairs/policy/federal-election-2016-ugly-irish-gay-marriage-defence-rejected/news-story/d979b9508fcdcfc721becc83ad483fab>

5   Andrew Bolt, 'Scare campaign is an insult to Australians', *Herald Sun*, 24 August 2016 <https://www.heraldsun.com.au/news/...to.../49bf25ca394ccbb18fcfd774942627d7> ; George Brandis, Plebiscite (Same-Sex Marriage) Bill 2016, Second Reading, 7 November 2016, Senate Hansard, p. 2054.

6   Paul Karp, 'Rodney Croome quits Australian Marriage Equality to oppose a plebiscite', *Guardian*, 2 August 2016, <www.theguardian.com/australia-news/2016/aug/02/rodney-croome-quits-australian-marriage-equality-to-oppose-plebiscite>.

10   The plebiscite is voted down

1   Paul Ritchie, *Faith, Love and Australia: The Conservative Case for Marriage Equality*, Connor Court Publishing, Brisbane, 2016.

2   Francis Voon, communication to authors, authors' possession.

11   Uncertain future

1   Christopher Knaus, 'Lyle Shelton gets more media mentions than all three leading Yes campaigners', *Guardian*, 21 September 2017, <www.theguardian.com/australia-news/2017/sep/22/lyle-shelton-gets-more-media-mentions-than-all-three-leading-yes-campaigners>.

2   Sarah Midgley, communication to Alex Greenwich, authors' possession.

3   'Same-sex marriage hopes rise as Senate Inquiry rejects discriminatory measures', *Guardian*, 15 February 2017, <www.theguardian.com/australia-news/2017/feb/15/same-sex-marriage-hopes-rise-as-senate-rejects-discriminatory-measures>.

4   'Clouds parting in gay marriage debate', *West Australian*, 15 February 2017, <www.thewest.com.au/politics/clouds-parting-in-gay-marriage-debate-ng-s-1676257>and Lane Sainty, '"Historic Agreement" moves the marriage equality debate forward', *Buzzfeed*, 15 February 2017, <www.buzzfeed.com/lanesainty/senate-marriage-inquiry-bill?utm-term=.qtvNQooVg#.fe61AWWQg>.

5   'Same-sex marriage hopes rise as Senate Inquiry rejects discriminatory measures'.

6   *Sydney Morning Herald*, 2 March 2017, <www.smh.com.au/politics/federal/malcolm-turnbull-wont-attend-this-years-gay-and-lesbian-mardi-gras-20170302-guome6.html>.

7   Authors' possession.

8   Ewin Hannan and Paige Taylor, 'Joyce declares strong business case for marriage equality', *The Australian*, 5 June 2017, <www.theaustralian.com.au/national-affairs/policy/joyce-declares-strong-business-case-for-marriage-equality/news-story/59ec290b8551c2a66f5700e957078b11>.

9   '"We are in the winner's circle": Pyne crows about influence of Liberal Party's left faction', *SBS News*, 26 June 2017, <www.sbs.com.au/news/we-are-in-the-winner-s-circle-pyne-crows-about-influence-of-liberal-party-s-left-faction>.
10 Joe Spagnolo, 'WA Liberal Dean Smith opens up about his same sex marriage bill and being gay', *Perth Now*, 8 July 2017, <www.perthnow.com.au/lifestyle/stm/wa-liberal-mp-dean-smith-opens-up-about-his-same-sex-marriage-bill-and-being-gay-ng-cbfb82e82d5a33670582ba23c9446a9b>.
11 Andree Withey, 'Queensland's first openly gay MP, Trevor Evans, wants same-sex marriage vote now', *ABC News*, 31 July 2017, <www.abc.net.au/news/2017-07-31/gay-marriage-same-sex-marriage-vote-openly-gay-mp-trevor-evans/8758852>.

13 Campaign headquarters
1   Sarah Midgley, communication to Alex Greenwich, authors' possession.
2   Shannan Dodson, communication to Alex Greenwich, authors' possession.
3   Georgia Kriz, communication to Shirleene Robinson, authors' possession.

14 Australia campaigns
1   Matt Gilbertson, 'Thousands gather on the steps of South Australian Parliament in support of marriage equality', *Advertiser* [Adelaide], 16 September 2017, <www.adelaidenow.com.au/news/south-australia/thousands-gather-on-the-steps-of-south-australian-parliament-in-support-of-marriage-equality/news-story/a49e28b48eb85bda07371870d63fc73a>.
2   Alex Greenwich and Shirleene Robinson, 'No matter how far or how wide you've roamed, you can still call for equality at home', *Huffington Post*, 13 October 2017 <www.huffingtonpost.com.au/alex-greenwich/no-matter-how-far-or-how-wide-youve-roamed-you-can-still-call-it-for-marriage-equality-back-home_a_23240719/>.
3   Andrew Bolt, '"Yes" campaigners have your number', *Herald Sun*, 23 September 2017, <www.heraldsun.com.au/blogs/andrew-bolt/yes-campaigners-have-your-number/news-story/8bdf2886d6f11fa91ce2d4ad015e2893>.
4   William Brougham, communication to Shirleene Robinson, authors' possession.
5   Andrew Brown, '"Our fears have been realised": Plebiscite sees spike in calls to counsellors', *Canberra Times*, 26 August 2017, <www.canberratimes.com.au/national/act/our-fears-have-been-realised-plebiscite-sees-spike-in-calls-to-counsellors-20170824-gy377x.html>.
6   James Maasdorp, 'SSM: Kevin Rudd says godson Sean "punched standing up for marriage equality"', *ABC News*, 14 September 2017, <www.abc.net.au/news/2017-09-13/kevin-rudd-godson-sean-punched-same-sex-marriage/8942368>.
7   Phoebe Wearne, 'Premier Mark McGowan urged to introduce laws to protect LGBT people from hate speech', *Perth Now*, 5 September 2017, <www.perthnow.com.au/news/wa/premier-mark-mcgowan-urged-to-introduce-laws-to-protect-lgbti-people-from-hate-speech-ng-811f408f5fe44722dfe8cd7d04999e06>.
8   Sarah Midgley, communication to Alex Greenwich, authors' possession.

15 Reinforcements
1   Neil McMahon, 'Q&A Recap: Magda Szubanski delivers emotional punch in same-sex marriage debate', *Sydney Morning Herald*, 24 October 2017, <www.smh.com.au/entertainment/tv-and-radio/qa-recap-magda-szubanski-delivers-emotional-punch-in-samesex-marriage-debate-20171024-gz6r2x.html>.
2   Julia Banks, 'Liberal MP: This is why I'm campaigning for "Yes"', *Sydney Morning Herald*, 24 October 2017, <www.smh.com.au/opinion/liberal-mp-this-is-why-im-campaigning-for-yes-20171024-gz6z6k.html>.

16 Results day

1 Heather McNeill, 'Same-sex marriage results: Perth's western suburbs deliver strongest Yes vote in WA', *WA Today*, 15 November 2017, <www.watoday.com.au/wa-news/perths-western-suburbs-deliver-strongest-yes-vote-in-wa-20171114-gzlkuv.html>.

2 'Social issues: equality campaign', Radio Adelaide, 16 November 2017, <radioadelaide.org.au/2017/11/16/equality-campaign/>.

3 Essential Report, 'Same-Sex Marriage', 13 March 2018, <www.essentialvision.com.au/same-sex-marriage-29>.

4 Liz Burke, 'Stunning fact that shows how comprehensive the Yes victory was', news.com.au, 17 November 2017, <www.news.com.au/lifestyle/gay-marriage/stunning-fact-that-shows-how-comprehensive-the-yes-victory-was/news-story/6e9173fef9322faa2cfd99ed9c58880a>.

5 Sarah Blake, 'Same-sex marriage vote result: joy, tears as expats gather in NYC', news.com.au, 15 November 2017, <www.news.com.au/north-america/samesex-marriage-vote-result-joy-tears-as-expats-gather-in-nyc/news-story/f5a694d3ce1a4ac6fb0ddb84860ffb6b>.

17 The Senate makes history

1 Paul Karp, 'Rival same-sex marriage bill to trigger Coalition showdown', *Guardian*, 13 November 2017, <www.theguardian.com/australia-news/2017/nov/13/rival-same-sex-marriage-bill-to-trigger-coalition-showdown>.

2 'LGBTIQ+ Senators get emotional during marriage equality debate', *SBS News*, 16 November 2017, <www.sbs.com.au/news/lgbtiq-senators-get-emotional-during-marriage-equality-debate>.

3 Matt Young, 'Penny Wong's moving speech on same-sex marriage Bill', *Fraser Coast Chronicle*, 16 November 2017, <www.frasercoastchronicle.com.au/news/penny-wong-makes-moving-speech-in-senate-over-same/3266776/>.

4 Sarah Hanson-Young, 'Marriage Amendment (Definition and Religious Freedoms) Bill 2017 Speech', Senate, 27 November 2017, <parlinfo.aph.gov.au/parlInfo/genpdf/chamber/hansards/d0612196-7e36-4c16-bdc8-e2f1f06b87b8/0018/hansard_frag.pdf;fileType=application%2Fpdf>.

18 The House finally represents

1 Kate Doak, communication to Alex Greenwich, authors' possession.

2 Bill Shorten, 'Second Reading Speech: Marriage Amendment (Definition and Religious Freedoms) Bill 2017', 4 December 2017, <www.billshorten.com.au/second_reading_speech_marriage_amendment_definition_and_religious_freedoms_bill_2017_canberra_monday_4_december_2017>.

3 Tony Wright, '"For my late son": Linda Burney's tear-filled speech to parliament on same-sex marriage', *Sydney Morning Herald*, 5 December 2017, <www.smh.com.au/politics/federal/for-m-late-son-linda-burneys-tearfilled-speech-to-parliament-on-samesex-marriage-20171205-gzyy1y.html>.

4 Shana Morgan, '"Old Aunt" Cathy McGowan's speech, call to accept all genders into marriage', *Border Mail*, 6 December 2017, <www.bordermail.com.au/story/5104344/old-aunt-cathys-call-to-accept-all-genders-into-marriage/>.

5 Cathy McGowan, 'Marriage equality speech – not "they" or "other" but "us"', 6 December 2017, <www.cathymcgowan.com.au/marriage_equality_not_they_or_other_but_us>.

6 Lane Sainty, 'Magda Szubanski slams "Gloating" Same-Sex Marriage Speech', *Buzzfeed*, 5 December 2017, <www.buzzfeed.com/lanesainty/magda-szubanski-says-turnbull-speech-was-gloating?utm_term=.wjZGayypY#.ws9JX55rx>.

19 To have and to hold

1 Patrick Williams, 'Married for 48 days before death parted them', *ABC News*, 8 March 2018, <www.abc.net.au/news/2018-03-07/heartbreaking-story-behind-australias-first-same-sex-marriage/9523098>.

2 Patrick Williams, 'Married for 48 days before death parted them', *ABC News*, 8 March 2018.

3 Felicity Caldwell, 'Before she passed away, Jo was finally able to call Jill her wife', *Brisbane Times*, 7 March 2018, <www.brisbanetimes.com.au/politics/queensland/before-she-passed-away-jo-was-finally-able-to-call-jill-her-wife-20180307-p4z37c.html>.

4 'Two lesbian couples celebrate first same-sex weddings in Australia', *Daily Telegraph*, 16 December 2018, <www.dailytelegraph.com.au/lifestyle/two-lesbian-couples-celebrate-first-legal-samesex-weddings-in-australia/news-story/d270395cc5230488a0674f6c222abaa9>.

5 'Tributes: Willow, Cas', *Herald Sun*, 3 January 2018, <tributes.heraldsun.com.au/notice/483552013/view>.

6 'Queensland delivers marriage equality for transgender people', Human Rights Law Centre, 13 June 2018, <www.hrlc.org.au/news/2018/6/13/queensland-removes-forced-divorce-for-transgender-people>.

7 Jaye Cartwright, communication provided to authors, authors' possession.

Index

This index uses the abbreviation AME for Australian Marriage Equality. The names of all the businesses in the book have not been indexed; they can be found through the entry for corporate Australia.

Index

Stracke, Wil 144–45, 203, 222–23, 268, 293, 299, 307
Stratton, David 246
Stricker-Phelps, Jackie 4, 21, 52, 64, 246, 294
Sullivan, Luke 306
Swan, Wayne 106
Szubanski, Magda
    and Janine Middleton 113
    during passage of Dean Smith bill 291, 294
    Q&A appearance 251–55
    speeches given by 260, 272, 282–83
    support for marriage equality 82, 249–50

Tasmania
    campaigning in 239
    rallies and celebrations in 31, 224, 239, 269
    support for marriage equality 74, 23, 84, 220
Tayeh, Jayson 118–19
Taylor, Lenore 77–78
text messages, used in campaign 194, 235–37
Thi Hy Dang 169, 178
Thomas, Geoff 59–60, 64, 67, 239–40
Thomas, Nathan 67, 100
Thompson, Nick 73
Thorpe, Ian 111, 207, 248, 294
Throsby, Stephen 87
Tkachuk, Georgia 218
Tomlins, Jacqui 5, 268, 293
Tran, Natalie 67
transgender Australians 1, 22, 87, 124–25, 243, 261, 270, 307–308
Tuazon-McCheyne, Adrian 5, 293
Tuazon-McCheyne, Jason 5, 268, 293, 299
Turnbull, Malcolm
    position on marriage equality 61, 67, 220, 291
    position on plebiscite 133–35
    as Prime Minister 186–87, 189, 201–202
    see also Liberal Party

unions, support from 145, 207, 212, 215–16, 231, 247
United Kingdom 35, 98–99, 185
Unites States 52, 85, 90, 119–20, 123–24, 188, 214

Van Houwelingen, Ron 306–307
Victoria
    campaigning in 107–109, 114, 232
    marriages in 305–307
    rallies and celebrations in 31, 223, 268
    support for marriage equality 74, 220–21
Voon, Francis 169–70, 270
Vote4Love 99–101

Wall, Louise 85
Wallace, Anthony 268
Wallace, Jim 12, 30
Washer, Mal 32, 61
Waters, Larissa 160
Weatherill, Jay 269
Weaving, Hugo 123, 246
West, Alex 221–22, 239
Western Australia
    campaigning in 233–34
    rallies and celebration in 31, 221, 224, 269
    support for marriage equality 74, 220–21
White, Jacob 221
Wilkie, Andrew 66–67, 129, 199, 298
Williams, George 23
Willow, Cas 305
Wilson, Tim
    and Coalition party room decisions 133, 195–98
    during passage of Dean Smith bill 289, 296–97
    friendship with Alex Greenwich 62, 86, 275
    political action in support of marriage equality 37, 45, 173, 179, 190–91, 193
    public appearances in support of marriage equality 46, 108, 185
Windsor, Tony 67
Witthaus, Daniel 60, 107
Woods, Lachlan 179
Wolfson, Evan 54, 89, 91, 163
women, acknowledged role in campaign 175–76
Wong, Penny
    and change of Labor party platform 34, 40, 57–58, 72, 74–76, 78–81
    during passage of Dean Smith bill 276–8, 279–80, 284, 296, 297
    during postal survey 221, 226, 241, 269
    political action in support of marriage equality 13, 51, 127, 154, 171, 173, 183

Xenophon, Nick 165
    see also Nick Xenophon Team

Yapp, Barbara 35
YES campaign
    bipartisan support for 219–21
    campaigning 203, 227–234, 237
    organisation 204–206, 210, 212–13, 215–18, 221–23
    public support for 226–27
    text message incident 235–37
    see also postal survey

Zborowski, Alex 179
Zimmerman, Trent 101, 193, 234, 287